Blunders and
Disasters
at Sea

Blunders and Disasters at Sea

David Blackmore

Pen & Sword
MARITIME

First published in Great Britain in 2004 by
Pen & Sword Maritime
an imprint of
Pen & Sword Books Ltd
47 Church Street
Barnsley
South Yorkshire
S70 2AS

ISBN 1 84415 117 4

A CIP catalogue record for this book is
available from the British Library

Typeset in 10/12pt Plantin by
Phoenix Typesetting, Auldgirth, Dumfriesshire

Printed and bound in England by
CPI UK

Pen & Sword Books Ltd incorporates the imprints of Pen & Sword Aviation,
Pen & Sword Maritime, Pen & Sword Military, Wharncliffe Local History,
Pen & Sword Select, Pen & Sword Military Classics and Leo Cooper.

For a complete list of Pen & Sword titles please contact
PEN & SWORD BOOKS LIMITED
47 Church Street, Barnsley, South Yorkshire, S70 2AS, England
E-mail: enquiries@pen-and-sword.co.uk
Website: www.pen-and-sword.co.uk

For Paula
Whose spousal support
and encouragement
were essential

And for Binkie
Whose sibling example
was always a spur

Contents

Prologue

Somewhere, sometime, deep in the mists of prehistory, one can imagine a proto-human clambering onto a piece of driftwood or floating tree trunk. After learning how to keep his balance, he discovered he could use his hands or a leafy branch to propel his craft forward. Delighted, he returned to his village to tell fellow clanspeople of the remarkable find.

'Now', he said, 'now we can cross the deep river to hunt those herds we can see grazing on the far bank! Now we can reach that island to harvest its bounty of gulls' eggs!'

Later, or possibly sooner, one of them became the first mariner to blunder and drown. Perhaps he thought he could paddle across the deceptively slow-flowing river before being sucked into whitewater rapids. Perhaps he was unaware of the offshore current on the far side of the island. Whatever the reason, he had started a long trail of waterborne stupidity and misfortune.

From the reed boats of ancient Babylon to modern ocean giants, mankind has been venturing onto the rivers, lakes, seas and oceans, which cover almost three-quarters of our globe. But these waters are some of nature's most magnificent and potent forces, demanding extreme caution and respect.

They are highly temperamental, sometimes resting in mirror-like calm, at others ranting and raging to throw up twenty-metre (sixty-five foot) waves. Their natural forces are compounded in time of war because the urgency and complexity of armed conflict frequently result in human error and miscalculation.

Because of such hazards, maritime mistakes tend to be irreversible to an extent seldom encountered on land. They frequently result in the loss of a ship, together with many lives. Moreover, with every technological advance, ships grow in size and the scale of disaster tends to grow in proportion.

PART ONE

Antiquity and the Classical Epoch

1176 BCE – AMBUSH IN THE NILE DELTA

The Hittites were a timocracy (as Plato calls a state run by a warrior class). By the thirteenth century BCE (Before the Current Era), their hegemony extended from the Aegean Coast to the Tigris River and from the Dardanelles to the mountains of Lebanon. They shared superpower status and a common border with Egypt.

The destruction of Troy, around 1260 BCE, had exposed the Hittite flank to seaborne invasion and, in 1210 BCE, King Suppiluliuma II fought a battle off Cyprus, possibly against the powerful seafaring coalition, which the Egyptians later called 'Peoples of the Isles' or 'Sea Peoples.' His defeat of the hostile fleet was recorded on clay tablets, making it the first naval engagement which can be accurately dated.

A generation later, the Sea Peoples advanced southward by both land and sea, overrunning the Aegean and Asia Minor, destroying the mighty Hittite Empire, and invading the Levant. In inscriptions on temple walls, the scribes of Pharaoh Ramses II reported:

> Behold, the northern countries, which are in their isles, are restless
> . . . they infest the river mouths. . . . The islands pour out their
> people all together and no country can stand against their arms . . .
> They are coming towards Egypt . . . their hearts confident, full of
> their plans.

Their first encounter with Egypt was on land; pictorial inscriptions show Egyptian chariots, led by Pharaoh Ramses in person, smashing through the invading army to fall on lumbering ox-carts loaded with women, children, and provisions.

The land column was defeated and scattered into the Judean hills, but the powerful seaborne force continued southward toward the Nile Delta, where Ramses set up a deadly ambush, hiding ships in tributaries of the main channel, and soldiers amid the tall reeds and papyrus which line its banks. His inscriptions say:

> I made the river mouth like a strong wall with warships, galleys, and
> skiffs completely equipped both fore and aft with brave fighters
> carrying their weapons . . . The net is made ready for them, to
> ensnare them. Entering stealthily into the river mouth . . . they fall
> into it. . . . They penetrate the channels of the river mouths . . . the
> full flame is in front of them . . . a stockade of spears surrounds them
> on the river bank.

This implies he set reeds and rushes aflame to halt the advance, but fire is not depicted on reliefs of the battle, which show the invading vessels – with prows carved into duck's bills, their crews clearly identified by short kilts and magnificent feathered headgear – sailing blithely into the main channel with rowing benches unmanned and marines at rest. They advanced as an undisciplined mass, with no scouts out in front.

Soon they came under a devastating shower of missiles launched by archers lining the shores, and others standing on Egyptian galleys. The surprise was so complete that the invaders were still under sail, while the reliefs show one of the enemy lookouts pierced by an arrow and hanging dead in his crow's-nest.

Other reliefs show Ramses' fleet moving in for the kill, ramming and grappling, while Egyptian marines, wielding shields and spears, swarm aboard the unprepared enemy decks. One of the Sea Peoples' ships has capsized, and its crewmen stand on an Egyptian galley with their arms bound. Others swim to shore, to be picked off by waiting Egyptian archers.

The first naval engagement for which there are both textual and pictorial records ended in total victory for Egypt, thanks to the invading admiral's overconfidence and lack of forethought. Ramses claims he was merciful to survivors, settling them in 'strongholds' under his control, and taxing them in cloth and grain. It is probable that a tribe called the Libu was settled in and gave its name to Libya, while the Peleset did the same for Palestine.

492 BCE – SHIPWRECK ON MOUNT ATHOS

In 499BCE, Ionia rebelled against Persian rule, calling for help from the mainland Greeks. Sparta refused military aid, but Athens and Eretria sent troops. With the advantage of surprise, the combined armies advanced rapidly inland, capturing, sacking and burning the city of Sardis. Then the mainlanders prematurely decided their part of the job had been done, and withdrew their expeditionary forces. The abandoned Ionians continued to fight defensively against overwhelming odds, but were brutally crushed.

Sitting in his opulent environment, with courtiers and suppliants prostrating themselves before him, Darius, known as The Great King, supervised the running of his vast Empire, constantly brooding on the saucy Greeks who had dared to intervene in his sphere of influence. He determined to punish Athens and Eretria and, although a small seaborne punitive expedition was all it would take to chastise them, he decided he might as well establish hegemony over all of Greece.

In 492 BCE, a powerful invasion fleet, commanded by his son-in-law Mardonius, conquered Thrace and Macedonia, and probably reached the Danube River. On the way back, Mardonius marched the army across the base of Halkidice Peninsula, planning to meet the fleet, which was rowing around it.

Halkidice has a very distinctive shape. Its main neck of land terminates in three smaller ones, which stick out into the Aegean like fingers. From west to east, these are Kassandra, Sithonia and Mount Athos. The latter, which is known to the Greeks as Aghion Oros (Holy Mountain), is 2,033 metres high. Each sub-peninsula terminates in an impressive and dangerous rocky cape.

As the fleet rounded these, a violent northerly gale drove it onto the jagged rocks off Mount Athos. Meanwhile, the ground force had been attacked by a wild Thracian tribe, the Briygi, and had suffered major casualties. Mardonius himself was injured, and retreated to Persia with the remnants of his fleet and army. According to almost-contemporary historian Herodotus, Persian naval losses were 300 ships and 20,000 men, but these figures are probably exaggerated.

480 BCE – SLEEPLESS AT SALAMIS

Two years later, Darius struck again with an even larger amphibious force. Mardonius was not given command, either discredited after his losses in Macedonia or because of his wound. Avoiding treacherous Mount Athos, it sailed directly across the Aegean. Eretria was easily subdued, and the Persians moved on to land their shallow-draught troop and horse transports on an undefended beach at Marathon, forty-two kilometres (twenty-six miles) from Athens. 10,000 Athenian heavy infantry, with 600 allies, rushed to the beachhead and defeated some 30,000 Persians.

Infuriated by this humiliation, Darius began elaborate preparations for a third and final expedition to crush the insolent Greeks. But in 487 BCE he died, and was succeeded by his son Xerxes – cousin and brother-in-law of Mardonius. The new King was so intent on avenging his father's loss of face that he ordered a slave to stand behind him at mealtimes, whispering in his ear, 'O Great King, remember the Athenians!'

Before Xerxes could deal with the Greeks, he had to put down insurrections in Egypt and Babylonia, but by 480 BCE he was ready. The ground force was too large to be carried by sea, so it marched around the Aegean, instead of sailing directly across as Darius' second expedition had. It was also too big to live off the land and would have to rely on ship-borne provisions. Xerxes ordered his engineers to dig a canal across Mount Athos Peninsula, so that supply ships could pass inshore of the rocks where his father's fleet perished.

The Persians Invade

As the vast army advanced, most of northern Greece surrendered without a fight, but the southern Greeks resisted. In a linked and bloody land-sea battle, a Persian ground force overwhelmed the Spartan garrison at Thermopylae, while the Persian navy drove the Greek fleet away from Artemesium.

After the twin battles, Xerxes rampaged southward without opposition. Most of the Greeks withdrew behind a palisade on the Corinthian peninsula, but Athenian leader Themistocles evacuated the entire Athenian population to the Island of Salamis. Next day the Persian navy entered the harbour of Piraeus, and the fortified Acropolis fell. Shortly afterward, the city went up in smoke, before the horrified eyes of its citizens.

Having captured Athens, Xerxes had to settle the matter quickly. The campaigning season was almost over and there would not be enough food or fodder to sustain his huge army and pack train through the winter. The main Greek force was deeply entrenched in a strongly fortified position but, despite storm and battle losses, the oriental fleet still enjoyed a huge numerical superiority, so an overwhelming assault on Salamis seemed an attractive possibility.

Themistocles knew that superiority in seamanship and ship-handling would allow sleek Phoenician triremes to outmanoeuvre heavier Greek ships in open waters, so he planned to lure them into the narrows, where numbers and ability would be less decisive. To this end he contrived a hoax. He had his trusted slave Sicinnus 'defect' to the Persian camp, to tell Xerxes the Greeks were quarrelling among themselves (true) and would fall apart if attacked (false).

Persian and Greek Dispositions

Being hungry for glory to match his forebears, young King Xerxes leapt into the trap. First, he sent his formidable 200-ship Egyptian squadron around Salamis to seal the southern exit from the Gulf. Then he assigned a detachment of marines to seize the islet of Psyttaleia at its northern mouth. Finally, he ordered the main fleet – Phoenician and Ionian vessels supplemented by a recently-arrived squadron from the Cyclades – to embark at sunset and remain overnight at sea, ready for a surprise assault at dawn.

Most of his aides accepted the Great King's decision without question. His word was absolute, and those who dared challenge his decisions normally fared badly. But one squadron commander had the temerity to suggest he should remember his recent repulse at Artemesium, saying – according to Herodotus – 'The Greeks are as far superior to us in naval matters as are men to women.' Interestingly, this gender-discriminatory remark was made by Queen Artemisia, Regent of Halicarnassus (Herodotus' home town) who commanded five war galleys.

Xerxes respected his female vassal's opinion, especially since she had distinguished herself in battle. He listened attentively, but decided to ignore her advice, saying the earlier disaster was doubtless due to the absence of his own inspiring presence. This time his seamen and marines would be stimulated by the sight of their monarch in magnificent splendour on a golden throne overlooking the Gulf.

Themistocles divided the Greek fleet into three divisions. Thirty or so Corinthian ships lying well forward in the Strait were to hoist sails and flee into the Bay of Eleusis, enticing the enemy to follow. The main fleet of about 220 galleys, mainly Athenian and Spartan, would then emerge from behind Cape Aigaleos to envelop the heads of pursuing Persian columns in the Narrows. Finally a detached squadron of about fifty ships from Megara and Aigena, some of the best in the fleet, was to hide just south of Salamis village (modern Ambelaki), to hit the columns in the flank after the main force had engaged.

The Battle of Salamis

It was a fine sight that Xerxes looked down on, as 550 triremes in line abreast rowed towards 300 Greek vessels inside the Gulf. But they were tired after their night at the oars and things soon began to go wrong. The columns lost cohesion when they had to pass on either side of Psyttaleia. Then, as they emerged, they saw the Corinthians backing water and hoisting sails in their feigned attempt at escape. Each Persian vessel surged forward, racing its neighbour for the honour of being first to strike an enemy.

When this mad dash had further distorted the Persian battle line, the trap was sprung. Greek trumpets blared, and the main fleet surged forward to grapple the incoming enemy. The Corinthians downed sail and rowed back to join them, and the detached squadron charged in from the flank to smash through banks of oars and thrust their wicked beaks into the fragile side-planks of enemy ships.

Boarding parties of heavily-armoured Greek *epibatai* (marines) were more than a match for felt-clad Persian sea soldiers, who resisted gallantly on blood-slippery decks. The poet-playwright Aeschylus, who himself fought on the Greek side at Salamis, sums it up from the Persian-Phoenician point of view:

> Then ship on ship rammed home her beak of bronze . . . and all along the line the fight was joined. At first the torrent of the Persian fleet bore up; but when the press of shipping jammed them in the narrows, none could help another, but our ships rammed each

other, fouled each other, and broke each other's oars. But those Greek ships, skillfully handled, kept the outer station, ringing us around and striking in, till ships turned turtle, and you could not see the water for blood and wreckage; the dead were strewn thickly on all the beaches, all the reefs; and every ship in all the fleet of Asia in grim confusion fought to get away.

The brilliant strategy – devised by Themistocles, and executed under the calm leadership and tactical command of Corinthian Admiral Adeimantos – had worked perfectly. After eight hours of combat, the Greeks had destroyed or captured more than 180 galleys, mostly Phoenician while losing only forty of their own. The enemy retreated, and Themistocles wisely let them go, choosing not to risk a stern chase into the open sea. Xerxes was so infuriated by the failure of his seamen and marines that he ordered survivors slaughtered as they scrambled ashore.

Aftermath

Winter was close at hand, and the army was far too large to be supplied and victualled during the barren months ahead. So Xerxes decided to return to Asia with two thirds of his troops, most of them irregular levies and half-hearted allies, leaving Mardonius in command of a smaller, but far more cohesive and efficient army. In the spring of 479 BCE, Mardonius advanced on Athens but, at the land battle of Plataea, virtually his entire force was annihilated. At roughly the same time, a Greek fleet caught the remnants of the Persian fleet beached under the promontory of Mycale in Ionia. In a surprise attack, all its ships were burned and destroyed.

429 BCE – WANT OF PRACTICE AT NAUPACTUS

In 435 BCE, a naval war broke out between Corcyra (Corfu) which enjoyed Athenian protection, and Corinth, one of Sparta's allies. Athenian leader Pericles imposed a trade embargo and blockaded the Corinthian fleet in its eponymous Gulf, saying, 'If they are kept off the seas by our superior strength, their want of practice will make them unskilful and their want of skill timid.'

However, the sanctions damaged other Spartan allies as well as Corinth, and Sparta grabbed the excuse to declare war. In 429 BCE, a battle fleet under Spartan Admiral Brasidas set out to link up with a convoy of invasion troops under Corinthian Admiral Machaon. They planned to break the blockade by driving the Athenians out of their naval base at Naupactus (medieval Lepanto).

Machaon slipped through the narrows, with a fleet of forty-seven war-galleys guarding the troop transports. As his ships hugged the south shore, they were shadowed by twenty Athenian triremes under Admiral Phormio. Although outnumbered by more than two-to-one, he was confident his crews and tactics would be superior to the enemy's. At dawn, the Corinthian fleet reached Patras and turned north to run for the invasion beaches. Phormio allowed it to reach the mid-point of the Strait, then pounced.

The Battle of Patras

Machaon immediately adopted a 'hedgehog' formation, ranging forty-two of his warships in a circle with their rams pointing outward, like the spokes of a rimless wheel. For safety, he placed the troop transports and cargo ships inside this circle, together with five of his most powerful triremes as a mobile reserve. It was early in the day, so there was little wind and the sea was calm.

Phormio made no attempt to break the defensive circle, but led his fleet in line astern, in a huge arc girdling the Corinthian fleet. This manoeuvre seemed to put his own ships in harm's way, by offering their vulnerable flanks to the enemy's rams. But Phormio had realized that Machaon must hold his formation steady, since any vessel succumbing to temptation and charging the passing Athenians would expose its own flank to the next in line, well before it had reached ramming speed. The effect of Phormio's tactic was thus to cause the Corinthian circle to tighten up on itself until the oars of neighbouring vessels almost overlapped.

Towards noon, just as the veteran Athenian admiral anticipated, the wind got up and began to push the closely-packed and stationary Corinthian ships into one another. At the same time the choppy swell made control difficult for their inexperienced oarsmen. Soon, station keeping was lost, the impregnable formation broke up in chaos, and Machaon ordered his ships to flee to safety at Patras on the southern shore.

This was the moment Phormio had been waiting for. Pipes sounded the charge, and sleek Athenian triremes surged forward, crashing their deadly three-metre (ten-foot) beaks into the delicate side-planks of the helpless enemy. Before the Corinthians could reach asylum, the Athenians captured twelve of their vessels and impressed them into their fleet. They would have inflicted even greater damage, but Brasidas arrived, commanding the concentrated fleets of Sparta and her other allies.

The Battle of Naupactus

Outnumbered by seventy-seven war-galleys to his own twenty, Phormio withdrew towards his base, pursued by the allies who outdistanced one another in their attempts to catch up. Then, just as he reached Naupactus, Phormio abruptly turned, swung round a merchantman anchored in the roadstead, and rammed the nearest pursuer amidships. The stern-chasing Spartans were strung out, allowing the rest of the Athenian squadron to wheel and attack the leading elements in detail, destroying another six for the loss of one, and putting the remainder to flight.

This two-phase battle proved the wisdom of Pericles' thoughts on lack of practice due to blockade, and effectively removed any Spartan naval threat to Athens for more than a decade.

413 BCE – DISASTER IN SYRACUSE HARBOUR

A traveller passing though Athens dropped into a barber's shop for a shave. As usual, they chatted about this and that, until the visitor casually deplored the terrible defeat of an Athenian expeditionary force at Syracuse. The unfortunate half-shaved stranger was promptly arrested as a defeatist scandalmonger, and held in irons until others arrived to confirm his story.

Three years earlier, when Athens was already at war with the Peloponnesian states of Sparta and Corinth and their allies, the powerful oratory of a man called Alcibiades had convinced the Assembly to open a new battlefront by attacking Syracuse. Many of those who voted in favour were merchants casting covetous eyes on the highly profitable maritime trade with Sicily and the West. Thucydides, principal historian of the conflict, says: 'Most of them . . . (had) no idea of the size of the island and of its population, and of the fact that they were embarking on a war not much less serious than that with the Peloponnesians.'

In the spring of 415 BCE, the expeditionary force embarked in 134 triremes. Their leaders were Lamachus, one of the most experienced and competent of Athenian field commanders, and two political appointees – Alcibiades, sponsor of the expedition, and Nicias who had vehemently opposed it in the Assembly.

A Half-Hearted Siege

Lamachus proposed striking hard and fast, but the politicians overruled him, wasting almost a year on diplomatic wrangling, and losing the advantage of surprise. Towards the end of the year, Alcibiades defected to Sparta and, on his advice, the Spartans sent General Gylippus to mastermind the Syracusan defence.

By the following spring, Nicias had run out of excuses, and Lamachus persuaded him to move. Eight thousand Athenian troops mounted an amphibious assault, while 25,000 seamen disembarked to build siege works. Then Lamachus was killed, leaving the expedition under the command of Nicias, who was a lacklustre commander even when his heart was in it. At year end, the siege was getting nowhere, and Nicias sent a plaintive message to Athens, saying:

> The time . . . has come for you to decide either to recall us, or else to send out another force, both naval and military, as big as the first, with large sums of money, and someone to relieve me of command, as a disease of the kidneys has made me unfit.

Withdrawal would have been sensible, but Athenian pride made them decide to reinforce failure. In the spring of 313 BCE, another strong force was dispatched in seventy-three triremes, under the command of Demosthenes, one of their best fighting generals. Before they arrived, Gylippus launched simultaneous land and naval assaults.

The seaward foray was repulsed, but the ground force took Cape Plemmyrium, giving Syracuse control of the harbour approaches. This forced the Athenian fleet to abandon its base and beach its vessels along the foreshore. Shortly afterward, the reinforcements arrived and beached their ships alongside the others.

Demosthenes evaluated the situation and decided to mount an immediate assault on the city. By moonlight, his force scaled the western cliffs and routed the surprised garrison. But, as often happens in night engagements, the attackers lost cohesion and fell into disarray. Some pursued the retreating enemy, some fell off the cliffs to die on the rocks below, and others stumbled back to crash into reserves moving up behind.

When morning came, it was clear the attack had failed. Demosthenes proposed withdrawing from their untenable position, but Nicias procrastinated, saying soothsayers had advised a delay of 'thrice nine days' until a propitious phase of the moon. While waiting, the Athenians kept their triremes afloat, ready for defensive action.

Battles in Syracuse Harbour

Before the waiting period was over, Gylippus attacked again. The Athenians' softwood hulls had soaked up water, making them heavy and sluggish, whereas the Syracusan ships, which had been beached to dry out, were handier. Athens lost forty ships and many valuable crews.

Thucidides reports that, when they retreated, the troops ashore 'raised in intolerable anguish one universal groan'.

Then Gylippus blocked the harbour exit with a boom of about two hundred old ships, anchored and lashed together, protected against incendiary missiles by hide-covered frames, and fronted by a palisade of spiked spars and timbers. Both Athenian fleets were trapped, and even superstitious Nicias had to agree that they must break out at once.

Twenty-two seaworthy battle galleys had to be left ashore for lack of crews, but 115 set out overnight with 16,000 at the oars and 11,000 marines on board. At dawn they attacked in four lines of twenty-five, with fifteen in reserve.

When they were about 300 metres (330 yards) away from the boom, scores of small Syracusan craft swarmed out of the mist, showering them with darts, firebrands, and jars of sulphur. Then artillery mounted on the boom began throwing huge boulders, but they pressed on and boarded to fight on the decks of the boom ships where, for a while, they seemed to be winning. But Gylippus had assembled 50,000 troops on Cape Plemmyrium and thousands more on the city promontory. These scrambled onto the boom from both ends replacing casualties and facing tired Athenians with fresh enemies.

Thousands died trying to break through the ring of Syracusan wood in the harbour and Spartan iron ashore until, in the words of Thucydides, 'Their losses were . . . total; army, navy, everything was destroyed.' Seven thousand who surrendered perished in intolerable squalor. The news did not reach Athens until the traveller came for his shave.

405 BCE – ADVICE REJECTED AT AEGESPOTOMI

Athens recovered from the disaster at Syracuse, and hostilities continued for another decade. Then Sparta, the great land power decided to acquire a fleet, and this changed the complexion of the conflict. In 405 BCE, Spartan admiral Lysander captured the city of Lampsacus, and seized command of the Hellespont, interdicting the Crimean grain route on which Athenian survival depended.

The 180-ship Athenian fleet rushed to Aegospotami, facing Lampsacus across the narrow Strait. Not only did the Athenians have a split command structure with multiple admirals, but their choice of campsite on an open beach was a tactical blunder. Plutarch reports on their disposition and how the exiled turncoat changed sides yet again:

> The Athenians grew extremely confident, lay carelessly and without order, in contempt of the enemy. Alcibiades, who was not far off,

did not think so lightly of their danger, nor neglect to let them know of it. . . . (He) came to the admirals and represented to them that they had chosen a very inconvenient station, where there was no safe harbour, and where they were distant from any town . . .

He also pointed out to them their carelessness in suffering the marines, when they went ashore, to wander up and down at their pleasure, while the enemy's fleet . . . strictly obedient to discipline, lay so very near to them. He advised them to remove the fleet to Sestos. But the admirals not only disregarded what he said, but . . . with insulting expressions, commanded him to be gone, saying that now not he, but others had command.

Despite the timely warning, the admirals still neglected to mount sentries, and made no attempt to discipline their motley crews. Meanwhile Lysander, lying across the Strait, cunningly lulled them into complacency by refusing to accept their challenges to battle for five consecutive days.

On the fifth day, he waited until they returned to their anchorage and their crews, as usual, wandered inshore to forage. Then a polished bronze shield flashed the signal to advance, his trumpeter sounded the call to battle-speed, and the Spartan fleet darted across the narrows at maximum oar-stroke. With almost no opposition, they took 172 beached Athenian ships as prizes, and slaughtered between 3,000 and 4,000 unarmed prisoners in cold blood.

Only the senior Athenian admiral, Conan, escaped with eight galleys and a favourable north-easterly wind, stopping briefly at the Spartan anchorage in order to circumvent a stern chase by carrying off all their sails. In this single action, Lysander destroyed Athenian maritime hegemony, and effectively won the Second Peloponnesian War.

255 BCE – SHIPWRECK ON SICILY

Superpowers Rome and Carthage were commercial rivals and military opposites. The pride of Carthage was a large and efficient navy, but its army was a medley of conscripts and adventurers. In contrast, Rome had a magnificent citizen army, but only a few small ships crewed by Greek mercenaries. They came to blows in three conflicts known as the Punic Wars, sparked when each attempted to control Sicily and gain a stranglehold on the strategic Strait of Messina.

Romans had no natural affinity for the sea, but geography dictated they had to fight Carthage on water as well as on land. They developed a fleet, and when superior Carthaginian seamanship prevailed, they desperately adopted an Athenian invention which they called the *corvus* (raven).

This consisted of a gangplank, mounted vertically on a turntable. When a hostile vessel closed in to ram, the device was dropped to drive its spike deep into the enemy hull. *Classiarii* – legionaries specially armed and trained for service as marines – then charged across the gangway to fight with the tactics of land warfare in which Romans excelled. The *corvus* decided several battles during the First Punic War but, like most secret weapons, lost its effectiveness when the enemy devised counter-tactics.

In the spring of 255 BCE, a 364-ship Roman fleet was carrying survivors from a failed invasion of Carthage. As it neared the coast of Sicily, a sudden squall blew up, catching the still-novice seamen off guard. Two hundred and eighty-four ships foundered, many because the weight of the *corvus* made them top-heavy. With them perished 100,000 of Rome's finest soldiers, seamen and marines – a disaster which is still the greatest single loss of life in the history of seafaring.

249 BCE – SACRILEGE AT DREPANUM

Six years later, an inexperienced Roman admiral, Consul Claudius Pulcher, planned to catch a Carthaginian fleet unawares in the harbour of Drepanum (modern Trapani at the north-westernmost tip of Sicily). However, before engaging in battle, he paused to follow the Roman tradition of asking priestly augurs to foretell the outcome. According to legend, the sacred fowls refused to eat – a very bad omen indeed – where-upon he cried blasphemously, 'Throw the damned birds into the sea; if they won't eat, let them drink instead.'

Pulcher then ordered his captains to row into the harbour in line-ahead but, according to second-century historian Polybius, positioned himself at the rear, ' . . . in order to hustle laggards'. Meanwhile, Carthaginian lookouts had sounded the alarm, and the pause for auguries had given Admiral Adherbal time to assemble his crews and order his fifty-ship fleet out to sea.

The leading vessels met in the harbour mouth. Both fleets were in disorder and crammed together without room to manoeuvre. With no admiral present to change its orders, the Roman centre kept pressing on the vanguard which was trying to extricate itself. Pulcher's decision to lead from the rear had resulted in an immense log-jam. When word of the confusion finally reached him at the rear of the long 123-ship column, he ordered a fast-rowing ship forward to order the retreat.

It was too late. Pulling back, the Roman captains desperately tried to form a battle line, but they had lost formation, and some were unable to manoeuvre because their oars had been broken in the earlier mêlée.

Having marshalled his own fleet, Adherbal took advantage of their disorder, seized the offshore station and drove them onto the rocks. Ninety-three were destroyed in Rome's greatest defeat of the First Punic War.

Aftermath

Superstitious Romans blamed the disaster on Pulcher's sacrilege and, shortly afterward, another catastrophe seemed to confirm divine displeasure. A huge Roman convoy of 800 transports, escorted by 120 warships was attacked and badly mauled by a Carthaginian squadron, after which a gale wrecked all surviving vessels on the coast of Sicily

In just over six years, battle casualties and storm losses had destroyed some 800 Roman warships and countless transports, taking the lives of upwards of a quarter-of-a-million men. Nevertheless, the Punic Wars continued sporadically for another century until Carthage was totally destroyed, and Rome gained absolute command of the Mediterranean.

NOVEMBER 61 –
SAILING TO ROME OUT OF SEASON

Several centuries of conflict and violence ended when Octavian (later Emperor Augustus) won a Roman Civil War and ushered in one of the least eventful periods of military history. He established frontiers along clearly-defined defensible boundaries, within which Romans and their subject peoples could live in peace and security.

Under the *Pax Romanum Maritimus* (Roman Peace at Sea), the Mediterranean and Black Seas were Roman lakes, seaborne trade was the imperial life blood and, with no wars to fight, the navy's primary task became the protection of trade routes sailed by a huge merchant marine plying between Rome and the Provinces.

Unprecedented freedom of movement encouraged the spread of ideas, including new religions. One was an offshoot of Judaism, founded by Jesus of Nazareth, and known as Christianity. Its members were persecuted as heretics by orthodox Jews, one of whom, Saul of Tarsus, underwent a change of heart, changed his name to Paul, and became a fervent Christian proselytizer. His influence on the new faith was second only to Jesus himself.

In the year 59, Paul was in the Jewish Temple at Jerusalem when a group of fanatical extremists accused him of being an apostate whose presence in that Holy Place was blasphemy. It looked as though he would be lynched, but a patrol of Roman legionaries rushed down from the ramparts to take him into protective custody. When their commander learned Paul was a Roman citizen he transferred him to Caesarea (modern Har Qesari), where Felix, the Roman Governor (Procurator) of Judea, kept him under house arrest hoping – according to Paul's biographer, a physician called Luke – to be bribed to release him.

After two years, Paul invoked the citizen's privilege of appeal to the Imperial court. This petition seems to have been premature, because Felix had just been replaced as Procurator by Porcius Festus, who commented, 'This man has done nothing to deserve death or imprisonment. He could easily have been discharged if he had not appealed to Caesar.'[1] However, once the request had been made, the Law required the accused to be transferred to Rome as quickly as possible.

Paul, together with Luke and some other prisoners, was handed over to an officer of the Imperial regiment called Julius. Embarking on a ship bound for Adramyttium (Edremit) they set sail, stopping first at Sidon (Saïda), where Julius allowed Paul to visit his friends. From there, the wind was against them so they had to sail under the lee of Cyprus. After crossing the Gulf of Iskanderun, they landed at Myra in Lycia.

There, the officer put his prisoners on board an Alexandrian ship bound for Italy. For a number of days they made a slow passage and had great difficulty in arriving off Cnidus. Then, as they still faced contrary winds, they sailed around Cape Salmone (Sidheros) onto the lee side of Crete finally reaching a place called Fair Haven somewhere on the south-west coast of the island.

By this time, it was well into the season known as *mare clausum* (sea closure) when navigation came to a virtual standstill due to the hazards of changeable and inclement weather. Knowing that sailing had become dangerous, Paul warned them, saying, 'I see this voyage is likely to involve hardship and serious loss, not only to the cargo and the ship but even of our own lives.' However, since the Fair Haven anchorage was unsuitable for overwintering, Julius let himself be persuaded by the captain and helmsman who proposed sailing to Phoenix, a harbour at the tip of Crete, facing both north-west and south-west. When a moderate southerly breeze sprang up, they weighed anchor and set off along the coast of Crete, staying close inshore.

However, before long a strong north-easterly gale blew up. The ship was caught by the offshore wind and driven hopelessly out to sea. This put them in a serious situation. Once blown out of sight of land, first century navigators had no means of knowing where they were, and might drift aimlessly for days. However, unable to face the wind, they gave up and let her drive along, lowering the sail and using ropes to brace the hull.

Next day, being terribly battered by the storm, they had to jettison the cargo. Two days after that they took the desperate measure of throwing much of the ship's gear and tackle overboard. Weeks went by with no sight of sun, moon or stars. The fierce storm continued to rage, and at last they gave up all hope of being saved. Paul then spoke up, saying, 'You should have listened to me and not set sail from Crete and suffered this damage and loss.' However, he told them to keep up their spirits, a vision had assured him that 'No-one's life is going to be lost, although we shall . . . have to run the ship aground on some island.'

When the fourteenth night arrived, they were still drifting out of control. But around midnight, the sailors sensed land was at last nearby. A sounding of twenty fathoms was quickly followed by one of fifteen so, afraid of being wrecked on the rocks, they let go four stern anchors and waited for dawn. At first light they could make out a sandy-shored bay suitable for beaching the ship. So the anchors were cut away and left in the sea, while the crew unlashed the ropes that tied the rudders, hoisted the foresail to the breeze, and headed for the beach.

Before they got there, they struck a reef, driving the ship hard aground. The prow jammed fast, but the stern began to break up under the beating of the waves. The guards proposed killing the prisoners to prevent their escape, but the officer restrained them, ordering swimmers to dive overboard and make for land, while telling the rest to cling to planks or wreckage. In this way, all 276 in the ship's company arrived safely on the island of Malta. When navigation re-opened, they embarked on an Alexandrian ship for an uneventful trip to Rome. Two years later, Paul was executed by Emperor Nero.

MARCH 549 – THE BATTLE OF THE TIBER BOOM

The West Roman Empire had fallen to Gothic barbarians, but the East Roman Empire, also known as Byzantium, lived on. Even while on the defensive against Persia in the East, Emperor Justinian was determined to recapture the West. Having re-established the Roman Province of Africa, he moved troops into Italy and seized Rome.

Totila, newly-crowned king of the Ostrogoths, set siege to Rome. To intercept Byzantine freighters and cut off supplies to the city, he assembled squadrons in the Bay of Naples and on the Lipari Islands. Then, to interdict the passage of any ships which escaped this blockade, he stretched a heavy chain across the mouth of the Tiber, anchored a massive wooden boom upstream from the chain, and protected this upper barrier with guard-towers on each shore.

Byzantine general Belisarius devised a daring amphibious operation designed to breach these barriers and carry supplies to the beleaguered city. First, to shelter detachments of soldiers and archers, he built high parapets on the decks of 200 large barges. Then he roped two of the biggest barges together, to form a platform for a tower higher than the Gothic ones guarding the boom. To its top, he hoisted a small boat packed with sulphur, and bitumen, and other combustibles.

The tower-carrying catamaran was towed upstream led by dromons (fighting galleys), accompanied by ground troops marching along the towpath, and followed by the barge convoy loaded to the gunwales with provisions and supplies. As a diversion, a contingent of cavalry left the port of Ostia along the road to Rome.

The heavily-guarded chain was breached by the weight of the dromons, and its defenders were either killed or retreated to the upstream fortifications. There the advance was stalled by the fiercely-defended towers.

Troop-carrying barges were brought up and archers, firing through embrasures in the parapets, forced the Goths to take cover while the fire-tower was guided to the bank and its boat-load of flaming combustibles dropped, incinerating one of the guard-towers along with 200 of its defenders. As ground troops advanced along the towpath, the Goths evacuated the second guard-tower, the boom was destroyed, and the way to Rome lay open.

At this precise moment, a breathless messenger arrived to tell Belisarius his base camp was under attack. His beloved wife Antonina was there and for once the wise commander lost his head. Instead of delivering the relief supplies, he pulled all 200 shiploads back to Ostia. It turned out to have been a false alarm, but he fell ill and his subordinates made no further attempt to victual the city which, without re-supply, was taken by the Goths.

PART TWO

The Medieval and Renaissance Ages

NOVEMBER 1084 –
LACK OF BALLAST AT CORCYRA

Byzantine Emperor Alexius was besieging the Norman garrison on Corcyra (modern Corfu) when he heard that Robert Guiscard, Norman Duke of Calabria and Apulia, was heading to its rescue with a 120-ship fleet. Alerted, he hired as many Dalmatian pirates as he could afford, and asked his ally Venice to send a large fleet. Both contingents rendezvoused with the Imperial navy at a mainland base. Robert promptly moved to a small harbour facing them from the tip of the island.

The first phase of the battle was hard-fought at close-quarters in the narrow waters between island and mainland. Combat was ferocious but inconclusive, and both fleets retired to their bases to recuperate. Two days later Robert sortied again, only to be firmly repulsed and forced to flee. Since it was the end of the campaigning season, the victorious allies paid off the pirates and sent most of their own ships home, keeping only the largest Imperial and Venetian vessels to maintain a blockade.

Robert heard of their departure and turned around to mount a third attack. The Venetians chained their remaining ships together in the defensive formation known as a 'sea-harbour', but the complacent Imperial squadron remained in loose order. The Normans attacked in five squadrons of five ships, one commanded by Robert himself and the others by his sons. The rest of his fleet stayed in reserve. The Imperial ships broke and fled before the Norman charge, but the Venetians held fast in their floating fortress.

Then a strange thing happened; the big Venetian warships (known as *usciere*) had either consumed or offloaded most of their stores, leaving themselves top-heavy. As armour-clad marines crowded towards the engaged side, their weight made the ships heel so dramatically that many of them slid overboard and were drowned. Resistance faltered, and several Venetian captains tried to cut the cables which held them in the sea-harbour. After suffering heavy losses of men and ships, the survivors surrendered to the Normans, who treated them with great cruelty.

NOVEMBER 1120 –
TIPSY NAVIGATORS AT BARFLEUR

Within four years of their invasion of England, the Normans had completely broken the great Anglo-Saxon earldoms and established a highly-centralized feudal kingdom. They still controlled immense territory in France, and these involved them in frequent armed conflicts with rival French landowners, and even their nominal suzerains, the French kings.

Twenty years into his reign, William the Conqueror's son, King Henry I, left Barfleur to return to England after yet another French campaign. His seventeen-year-old son, another William, was carousing and was left behind. His friends urged him to take the fast-sailing royal yacht, *White Ship*, and catch up with his father. Leaving the tavern, they staggered down to the dock, far too drunk to worry about high winds and rough seas.

Merrily they crammed on as much sail as the yacht could carry, boasting about how quickly they would overtake the king. But none of them took the con, and they had barely left the harbour when *White Ship* ran on the rocks off Pointe de Barfleur. Sobered-up, they tried desperately to push themselves off but, despite their best efforts, several were swept overboard, and waves continued to pound the yacht against saw-toothed rocks.

Eventually they managed to launch a small pinnace and, anxious to save the heir to the throne, pulled the young prince on board. They pushed away from the ship, but Prince William refused to leave without his bastard sister, the Countess of Perche. With difficulty, the oarsmen came back alongside, whereupon a mob of panic-stricken sailors and courtiers tried to clamber into the little boat. It capsized and all were drowned. Then *White Ship* went down and only the ship's butcher survived to tell the tale. It was said that Henry never smiled again.

May 1213 – Unguarded at Damme

When he came to the throne in 1199, King John of England inherited a vast swath of northern, western, and southern France, extending from Flanders on the English Channel, down the Atlantic coast, and along the Pyrenees, to Provence on the Mediterranean Sea. In contrast, Philip II of France controlled only about one-thirtieth as much territory.

However, between 1202 and 1205, Philip won control of Anjou, Brittany, Maine, Normandy, and Touraine, cutting land communication between England and the remaining Norman possessions south-west of the River Loire. These could only be reached by a long sea voyage around Cape Finisterre, and this led John to create the nucleus of a navy.

Instead of relying on converted merchantmen, as previously supplied by the 'Cinque Ports' under the terms of their charters, he organized a fleet of royal galleys at ports in southern England. Every Englishman over the age of twelve was liable for military duty, and many were impressed into naval service under full-time officers. They trained by fighting pirates and mounting hit-and-run raids on French ports and shipping.

In 1209, following a disagreement with the Pope over the appointment of bishops, John was excommunicated. Philip promptly assembled a fleet and army for a Holy Crusade against the heretic king. However, John reconciled with the Vatican in 1212, and the papal legate forced Philip to cancel the invasion.

John immediately set about building alliances to counter the designs of the French king, scoring a diplomatic coup when Renaud de Dammartin – Count of Boulogne and commander of Philip's aborted invasion – changed sides to support him, and another when he concluded a treaty with the Count of Holland in May 1213.

Philip had used the ships assembled for his English invasion to transport an army to Flanders. Landing near Bruges, he moved inland. Count Ferrand of Flanders appealed for English support. By this time, John had amassed a substantial war chest in preparation for renewed warfare. With these funds he gathered land forces at Canterbury and Dover, and paid a 500-ship fleet to assemble at Portsmouth on the south coast.

On 28 May, they set out for Flanders with 700 knights and several thousand men-at-arms on board. The force was commanded by William Longespée, Earl of Salisbury, with the Counts of Boulogne and Holland as his lieutenants. Two days later, after fighting contrary winds, they made landfall off the estuary of the River Zwyn, up which Salisbury sent an exploratory patrol.

The reconnaissance reported a huge number of French vessels, most of them loaded with stores and supplies, beached in the estuary, or lying at anchor in the harbour of Damme, the seaport for Bruges. Only a few seamen were on sentry duty, as most of the French army had moved inland to besiege Ghent, while the rest had set out to forage and plunder.

Salisbury ordered an immediate attack, and the small guard force was easily overwhelmed. The English cut 300 ships adrift, destroyed or captured over 400 more, and took a vast quantity of valuable booty, including the priceless personal belongings of the French barons. In its first major operation, the English Royal Navy had achieved a brilliant triumph, and removed all threat of invasion.

The ground force was less successful. It had landed at Damme to support the Count of Flanders, but was almost trapped by Philip, who rushed back from Ghent with the main French army. Just in time, knights and soldiers re-embarked and returned to England to form the nucleus of John's campaign in France. Philip was unable to move his remaining transports out of the Zwyn and, to avoid having them captured by another sortie, was obliged to burn almost 1,000 of them, bringing his total losses to some 1,700 ships.

NOVEMBER 1274 – TYPHOON AT DAZAIFU

Late in the thirteenth century, the Mongol emperor Kublai Khan sub-jugated Korea and began a forty-five-year conquest of China. He also sent emissaries to Japan, demanding tribute and homage. The Japanese regent, Hojo Tokimune, replied that Nippon (Japan) enjoyed divine protection and would never submit. In response, Kublai ordered the king of Korea to construct a fleet and gather troops and supplies for an amphibious invasion of the islands.

During the next five years, he continued diplomatic efforts to secure Japanese submission, but they remained defiant. By the autumn of 1274, an invasion force of 23,000 Chinese, Korean and Mongol soldiers had assembled. Setting out in 900 ships, they occupied Tsushima and Iki Islands as staging posts for an unopposed landing at Hakata Bay on the main island of Kyushu.

The Japanese samurai mounted stiff resistance. They were formidable warriors, but their military tradition stressed formalized single combat against opponents of equal rank. The Mongols, in contrast, were a disciplined military machine which manoeuvred skilfully in mass formations. The samurai could not match Mongol tactics and were driven steadily back to the ancient stone fortification of Dazaifu. When night fell, the invaders withdrew to their anchored fleet, planning to renew the attack in the morning. However, shortly after they finished boarding, a typhoon struck without prior warning.

Navigation became virtually impossible as heavy rains, cyclonic winds and rough waters battered the Mongol fleet. Many ships dragged their anchors and were blown ashore to shatter on the rocks, many others foundered where they lay. The storm only lasted a few hours, but 300 ships had been sunk, taking a third of the soldiery with them. The remnants retreated to Korea to regroup.

AUGUST 1281 – SHINTO PRAYERS AT IMARI BAY

Determined to finish the job, Kublai set up an invasion-planning bureau, known as 'The Office for Chastisement of Japan'. However, before a new campaign could be launched, he had to divert forces to combat the Sung Empire in South China. His fleet moved in parallel with the army and, at the Battle of Yaishan in 1279, won control of the South China Sea.

Escaping from this battle, a huge Chinese junk raced across the Bay of Canton, closely pursued by a squadron of Mongol warships. It was the imperial flagship and, sooner than allow his monarch to be captured and humiliated, the Chinese admiral leapt overboard with the infant emperor in his arms. The drowning ended the Sung dynasty, establishing Kublai's Yüan regime as the first to rule united China since the fall of the Tang almost four centuries earlier.

The Japanese were still recalcitrant and executed all Kublai's envoys, so he decided to mount another invasion, this time in overwhelming force. He augmented the captured Sung fleets with new construction, and embarked about 120,000 troops on 3,200 ships at ports in South China. They were to rendezvous at Iki Island with 1,200 Korean ships carrying another 40,000 soldiers.

The Koreans sailed first but, after taking Tsushima and Iki at the beginning of May 1281, did not wait for the larger Chinese contingent and sailed on to Hakata. There, they found the Japanese waiting for them behind newly-built stone defences. Thwarted, they fell back on Shikanoshima Island in the middle of Hakata Bay, only to be raided by fishing boats carrying Japanese warriors, who leaped onto their decks wielding terrible samurai swords. Captured Korean ships were set ablaze and drifted down on the rest of the fleet. The survivors retreated to Iki Island.

The huge Chinese force arrived there towards the end of July, and the combined fleets, still with about 4,000 ships, returned to Japan carrying some 140,000 troops divided into two armies. Mounting a pincer movement to outflank the formidable Japanese defences, one army landed at Hakata Bay to their north, the other at Imari Bay to their south. Both were met by fierce resistance and fighting continued for weeks, with the Mongols returning to their ships at sunset to avoid night raids by the Samurai.

After six weeks of violent combat, the Japanese called on their gods. Throughout the countryside, at Shinto shrines and Buddhist temples, priests, warlords, politicians and ordinary people pleaded for deliverance from the foreign invaders. As if in response to these millions of supplicants, a small storm gathered in the North Pacific Ocean, rapidly developed to typhoon strength, and curved northward towards the Mongol fleet.

On the evening of 15 August, just after the Mongol soldiers had re-boarded their ships, the storm struck. One of the samurai warriors reported that its arrival was 'as if a green dragon raised its head from the waves . . . sulphurous fumes filled the firmament'.

The combination of high tides, powerful currents, mountainous waves, and howling 120 km/h (75 mph) winds was lethal. Japanese sources indicate that virtually all 4,000 ships were lost, along with over 100,000 Mongol lives. One report claims that 'a person could walk across Imari Bay from one point of land to another on the mass of wreckage'.

After the typhoons of 1274 and 1281, the legend of the kamikaze

(Divine Wind), which comes as heavenly protector whenever their home islands are threatened, became deeply embedded in Japanese folk memory, to be invoked again in the closing days of the Second World War.

JUNE 1340 – IMMOBILITY AT SLUYS

In 1328, after Charles IV of France died childless, Edward III of England claimed to be ruler of all France on the grounds that his mother, Eleanor of Aquitaine, was the dead king's aunt. To forestall him, the French nobility quickly crowned a distant cousin with a much weaker claim, naming him Philip VI. This launched a long drawn-out dynastic dispute between the French royal house and the English crown, which became known as the Hundred Years War.

The English held royal France in a triple-pronged pincer, formed by Edward's fiefdoms of Anjou and Aquitaine in the south, closely-allied Flanders in the north, and friendly Brittany in the west. In 1337, Philip announced the forfeiture of all English lands south of the River Loire, and half-heartedly invaded them. In response, Edward mounted raids into northern and north-eastern France from England and Flanders respectively.

Two years later, spies reported that Philip and his allies were assembling a mighty fleet and army, intending to crush Flanders, preparatory to invading England itself, so Edward decided on a pre-emptive strike. John's royal fleet had long since been disbanded, and the English Navy consisted of some 200 impressed merchant vessels, once again supplied by the Cinque Ports, on which carpenters had installed 'castles' (fighting platforms) fore and aft.

These ships were qualitatively and numerically inferior to the 400-ship Franco-Spanish-Genoese fleet, which had assembled in an arm of the Scheldt River, near the town of Sluys. Although their ships carried crossbowmen, the French despised distance weapons, believing the only chivalrous form of naval warfare was hand-to-hand combat between armoured knights, essentially fighting a land battle on board ship.

On Friday 23 June 1340, Edward sent two knights ashore to make contact with his Fleming allies, who told them the French commander-in-chief, Admiral Hugues Quiéret, had divided his fleet into three squadrons. Two of sail, led by himself and Vice Admiral Balmuchet, had chained themselves together and anchored in parallel lines, one behind the other. The third squadron, consisting of rowed galleys under Admiral Barbenoire, was stationed behind them as a mobile reserve.

Barbenoire, who was a highly experienced Genoese sea soldier, condemned this defensive arrangement, saying it sacrificed their advantages of mobility, numbers, seamanship and manoeuvre. He recommended moving out to confront the English in open water, but the king overruled him.

Edward realized that Quiéret's static disposition gave him numerical advantage over each individual enemy rank. He and his Vice Admiral, Sir Robert Morley, divided the fleet into groups of three, each consisting of two ships with castles crammed with archers, followed by a third loaded with men-at-arms.

The Battle of Sluys

Soon after dawn on Saturday morning, the blaring hunting horns of the advancing English were answered by French trumpets, as each of Edward's groups took on an anchored enemy with three-to-one local superiority. Ranging themselves on either side of a foe, the archer-boats swept his decks, filling the air with the hiss of flying arrows and the thud of their impact on human bodies. Return fire was ineffective because English longbows outranged and shot faster than French crossbows. As each French crew was depleted, each third English ship grappled and launched its boarding party. After the front rank of French ships had disintegrated, the English moved against the second, many of whose crews abandoned ship and headed for the shore, only to be clubbed to death in the shallows by vengeful Flemings.

By midday, the outcome of the battle had essentially been decided, but ship-by-ship deck fighting between English men-at-arms and French, Genoese, and Castilian knights continued throughout the day and into the night. By the time it died down around midnight, upwards of 20,000 Frenchmen and their allies were dead, and virtually their entire fleet had been destroyed. Only thirty of Barbenoire's galleys had managed to extricate themselves and row to safety.

Aftermath

None of the surviving French nobles had the courage to tell irascible Philip of the disaster. Eventually, they pushed forward the court jester who cried, 'Oh the cowardly English, the cowardly English.' When Philip asked what he meant, he replied 'Unlike our brave Frenchmen, those fools did not dare jump overboard.' Because England controlled the Channel for the balance of the Hundred Years War, it was unscathed by the fighting which devastated France.

JANUARY 1500 – IMPERIAL FIAT

Mistakes by shipmasters, watch officers and naval architects have wrecked individual vessels, while blundering commodores have destroyed squadrons and admirals have decimated fleets, but it took an emperor to demolish an entire navy and annihilate a proud maritime tradition.

After conquering the Sung in 1279, Kublai Khan founded a Chinese dynasty called the Yüan. In spite of his losses to kamikaze winds, Kublai and his successors developed ocean-going seapower at the expense of river- and lake transport. Their large merchant fleet took over the Indian Ocean spice trade from Arab merchants.

In 1356, Chu Yuan-Chang, a Buddhist monk, led a popular uprising against the Yüan. Civil War raged for three decades, but in 1388 the last Yüan emperor was driven from his capital of Karakorum and the Ming dynasty seized power. The early Ming emperors preserved and built upon Yüan maritime policy and technology.

This technology was state-of-the-art. It included the magnetic compass, stern-post rudder, and fore-and-aft lugsails, which were much more efficient for beating upwind than the square-rig and lateen sails favoured by Europeans and Arabs. They had developed map-making techniques, and discovered how to make ships virtually 'unsinkable' by compartmentalization. As early as 1299, Venetian traveller Marco Polo reported seeing four-masted junks with watertight bulkheads, cabins for sixty merchants, and crews of 300.

The Great Expeditions

In 1403, the third Ming emperor, Zhu Di, ordered construction of a huge imperial navy, and embarked on an ambitious programme of ocean exploration with a fleet of some 350 warships and support vessels. Many of these new ships were immense, as can be seen from comparison of the flagship with two well-known vessels;

Ship	Length	Beam	Masts	Crew
Columbus' *Santa Maria*	18 m (59.0 ft)	6.5 m (21 ft)	3	52
Nelson's *Victory*	69 m (226.5 ft)	15.7 m (57 ft)	3	820
Zheng He's *Treasure Ship*	145 m (475.7 ft)	59.0 m (193 ft)	9	1,000

The encyclopaedic *Li-Tai Thung Chien Chi Lan* (Essentials of the Comprehensive Mirror of History), published in 1767, tells us:

> The emperor . . . commissioned Zheng He, Wang Ching-Hung and others. . . . With a force of more than 37,000 officers and men under their command, they built great ships and set sail from . . . Suchow, whence they proceeded by way of Fukien to Chan-Chheng (Vietnam) and thence on voyages throughout the western seas. . . . Zheng He was commissioned on no fewer than seven diplomatic missions, and thrice made prisoners of foreign chiefs. . . . The different peoples, attracted by the profit of Chinese merchandise, enlarged their mutual . . . trade, and there was uninterrupted going to and fro.

Senior Admiral Zheng He (pronounced jung huh), was a eunuch who had been in Imperial service since the age of thirteen and was originally a soldier. Between 1405 and 1433, he traversed the South China Sea, the Indian Ocean, the Persian-Arabian Gulf and the Red Sea, and his voyages may have extended into the Atlantic and Pacific Oceans. The official Ming history records visits to Java, Sumatra, Vietnam, Thailand, Cambodia, the Philippines, Ceylon, India, Bangladesh, Yemen, Arabia, Somalia and Mogadishu. It also mentions 'Franca' (believed to be Portugal and France) and a people called 'Hollanders'. If he really did meet Europeans in their own countries by ship, he must have rounded the Cape of Good Hope.

In a book published in 1434, Venetian merchant Nicolo da Conti claimed to have travelled to Australia with a Chinese fleet. He somehow acquired some Chinese maps and star charts. These have now been lost, but were said to show the outline of North America. In a presentation to the Royal Geographical Society on 15 March 2002, British naval officer and historian Gavin Menzies claimed to have located the remains of nine large Chinese junks wrecked in the Caribbean in 1421.

Retreat into Isolationism

Even if Zheng did not circumnavigate Africa before Magellan, visit America before Columbus, and reach Australia well in advance of James Cook, his voyages were magnificent achievements. However, soon after his death, Confucian scholar-officials began to challenge their value. They trumpeted the superiority of domestic agriculture to foreign trade, of canal shipment over sea-borne transportation, eschewed contamination by alien concepts, and advocated the social purity of cultural isolationism.

Xenophobic anti-maritime politicians steadily won power and influence at the Imperial court, and their attacks led to a gradual loss of interest in overseas contacts, geographical sciences and naval technology. By 1474, they had succeeded in reducing the fleet to about one-third of its early Ming size. Finally, in 1500, they gained the ear of Emperor Ming Xiao Zong, first persuading him to remove Imperial support from overseas trade, then to order the destruction of Zheng's logs and nautical charts, and make it a capital crime to build or go to sea in any vessel with more than three masts.

Coastal commerce and trade with India and East Africa continued in smaller vessels but, thanks to official hostility and neglect, ocean-going technology fell into decline, the pool of deep-water sailors steadily diminished, and shipyards forgot how to construct large craft. Within a few decades, China's commanding lead was lost, never to be regained, although it would be centuries before ships matching the size and sophistication of *Treasure Ship* were built in the west.

JULY 1545 – OPEN GUNPORTS AT SPITHEAD

Henry VIII, King of England, was dining with Viscount Lisle, his Lord High Admiral, aboard the mighty warship *Henri Grace à Dieu* in Portsmouth harbour, when a messenger burst in. 'Sire, the French fleet is returning! It has rounded the Isle of Wight and is entering the Solent!' Vice Admiral Sir George Carew was promptly alerted to prepare *Mary Rose* and the rest of his squadron for action.

The Introduction of Gunpowder Weapons

A hundred and thirty years earlier, in 1414, the most heavily armed ship in the English Royal Navy had been *Holigost* which carried six small 'gonnes' on its castles, but escalation had been rapid. By the end of the century, Henry VII's fleet included *Regent* and *Sovereign*, each of which carried 285 serpentines – 38 mm (1½ inch) anti-personnel weapons – swivel-mounted on the rails and bulwarks of forecastle and quarterdeck.

The size and weight of naval ordnance was still limited, because ships mounting cannon on their weather decks could become top-heavy and capsize. In consequence, even this number of small guns had done little to change ship design or tactics, merely substituting bullets for arrows.

Then a French shipwright named Descharges[2] invented the port – an opening in the ship's side, fitted with a hinged waterproof door, originally intended to facilitate the loading of cargo. This produced revolutions in naval architecture and tactics. By using ports for artillery to fire through, shipwrights were able to place the heaviest weapons in the bowels of the ship, well below its centre of gravity, where they steadied rather than destabilized it.

In 1511, the idea was seized on by King James IV of Scotland for his new flagship, *Great Michael* which, in addition to three long bow-guns and about 300 bulwark-mounted anti-personnel weapons, carried twenty-four heavy cannon firing broadsides through side-ports.

This started a naval arms race, and Henry VIII of England adopted the concept for three new ships under construction. *Henri Grace à Dieu*, usually called *Great Harry*, carried 141 light pieces and forty-three heavy guns in below-deck broadsides. Slightly smaller were *Peter Pomegranate* and *Mary Rose*, each armed with ninety-one guns of which twenty or so were heavy culverins in broadsides. They were mostly muzzle-loaded, although some of the anti-personnel weapons were breech-loaders.

Mary Rose, named after Henry's favourite sister, was laid down in 1509 as a four-masted carrack of some 600 tons. She was the flagship of Sir Edward Howard at the Battle of Brest in 1513, during which she sank the French flagship. After the battle, Sir Edward told the king, 'Your good ship, was the flower I trow of all ships that ever sailed.' In 1536, she was extensively overhauled and modernized, including the installation of a larger number of heavier guns.

Along with *Great Harry* and *Peter Pomegranate,* she was the nucleus of the Royal fleet, which Henry VIII increased (as far as can be told from inadequate records) to about fifty-three heavy fighting ships armed with 2,185 guns. These vessels, which were among the first integrated weapons systems in purpose-built hulls, represent the true beginning of English sea power.

Henry VIII's Foreign Relations

In October 1540, an alliance between Francis I of France and Holy Roman Emperor Charles V broke down, freeing Henry from fear of a Franco-Imperial invasion and allowing him to turn on his neighbour James V of Scotland. In 1543 he formed an alliance with Charles against France, but Francis took the initiative, sending troops to Scotland and forcing Henry to fight on two fronts at once.

In May 1544, Henry sent Edward Seymour, Earl of Hertford, to ravage the Scottish lowlands while he personally led an army into France. In September, Boulogne surrendered, but, on the very same day, Charles repudiated the alliance, leaving him to face France alone.

Francis assembled a huge army and navy for his counter-offensive, setting siege to Boulogne, sending reinforcements to Scotland, and preparing to invade England itself. Henry returned to England to prepare its maritime defences. In 1545, *Chronicles of the Tudor Kings* reported the repulse of Francis' first assault:

On 18 July at 9 o'clock at night began thunder and lightning with some rain which continued all night until 8 o'clock the next morning, and that afternoon all the French king's navy came out of Newhaven and Dieppe and arrived off the coast of England in Sussex, before Brighton, in all over 300 ships besides 24 galleys which they had. And there they set certain of their soldiers on shore to burn, but the beacons were fired and the men of the country came down so thick that the French men fled and did little harm.

Two days later, the French returned, with 300 sailing warships and twenty-four rowed galleys, heading directly for Portsmouth Harbour. The English fleet set out to meet them with, probably, about 105 ships. They also had a few oared vessels, but heavy sailing warships formed the majority of both fleets. They moved sluggishly in extremely light and variable winds.

The Battle of Spithead and the Fate of *Mary Rose*

Leading the English *Mayne Battall* (the starboard squadron) was *Great Harry*, wearing the flag of Lord High Admiral Lisle. She was engaged by four galleys which had rowed ahead of the French fleet. After firing, they feigned a retreat, hoping to entice the English into open water where numbers would be decisive. But Viscount Lisle intended to fight a holding action in the channel, and was not drawn.

Suddenly, from behind the big warship, a number of English 'row-barges' darted out. These vessels, which were rigged like pinnaces, had sixteen oars to a side, carried a pair of bow-chasers and two heavy broadside guns under a half-deck. They were longer, narrower, faster and more nimble than the Mediterranean-style rowing galleys of the French. Giving them a nasty shock, they turned their feigned withdrawal into a rout.

At this stage of the battle, a slightly stronger wind came up, allowing *Mary Rose* to pass through the press of English ships toward her station alongside *Great Harry* as leader of the *Vauverde* (the port squadron). All her gunports were open and ready for action. Newly rebuilt and bedecked with banners, including the flag of Vice Admiral Sir George Carew, she was a splendid sight, but all was not well on board.

She was vastly overloaded; her normal complement of seamen, archers, gunners, marines and trumpeters was 415, but on this fateful day she was carrying some 700 men. Most, if not all, of the extra personnel were heavily armoured soldiers, ready for the combat on deck which was expected to decide sixteenth century naval battles. They were crammed into the fore- and after-castles, or crowding the main deck where they impeded the movement of seamen scurrying to set sails.

Moreover, there seemed to be a command problem with this huge crew

– insubordination, incompetence, or both. It was so obvious that Sir Gawen Carew, uncle of Sir George, sailing nearby in *Matthew Gonnson*, called out 'What's the trouble?' to which his nephew shouted back 'I have the kind of knaves I cannot rule.' Moments later, while increasing her spread of canvas to take advantage of the still-increasing wind, *Mary Rose* suddenly began to heel over.

Possibly mismanagement in the hoisting or handling of sails caused the abrupt roll, or perhaps a sudden gust of wind caught her tall castles as well as the just-increased spread of sail. As she tipped, some 500 heavily armoured fighting men slid down the sloping deck into the lee scuppers, adding their weight to that of the heavy broadsides, while those high up on the castles gave leverage to the list. Additionally, some guns in the starboard battery were probably not lashed down properly, and rolled across the deck to increase the imbalance.

Within seconds, a torrent swept through her open gunports and she was doomed. Weighed down by armour, trapped below decks, or entangled in the complex rigging, some 700 perished. There were only thirty-five survivors, all of them humble sailors wearing light clothing without armour.

The English fleet survived the battle by refusing to be drawn into open water, where French numerical superiority would have been decisive. The French landed on the Isle of Wight to burn and loot, and at every tide their galleys came in to shoot at ships in Portsmouth harbour, but they left at the end of July having achieved nothing. Next year, France and England concluded a peace, and the year after that both Henry and Francis died, signalling the end of one era and beginning of the next.

Post mortem

How could such a disaster have happened to the pride of the English Royal Navy? In addition to the possibility of inferior sail-handling, *Mary Rose* may have had design flaws. Whereas modern naval architects know that the metacentre of a vessel must be above its centre of gravity for the vessel to be stable, the problems and mathematics of this concept were little understood in the sixteenth century. Instead, most shipwrights relied on experience and eye-judgement to tell them how to proportion a vessel.

From contemporary paintings, it can be seen that *Mary Rose*'s lower main battery had gunports near the waterline, while her sternchaser ports were even closer. Her designers may have placed her heavy guns even lower than customary to counter-balance the extremely tall fore- and after-castles they planned to give her.[3]

JULY 1588 – THE SPANISH ARMADA

Sir Francis Drake, sometime pirate and currently Vice Admiral of Queen Elizabeth's Royal Navy, was enjoying a game of bowls on Plymouth Hoe when he was told that the long-awaited *Armada Invincibile Espagnol* (Invincible Spanish Fleet) had been sighted, the sails of its 130 ships seeming to stretch across the English Channel from shore-to-shore. Thanking the messenger, he continued playing.

This tale has been told to generations of English schoolchildren as an example of calmness under pressure but, in fact, Drake knew there was no need for haste – the English ships had been on standby alert for weeks, tactics had been discussed and rehearsed, and they could not sail until the tide turned in several hours.

In the latter part of the sixteenth century, Spain was an international superpower, with immense income from colonies in the New World and much of Europe. Powerful on land, Spaniards were not natural seafarers or shipwrights, so their navies tended to be weak, relative to other Europeans.

The Rival Fleets Prepare

Angered by the predatory activity of English privateers, notably Drake, King Philip III determined to invade England and add it to his Empire. He had four major objectives – collection of reparations for damage caused by the privateers; forcible conversion of Protestant heretics to the Church of Rome; removal of a serious rival for maritime trade; and an end to English support of Netherlandish rebels.

He ordered the Duke of Parma, Governor of the Spanish Netherlands, to assemble an army of 30,000 soldiers, and prepare sufficient boats and barges to carry them across the English Channel. Meanwhile he would assemble a powerful fleet to sweep the Channel free of English warships, protect Parma's crossing, and convoy another 30,000 troops to join the invasion.

As Commander-in-Chief, Philip was extremely inefficient and ineffective. Slothful and ignorant of maritime affairs, he wasted time and energy on macro-planning, while ignoring such micro-details as building, crewing and victualling the fleet. Without supervision, corrupt traders supplied poor quality provisions and inferior equipment. Moreover, when Spain's foremost naval commander, the Marquis of Santa Cruz, died, the king forced a landsman, the Duke of Medina Sedonia, to reluctantly take over.

The fleet waiting to meet the Armada was commanded by Lord High Admiral Howard of Effingham. The number of fighting ships was even, but the English were superior in number and weight of guns, their ships were more manoeuvrable, they excelled in gunnery, and their tactical doctrine was more up-to-date, designed to capitalize on the potential of broadside artillery.

Many myths have grown up about the Armada, the most common being that of little English ships bravely darting in like gadflies to harass vastly superior numbers of much larger and more-heavily gunned Spanish galleons. In fact, the English fighting ships were similar in size to all but seven of the Spaniards.[4]

The Battles in the Channel and off Calais

A four-day running battle began on 23 July. A few days later, *The English Mercurie: Published by Authoritie For the Prevention of false Reportes,* reported:

> They came in Sighte of the Spanish Armado . . . sailing in the Form
> of a half-Moon, the Points whereof were seven Leagues asunder.
> The Lord High admirall . . . after a Council of Warre had beene
> held, directed the Signall of Battell to be hung out. We attacked the
> Enemy's Reare with the Advantage of the Winde. . . . By God's
> blessinge there was no doubte but this unjuste and dareing
> Enterprise of the Kinge of Spayne would turne out to his everlasting
> Shame and Dishonour.

In the first days of this fight, the English scored numerous hits from beyond the range of Spanish guns, but at too great a distance for their light cannon balls to cause serious damage. Then both sides ran out of ammunition. Meanwhile, Drake had sighted a straggler and, following his instinct for plunder, dropped out of the battle and returned to port with it. The *English Mercurie* continued:

> The St Francis Galleon (*San Francisco*, Vice-Flagship of the
> Andalusian Squadron), of which Don Pedro de Valdez was
> Captaine, fell in with Vice-Admirall Drake, who tooke her after
> stout Resistence. She was disabled from keepinge up with the reste
> of the Fleete by an Accident . . . the Captours found on board five
> thousand Golde Ducats, which they shared amongst them after
> bringing her into Plymouth.

Folk myth holds Vice Admiral Drake, the deserter for personal profit, to be hero of the Channel Battle, virtually ignoring Commander-in-Chief Howard and his Rear Admirals Hawkins and Frobisher, who stayed at their posts. However, Drake did return in time for the final phase of the fight.

On 27 July, the Armada anchored off Calais; it was still virtually intact but Parma refused to embark his troops until the English Fleet had been destroyed and a Dutch blockading fleet driven away. Two nights later, the English drifted eight fireships into Calais harbour on the rising tide. The Spanish reacted rapidly, slipping their anchor cables and moving away, but several were lost by grounding or collision. Survivors were scattered in the roads and outside the harbour.

By this time Howard's Squadron, resupplied with powder and shot from shore bases, had been joined by Seymour's Narrow Seas Squadron. Realizing the Spaniards had no more cannonballs for their big guns, the combined fleets closed the range until near enough for their shot to penetrate Spanish hulls. Their energetic assault and heavy cannonade drove the Spaniards onto the Flanders coast.

Circumnavigation of the British Isles

Having lost some twenty ships by grounding or cannon fire, Medina Sedonia decided not to risk returning through the Channel, where he would face contrary winds as well as the English. Instead, even though the *Armada* had no chart or pilot for Scotland and Ireland, he chose to take advantage of a southerly wind to sail northward around the British Isles and home via the Atlantic Ocean. The English, once again desperately short of ammunition, pursued as far as the Firth of Forth, where Scottish territorial waters begin.

A few unnamed Spanish ships were wrecked on the English Coast, and *La Florida* foundered off the Scottish Isle of Mull, but the majority circumnavigated Scotland, only to encounter gales as they rounded Ireland into the North Atlantic. Many disappeared without trace, but the fate of several is known. Don Alonzo de Luzon, a regimental commander aboard a ship of the Levantine Squadron, reported:

> On the 14th September 1588 the 1100 ton ship *La Trinidad Valencera* entered Glenagivney Bay, County Donegal, Ireland in a sinking condition. Around four hundred and fifty men were brought ashore before the ship broke up and sank. The crew who remained on board drowned. . . . I and my whole company yielded ourselves, within six or seven days of our landing, to the captains that carried the Queen's ensigns . . . after which one promise was not kept . . . for the soldiers and savage people were allowed to spoil us of all we had.

Colonel de Luzon, Ensign Juan de Nova and other officers were separated from their men, stripped of their clothing and marched 160 kilometres (100 miles) to the English garrison at Drogheda. Meanwhile, three more of the Levantine Squadron, *La Lauria, La Juliana* and *Santa Maria de Vision* had found their final resting place in the Bay of Donegal, while *Santiago* of the Supply Squadron had foundered in Broadhaven, County Mayo. Most survivors were brutally massacred by the local Irish.

Another Levantine galleon, *La Rata Santa Maria Encoronada*, commanded by Don Alonzo Martinez Levia, proved hard to control in gale force winds, and was badly battered before finding shelter in Blacksod Bay, County Mayo. The crew obtained fresh water and supplies and made minor repairs, but the wind was still blowing strongly and the ship was blown ashore on Fahy Strand. Shortly afterward, *Duquesa Santa Ana* of the Andalusian Squadron entered Blacksod Bay, and took Don Alonzo and his men on board.

Setting sail again, they encountered even stronger winds, which drove them northward until they were driven ashore in Loughro Mor Bay, County Donegal. Don Alonzo took command of about 1,000 survivors and marched northward, pulling a number of salvaged cannon. By chance they stumbled into Killybegs, where three galleons had been driven by the gale. *La Lavia*, Vice-Flag of the Levantine Squadron, and *San Juan* of the Biscayan Squadron, had foundered with all hands, but *Girona*, a large galleass of the Guipúzcoan Squadron, had merely damaged her rudder.

As senior officer present, Don Alonzo assumed command. Deciding not to risk facing the onshore gale again, he headed north-eastward, intending to refit in anti-English Scotland before heading for Spain on the lee side of Ireland. Even on this course bad weather was encountered, resulting in new damage to the rudder. Unable to steer, even the power of 224 oarsmen was insufficient to hold the galleass offshore and she ran aground on Lacada Point, County Donegal. Of the crew of 531 and upwards of 1,000 fugitives from other ships, only three, five, or nine survived (accounts differ). Given shelter by Sorley Boy MacDonnell of Dunluce Castle, they settled nearby and married local women.

Patrona Zuriga, a larger galleass with 350 oarsmen, was luckier. She was forced into Liscannor Bay in County Clare, where she was able to take on fresh water and provisions, and repair storm damage. She was one of sixty-seven vessels, including the Duke of Medina Sedonia's flagship *San Martin* which eventually reached Spanish ports. Ships and men were in a sorry state. Virtually every vessel had storm or battle damage, or both, while many of the surviving soldiers and seamen died of wounds, exhaustion or disease within weeks of their return.

The encounter in the English Channel was the first to be decided by gunpowder alone. It heralded the artillery duels which would dominate naval combat for the next three-and-a-half centuries. However, it was stormy weather, rather than English cannon, which defeated the Armada, costing it fifty per cent of its ships and seventy per cent of its men.

JANUARY 1614 – FIRE ON THE HUDSON RIVER

Eager to establish a lucrative fur trade with native Americans, a consortium of Amsterdam merchants commissioned master mariner Adriaen Blok to explore the region discovered by Henry Hudson. Blok brought home a rich cargo and was sent back with a new and larger ship, the *Tijger*, and her consort, the *Fortune*. He anchored in the Hudson River and began trading with the aboriginals on what is now Lower Manhattan, sending *Fortune* to establish another trading post further upriver.

The Manhattan trading venture was successful and, by January 1614, *Tijger* was loaded with furs and preparing to sail home. However, someone had been careless with a lantern or the galley fire. In the first recorded disaster in New York harbour, the full cargo of oily pelts flamed furiously, and *Tijger* burned to the waterline.[5]

Just in time, Blok and his crew escaped in the ship's boat, but their predicament was serious. They had no shelter and no personal belongings except the clothes they were wearing. Moreover, they had no means of contacting *Fortune*, since it was an exceptionally hard winter and the Hudson was blocked by ice. Without help from native Americans they were doomed. Fortunately, they had been fair traders, so the Indians were friendly.

Blok had had the foresight to save a few lengths of rope, some spare sail canvas, and the shipwright's tool kit. With native help, they built crude huts for shelter, creating the first European settlement in what was to become Nieuw Amsterdam and, later, New York City. Whenever the weather permitted, he sent out logging parties of seamen and Indians to fell oak and hickory trees, cutting them into planks and beams to build a small yacht of sixteen tons displacement.

Onrust (translation: *Restless*) was the first seagoing vessel to be constructed by Europeans on American soil. She was too small for an Atlantic crossing, but Blok used her to explore the coast before rendezvousing with *Fortune* at Cape Cod.[6] Leaving her captain in command of *Onrust*, with orders to continue exploration, he returned to Holland with the news that fur trading and settlement in the New World were real possibilities, and with maps to show where such ventures might be set up.

AUGUST 1628 –
OPEN GUNPORTS OFF STOCKHOLM

In the early part of the chaotic period known as the Thirty Years War, Gustavus Adolphus, king of Sweden, known as 'Lion of the North', reorganized the government, revitalized the army, and enlarged the navy. For the latter, he engaged naval architect Master Henrik to design a magnificent and powerful addition to the fleet. Henrik died in 1619, and shipbuilder Hein Jacobssen took over the half-completed vessel, which was christened *Vasa*.

The ship's Master, Jöran Matsson, afraid the ship might be top-heavy, arranged a stability test in which thirty seamen rushed from side-to-side. The effect was so disconcerting that the experiment was aborted, and Matsson reported the ship as unable to withstand heavy weather. Admiral Fleming dismissed his fears saying, 'You don't have to worry; this builder is experienced and knows what he's doing.'

Sudden Disaster

On a sunny August evening in 1628, hundreds of civil and military dignitaries crowded on board Sweden's newest and most potent warship, anxious to have the prestige of sailing on her maiden voyage. Many had brought wives and children along. The anchor was hauled up and *Vasa* moved slowly out to sea. She was a magnificent sight, with extravagant carvings and brilliant gold, green, red and blue paintwork, made all the more impressive by an accompanying flotilla of rowing boats and yachts bedecked with flags.

As *Vasa* left Stockholm harbour, she was shielded by the cliffs of Söder and light winds hardly filled her sails. But once the headland had been passed, the wind freshened and she heeled alarmingly. Captain Söfring urgently yelled 'let fly the topsails' but, long before the topmen had time to respond, a stronger gust threw her hard over.

A collective groan rose from accompanying boats and watchers on the headland as – shades of *Mary Rose* – her lower gunports submerged and water flooded in, causing her to capsize and sink like a stone, taking between 300 and 400 men, women, and children with her.[7]

Aftermath

The Swedish Council of State immediately convened an investigation under Admiral Carl Gyllenhielm, who quickly determined that captain and crew had behaved in a seamanlike manner. Discussion then turned to *Vasa*'s design. Jöran Matsson told the Court about the stability test he had reported to Admiral Fleming, while Captain Söfring testified he never felt she was seaworthy, due to her heavy superstructure. Builder Hein Jacobssen responded he would have added ballast, if told of the problem, but Söfring pointed out that this would have increased the ship's draught, when her gunports were already a bare metre above the waterline.

Later, in his own testimony, the builder denied any design fault, saying he had scrupulously followed Master Henrik's original blueprints, which were based on a Dutch-built ship in French service. Moreover, he said, the design had been approved by Gustavus Adolphus himself. Rather than point a finger at the monarch, or even at Admiral Fleming, the Court adjourned without placing blame or naming a scapegoat.

June 1667 – Raid on the Thames Estuary

During the seventeenth century, the British and Dutch fought three, essentially naval, wars over commercial interests in the East Indies, Africa, and North America. The second of these began in 1665 and, under an earlier treaty, France was obligated to join in on the Dutch side. However, after the Great Plague and Fire of London in 1666, Britain initiated peace talks. While these were still underway, Dutch admiral Michael Adriaanzoon de Ruyter planned surprise naval raids on English naval bases.

King Charles II was alerted to the Dutch plans but – convinced they were as war-weary and cash-short as Britain – not only took no precautions, but actually demobilized. A number of ships were decommissioned, while others were reduced to skeleton crews. An existing fort on the Medway River was closed down and plans to build a second were scrapped. A chain boom had been prepared to block that river east of Chatham, but its tenders were laid up for lack of funds to pay their crews.

De Ruyter's fleet set out on 14 June, with fifty-one ships-of-the-line, three frigates, fourteen fireships and about a dozen smaller craft. On board was a renegade English sea captain, Robert Holland, who was familiar with navigating the treacherous sandbars and mudflats of the Thames Estuary. On 17 June they reached Sheerness at the mouth of the Medway, where the fort's garrison fled after only two men were killed by Dutch fire. The English warship *Unity* was not much braver, firing a single broadside before retreating up river.

Next day, the Duke of Albemarle reported, 'I went to visit the chain, which was the next thing to be fortified for the security of the river, where I found no works for the defence of it.' He supplemented the boom by anchoring *Unity*, four fireships and half a dozen small craft behind it, but these last-minute defences did little good.

Reaching the boom, Captain Jan van Brakel in *Vrede* forced *Unity* to surrender, while *Pro Patria* charged the chain, breaking it and opening the river and naval dockyards to de Ruyter's ships. In quick succession, they attacked and destroyed the undermanned capital ships *Matthias* and *Charles V*, burned six smaller ships, and went on to capture the English flagship *Royal Charles* which had been abandoned by her crew.

While Dutch men-of-war engaged the batteries of Upnor Castle and ravaged the Chatham naval dockyard, fireships crashed into line-of-battle ships *Royal London, Royal James* and *Royal Oak*. The first two were quickly abandoned, but Captain Archibald Douglas and the crew of *Royal Oak* fought on amid the flames and were burned to death.

Then de Ruyter withdrew, taking all his prizes, and wearing a broom at his masthead to symbolize a clean sweep. Thanks to complacency, incompetence, cowardice and stupidity, the British Royal Navy had suffered an amazing humiliation in its own back yard, where it should have been invulnerable.

De Ruyter's withdrawal was described as having taken place when 'the state of wind and tide were such that even the best of Chatham pilots would not have liked to undertake it'. After leaving the Nore, he sailed down the Channel, intending to give the Royal Naval base at Plymouth the same treatment as Chatham. However, before he got there, the Treaty of Breda brought an end to hostilities.

JUNE 1676 – SIGNAL CONFUSION OFF ÖLAND

Three decades after the loss of *Vasa*, Sweden was still commissioning narrow vessels with stability problems. Completed in 1672, *Kronan* was one of the most powerful warships afloat, carrying 128 guns. With so much armament in a slender hull, she soon developed a reputation for being a 'cranky' sailer.

When his father-in-law, Philip of Spain, died in 1665, Louis XIV of France claimed to have inherited the Spanish Netherlands. Initially, Sweden and England were among those opposing the claim but, after a short and inconclusive war, Louis skilfully separated the Dutch United Provinces from these allies by concluding secret treaties with each of them. On 1 June 1676, combined Dutch-Danish fleets set out to challenge Sweden.

Commanded by the formidable Martin Tromp, the allies had twenty-five ships-of-the-line and ten frigates, carrying 1,727 guns. Swedish Admiral Creutz, who had never commanded a fleet before, had twenty-six battleships and twelve frigates, mounting 2,184 guns. In addition to lack of combat experience, the Swedish system of passing orders by gun signals was, to say the least, confusing, especially in action when other guns were firing.

The Battle of Öland
The two flagships, Tromp's *Christianus Quintus* and Creutz's *Kronan*, had just engaged, when Vice Admiral Uggla, commanding the Swedish van,

fired a single forward gun. This was the signal to recall advanced units. From Creutz's vantage point, however, it seemed the gun was aft, in which case the signal would mean 'reverse course'. Instead of questioning the unusual order, he assumed his Vice had seen something he could not, broke off the action, and ordered the entire fleet to go about.

The turn brought the ships close-hauled and unable to carry as much canvas as they had been with a following wind. However the admiral, who had personal command of *Kronan*, did not shorten sail, nor did he order gunports on the new lee side to be closed. As *Kronan* heeled alarmingly, she began to ship water. However, before she could flood and sink like *Mary Rose* or *Vasa*, the 'safe lamp' in the magazine overturned and smashed (it can't have been suspended on gimbals). Seconds later, a terrible explosion tore the ship apart, her two halves settling into fifteen fathoms (twenty-eight metres; ninety feet) of water about 200 metres (660 feet) apart.

Uggla assumed command. His flagship, *Svärd*, had lost her mainmast but stayed in action, damaging Tromp's *Christianus Quintus*. Then a Dutch fireship set light to *Svärd*, which also blew up. Attempting to escape, the third of Sweden's big ships, *Apple*, ran onto a reef. Both Swedish flagships, six other ships, both admirals and some 4,000 officers and men had been destroyed, along with control of the eastern Baltic.

MAY 1678 – INNOVATIVE NAVIGATION

French Admiral Jean d'Estrées could not be bothered with all the fancy charts and calculations involved with fixing a position. Instead, he developed his own unique system of navigation. This involved sailing along a fixed latitude until he believed he had gone far enough, then sailing north or south and sailing until he reached (or bumped into) the intended destination.

During the night of 11 May 1678, d'Estrées was leading a large fleet towards (he believed) the Dutch stronghold of Curaçao when an accompanying buccaneer vessel fired a warning gun. The admiral was far too haughty to respond to a mere subordinate, let alone one who was not even a naval officer. So he continued on his course, running the entire fleet aground on the reefs off the Las Aves Islands, almost 150 kilometres (ninety miles) east of his intended landfall.

Seven ships-of-the-line and five other vessels were wrecked on the rocks, although most of their crews survived and, eventually, 364 cannon and 3,000 shot were salvaged. Incredibly, instead of being court-martialled and cashiered, d'Estrées was promoted and given greater responsibility by his close friend King Louis XIV.

PART THREE

Early Modern Times

OCTOBER 1707 –
LACK OF A RELIABLE TIMEKEEPER

A daring but foolhardy seaman aboard HMS *Association*, flagship of Admiral Sir Cloudesley Shovell, approached the Officer of the Watch, saying he had been keeping track of the ship's course and estimated she was heading for the needle-sharp rocks off the Isles of Scilly.

In an era when navigation was the prerogative of the officer class, he was taking a tremendous risk, especially since the fleet navigating officer had calculated a completely different position. According to popular but unsubstantiated belief, the unfortunate man was promptly arrested, charged with Contradicting an Officer and Subversive Navigation, and hanged.[8]

Bombardment of Toulon

Eleven weeks earlier, with the War of Spanish Succession in its seventh year, Prince Eugène of Savoy had decided to abandon an Allied siege of French Toulon. Before leaving, Shovell, commanding the associated seaward blockade, resolved to cripple the French fleet.

At daybreak on 10 August, a flotilla of bomb-ketches lobbed hundreds of shells into the dockyard, destroying numerous warehouses and facilities. They hit very few ships, but the French Admiral panicked and did the job for them by ordering his entire fifty-ship fleet to scuttle itself. This left the Allies in absolute control of the Mediterranean but, with Toulon still in French hands, they had no winter port from which to exercise their power.

Shovell's Last Voyage

On 29 September, leaving a small squadron at Gibraltar, where facilities were too small to service the entire fleet, Shovell sailed for England with fifteen ships-of-the-line and five smaller vessels. He was scheduled to be given a hero's welcome at Portsmouth.

By noon on 22 October, a series of storms and cloudy weather had left the fleet's navigators unsure of their whereabouts. They could be reasonably confident of their north-south position but, in the absence of an accurate timekeeper, could only estimate their east-west location.[9]

The weather was foul, visibility was minimal, a strong wind was blowing, and night would soon be falling. It would have been prudent to delay entering the Channel until dawn, but home was in sight and they had been a long time away. The admiral, who was worried about the possibility of hitting rocks in the dark, consulted the fleet's navigating officers who – relying on dead reckoning and soundings – reached a consensus which placed them safely west of Ile d'Ouessant (Ushant), off the Brittany Peninsula, and well to the south of any hazards.

Shovell detached three ships to Falmouth and decided to forge ahead to Portsmouth with the rest. However, there was a strong northerly set to the current, and it was not long before lookouts on the vanguard spotted breakers off the Scilly Isles – exactly as forecast by the hanged seaman. It was early evening, with enough daylight remaining for them to steer clear of the rocks.

The main fleet, however, did not reach the Scillies until after dark. Most of the ships managed to veer away but, with a fearful crunch, *Association* impaled herself on the rocky ledges of St Agnes and sank, losing her entire crew. Four ships-of-the-line and a frigate did the same. *St George* and *Firebrand* were able to free themselves from the rocks, but damage to the latter was so great that she foundered before reaching safe harbour, drowning another full crew. *Eagle* and *Romney* also went down with all hands, except *Romney*'s quartermaster who was rescued. Total losses were over 2,000.

Aftermath

The Spectator newspaper summed up the disastrous navigational miscalculation, saying, 'It was very unhappy for an Admiral, reputed one of the greatest sea commanders we ever had, to die by an error of his profession.' Shovell's disaster spurred efforts to find a precise means of measuring time at sea, but it was six decades before an accurate chronometer was developed.[10]

FEBRUARY 1744 – WRONG MAN CONVICTED?

In 1740, another major European war had broken out, this time over succession to the throne of the Holy Roman Empire. Austria, Britain and Holland were on one side; Bavaria, France, Naples, Prussia and Spain on the other. Land warfare raged in Silesia, Italy and the Netherlands, while naval campaigns were waged in the Atlantic, Pacific and Indian Oceans, the English Channel, and the Mediterranean, Caribbean and North Seas.

Towards the end of 1743, the British Mediterranean Fleet, commanded by Admiral Thomas Matthews, intercepted a Spanish squadron under Don José de Navarro. They pursued it into the French port of Toulon, where it rendezvoused with a convoy of troop transports. A French fleet under Admiral de la Bruyère de Court was already there. France and Britain were still officially at peace but, to prevent seaborne reinforcement of the Spanish ground forces in Italy, Matthews mounted a loose blockade on Toulon harbour.

As feared, France <u>did</u> join forces with Spain and, on 8 February 1744, twelve Spanish and fifteen French ships-of-the-line broke out of Toulon, with French Vice Admiral Gabaret in the van, Commander-in-Chief de Court in the centre, and Spanish Admiral Navarro to the rear. Twenty-eight ships of the British fleet set off in pursuit. Commander-in-Chief Matthews led the centre, while Rear Admiral Rowley had the van, and Vice Admiral Lestock the rear. The greatest example of tactical disorder in British naval history was about to begin.

The Battle off Toulon

On the 11th they caught up but, after a three-day chase, the three squadrons were spread out and disorganized. It would have taken most of the afternoon to assemble them into conventional line-ahead, making action impossible before the morrow. But Matthews believed the sortie was a diversion, intended to draw him southward while the Spanish troop convoy slipped out and headed eastward.

If he engaged immediately, there would still be time to intercept the slow-moving transports, but if he delayed they would probably reach Italy with their troops. Ignoring the rigidly enforced *Fighting Instructions,* he exercised his initiative, cleared for action and signalled 'Engage the Enemy'. He had the advantage of a light wind, but a heavy swell was running.

Spread out and in random order, Matthews and Rowley fell upon the Franco-Spanish, but Lestock lagged far astern. Either the Admiral's signals were unclear or, more probably, the Vice Admiral – who was on extremely bad terms with him – deliberately chose not to understand them. During six hours of confused combat, Navarro's flagship, the mighty *Real Filipe* of 114 guns, was disabled, while the sixty-gun *Poder* was brilliantly boarded and taken. Victory seemed possible, but then night fell.

Aftermath

The fleets remained in loose contact throughout the 12th and 13th and there were occasional exchanges of gunfire, but without Lestock's squadron, which still held back, Matthews was outnumbered. In consequence the three-day action was inconclusive, with the Franco-Spanish inflicting more damage than they received.

The Royal Navy expected more decisive results than this, so the admiral and his vice were recalled for court martial. In patently unfair verdicts, Matthews was found guilty of 'Divers Notorious Breaches of His Duty', but Lestock, who enjoyed considerable political influence, was acquitted of 'Gross Disobedience and Disregard of Orders'.

APRIL 1756 – INFLEXIBILITY OFF MINORCA

The playwright Voltaire wrote: '*Dans ce pays-ci il est bon de tuer de temps en temps un amiral pour encourager les autres*' (In this country it is proper to kill an admiral from time to time to encourage the others). He was speaking of another politicized English naval court martial, this time in 1757, the second year of the Seven Years War.

In that war, a coalition of Austria, France, Russia, Saxony and Sweden ganged up on Prussia, whose only major ally was Britain. Land campaigns were mounted in Eastern Europe, India and North America, while naval operations – which were another instalment of the long Anglo-French struggle for maritime supremacy – spread globally across the Atlantic and Indian Oceans and into the Mediterranean, Caribbean and South China Seas.

Early in 1756, a French invasion force assembled at Toulon under the command of Admiral Count Augustin de la Gallissonière. British Intelligence reported its objective to be the naval base on Minorca and, in April, Admiral John Byng set sail from England, carrying troops to reinforce the garrison. His ten ships-of-the-line were undermanned and ill-equipped, and his personal correspondence implies he was convinced of failure.

The Battle off Minorca
In mid-April, de la Gallissonière's force – twelve ships-of-the-line and 150 transports – landed troops to besiege the small British garrison in Port Mahon. A few days later, Byng appeared off the island with thirteen ships-of-the-line, having picked up three extra ships at Gibraltar. He enjoyed the weather gauge, and planned to engage the blockading French squadron ship-to-ship in line-ahead.

His imaginative Flag Captain, an early proponent of the mêlée school, suggested they abandon the prescribed formation in order to break through the French centre. However, Byng was a formalist tactician who intended to conform precisely to the hallowed *Fighting Instructions*.

Thus, instead of running parallel to the enemy, he came in at an angle, allowing the French to partially 'cross his tee' (a manoeuvre in which one line crosses the head of another, allowing all friendly guns to bear, while only those of the leading enemy are effective). His five leading ships were hammered, one of them being totally disabled and blocking the advance. At this stage, instead of freeing the uncommitted warships to sail individually around the obstruction, Byng rigidly attempted to continue in line-ahead, giving the virtually undamaged French time to withdraw in good order.

He hung around offshore for four days, making no attempt to communicate with the threatened fortress. Then, having unilaterally decided there was no point in landing the relief battalion since, in his opinion, it was too small to affect the outcome, he turned his squadron around and headed for Gibraltar. Ten days later, French Marshal Louis de Richelieu accepted the surrender of Port Mahon's superb harbour and well equipped naval depot.

Aftermath

The Government needed a scapegoat, so Byng was recalled for court martial but, since he had followed the *Fighting Instructions* to the letter, was tried under an obscure clause in the *Articles of War* which required every officer 'To Do His Utmost'. He was found guilty, but the Court made a unanimous recommendation for mercy. However, lacking political connections – and in spite of huge public outcry – he was executed by firing squad. There was little doubt the charge was accurate, even if the sentence was as draconian as his tombstone asserts:

> To the perpetual disgrace of public Justice. . . . The Honourable John Byng, Admiral of the Blue, fell a martyr to political persecution . . . at a time when courage and loyalty were insufficient guarantees of the honour and lives of naval officers.

August 1782 – Barrels of Rum at Portsmouth

The greatest fleet ever assembled near British shores lay at anchor off Spithead. It included over 300 merchantmen and more than fifty men-of-war, among them, *Royal George* and her sister ship *Victory*, the biggest in the Royal Navy. They were about to sail to relieve Gibraltar from Spanish siege.

Royal George was teeming with over 1200 people. Clumps of townsfolk and well-wishers were saying their last goodbyes on the upper deck while, in the Great Cabin, Rear Admiral Richard Kempenfeldt, whose flag flapped at the masthead in a gentle summer breeze, was entertaining distinguished guests.

Below, the gundecks were sweltering, despite a cross-breeze through open ports on both sides, and the noise was deafening as crewmen haggled with peddlers, hucksters and money-lenders, or socialized with wives, lovers and prostitutes. Although there was a fleet-wide ban on shore leave, the three senior warrant officers – boatswain, master and gunner – had slipped ashore.

Maintenance & Victualling

Royal George had spent fifteen of her twenty-six years of service 'In Ordinary' (laid up), with her hull prey to the ubiquitous teredo ship-boring worm. She badly needed hull repairs and replacement of a water-cock on the starboard side. For those purposes, the fifty-four guns of her starboard batteries had been run to port to tip her over – ignoring the warnings of William Nicholson, Master of the Dockyard, who said that, with 548 tons of stores and eighty-three tons of ammunition on board, the ship would be somewhat unstable.

Just after 9:00 a.m., the cutter *Lark* came alongside to deliver rum for the daily 'tot', which would be issued to every seaman during her long voyage to the Mediterranean. In the absence of the warrant officers who would normally supervise unloading, the dutymen decided not to rig the usual tackle and laboriously haul the heavy barrels up to deck level. Instead, as seamen always will, they took the easy route, passing the barrels through open gunports, which the list had brought down to the level of the cutter's deck. Then, rather than make the effort to haul them across the sloping deck; they lazily stacked them near the entry.

Shortly afterward the carpenter happened to come by and noticed rats and mice scurrying away from water slopping around the deck. Rushing to the quarterdeck, he warned the officer-of-the-day that the weight of stacked casks, added to that of two batteries of guns, had brought the ports perilously close to the water. He was brusquely told to mind his own business and go away.

Minutes later, the conscientious warrant officer returned to report the lower gundeck already flooding. This time Lieutenant Hollingberry snapped irritably, 'Damme, Sir! If you think you can manage the ship better than I can, you had better take command'. The carpenter then reported to Captain Waghorn who ordered the drummer to beat to quarters for 'Righten Ship', but it was too late. While hundreds of seamen struggled to push 108 guns – the massive 32-pounders each weighing 3,500 kilogrammes (3.4 tons) – up the steeply-sloping decks, *Royal George* slipped to the bottom of Portsmouth harbour, taking the admiral and some 900 other souls with her, including the carpenter and the captain's son.

Aftermath

The inevitable court martial, ignoring evidence by seamen-witnesses, brought down a whitewashing verdict:

> It appears to the Court that the ship was not overheeled . . . that the Captain, Officers, and Ship's Company used every exertion to right the ship . . . and the Court is of the opinion, from the short time

between the alarm being given and the sinking of the ship that some material part of her frame gave way, which can only be accounted for by the general decay of her timbers. . . . Captain, Officers and Ship's Company are acquitted of all blame.

Lieutenant Hollingberry survived and was later promoted to Captain, but Captain Waghorn had been disgraced and remained ashore on half-pay until his death five years later. Various attempts at salvage were abandoned, but *Royal George*'s cannon were raised and melted down, to be used in the construction of Nelson's column in Trafalgar Square, London. The wreck sat in the middle of the Royal Navy's main anchorage as a hazard to navigation until blown up by Colonel Paisey of the Royal Engineers in 1842.

JULY 1790 –
BIRTHDAY DEFERRAL AT SVENKSUND FJORD

The fifth Russo-Swedish War began in 1788, when King Gustavus III invaded Russian Finland. Two years later, to pre-empt a Russian assault on his capital, Stockholm, he decided to attack the Russian capital of St Petersburg. Crown Prince Carl set out with a sailing fleet of twenty-two ships-of-the-line and twelve frigates, while Gustavus left independently with an oar-propelled fleet of twenty-seven fighting galleys, nineteen troop transports, and 256 gunboats. They were to rendezvous at Vyborg in Finland, which was to be their base of operations for the campaign.

Gustavus arrived first and disembarked his 14,000 troops, but Carl was intercepted by a Russian fleet. After an indecisive but bloody battle, his ships joined the galleys at Vyborg, where they were blockaded by Russian Admiral Prince Nassau-Siegen. By the end of the month, the Swedes were running short of food and decided they would have to break out or starve.

The Battle of Vyborg
The Swedes started by sending a fireship downwind toward the blockade, but had overlooked the effect of a counter-current, which carried it back against one of their own ships. This caught fire and then collided with a nearby frigate. Both vessels blew up, throwing the Swedish fleet into confusion. Several ships collided and others opened fire upon each other. Those which managed to extricate themselves came under enemy gunfire.

The Russians captured two ships-of-the-line, and the rest of Prince Carl's sailing fleet was practically wiped out, but King Gustavus took advantage of widespread confusion among the sailing ships of both sides to escape with almost all his oared galleys and about ninety gunboats. He found shelter in nearby Svenksund Fjord, protected by the guns of Seaborg fortress.

Nassau-Siegen expected to make short work of the oared squadron and, knowing how much his sovereign, Catherine the Great, loved (and rewarded) extravagant personal tributes, decided to wait six days in order to present her with a victory on her birthday. Meanwhile, he was so confident of winning that he had his flagship modified to provide accommodation suitable for the captured Swedish king.

The Battle of Svenksund

On Catherine's birthday, Nassau-Siegen advanced arrogantly in crescent formation, and with little thought for the quality or disposition of the enemy. But Gustavus had made good use of the respite to prepare his defence. He had 195 ships against the Russian's 151 and arrayed them in a U-shaped curve, spanning the two arms of Svenksund Fjord. The flanks of this strong position were protected by low rocks.

The Russian Admiral's delay, plus his disdain for the enemy, cost him dear. In the greatest sea fight in Scandinavian history, the deadly concentrated fire of expert Swedish gunners devastated his incoming ships. Fifty-three Russian galleys were sunk or captured, with at least 9,500 casualties. The Swedes lost no ships and suffered a mere 300 casualties.

The threat to Stockholm had been removed and, just over a month later, on 14 August 1790, the peace treaty of Areloe restored the *status quo ante*. Another Russo-Swedish War broke out in 1808. In it, oar-propelled warships were employed in action for the last time in history.

JANUARY 1795 – HUSSARS ON THE IJSSELMEER

It was not often that a battle fleet could be threatened by cavalry, so Hendrik Reyntjes, captain of the Dutch warship *Admiraal Piet Heyn* was surprised and amazed when his servant told him, 'A French hussar stood near our ship. I looked out of my porthole, and indeed, there stood an hussar!'

Political Background

Holland faced internal division and external invasion. Rival factions known as *Orangists* (supporters of hereditary rulers called *Stadhouders*), *Regents* (an oligarchy of merchants) and *Patriots* (pro-French revolutionaries) were on the verge of a three-way civil war. Meanwhile, French forces were advancing across the border.

The Revolution and subsequent Terror had taken a toll on the morale, discipline and efficiency of the French military. Much of the officer corps had been exiled or guillotined, colonels being replaced by corporals, generals by sergeants. One of the latter was *Général* Charles Pichegru, whose invading Army of the North bore little resemblance to the super-efficient French forces of the coming Napoleonic age, but was still adequate to push back the badly coordinated coalition of Austrian, British, Hanoverian and Netherlands troops which faced it.

Invasion of the Netherlands

In October, Pichegru was ordered to invade Holland, seize the channel ports, and prevent the Dutch fleet from sailing to join the British Royal Navy. He had to cross three serious water barriers, the Maas, the Waal and the Lek, which heavy autumn rains had turned into raging torrents, while the retreating British had destroyed almost all of the bridges. Then, just as he was considering withdrawal, the weather changed.

Heavy frost froze rivers, lakes and estuaries and the advance was renewed. By the middle of January, Pichegru had crossed all three water obstacles, pushing demoralized coalition forces ahead of him. The Duke of York, commanding the British contingent, abandoned his troops and fled to England, and the *Stadhouder*, Prinz Willem V, followed him into exile.

Before leaving, Prinz Willem ordered *Luitenant-Admiraal* Jan Hendrik van Kinsbergen to assemble the Dutch fleet – fifteen ships-of-the-line, a couple of merchantmen and several smaller vessels – in Holland's inland sea, the Ijsselmeer, where they would be protected against land attack by tidal creeks, salt marshes and mudbanks. They were to sail for England as soon as he had negotiated terms with London. Unwittingly, the *Stadhouder* was sending them into a trap.

The Ijsselmeer was frozen, so the fleet anchored in the still-open Marsdiep (a strait between the North Sea and Ijsselmeer). Just after it arrived, a fierce north-westerly gale came in. The fleet sheltered in the lee of Texel Island, while driving snow and sleet brought visibility down to zero. When the weather finally cleared, the Marsdiep had also frozen, and its exit was blocked by an immense ice-pack stretching from shore to shore and which was quite impassable.

Attack on the Dutch Fleet

This intelligence reached Pichegru on 17 January 1795. He immediately ordered Général de Brigade Johan Willem de Winter, a Dutchman in French service, to secure the Dutch fleet's surrender. De Winter dispatched a mixed battalion of infantry, cavalry and horse-artillery under *Commandant* (Major) Louis Joseph Lahure, a twenty-three-year-old

Belgian émigré. They arrived late on 22 January and bivouacked for the night.

Seeing their campfires, Captain Reyntjes, oldest and most senior officer in the Dutch fleet and in temporary command of it, prepared to spike all guns and scuttle the ships, but around midnight a dispatch rider galloped in to report that the Patriots had taken control of the government and ordered a pause in hostilities. But for this timely ceasefire there might have been an epochal fight between a land army and a fleet, but only after the arrival of heavy siege artillery and infantry scaling-ladders.

In the morning, a frost-filled fog hung over the Marsdiep, and news of the truce had not yet reached detached forward French commanders such as Lahure. Uncertain as to how his small force could compel a battle fleet to surrender – the puny 6-pounder guns would barely dent the massive timbers of men-of-war, while ladderless infantry had no hope of scaling their tumblehome sides – he decided on a bold course of action.

He would try to intimidate them with threats of greater force coming up behind, so he set out onto the ice with a small squadron of Hussars and a large Tricolore flag, wondering what his reception would be. Because of the way they were dispersed, even if he could keep away from the broadside of one icebound Dutch ship, his force was likely to be in the sights of another, although the thick fog would provide some protection.

Subsequent French military propagandists sponsored the unlikely story of 'Ragged men . . . thundering on their horses across the ice to capture with naked swords the battlefleet of Holland'. In fact, it was a lot more mundane. Twenty-one years later, by which time he was himself a general and a baron, Lahure tried to set the record straight:

> I departed immediately with a company of *tirailleurs* in wagons and a squadron of light cavalry; before dawn I had taken position in the dunes. When the ships saw us, they prepared their defences. I sent some of my *tirailleurs* ahead, and followed with the rest of my forces. The fleet was taken. The sailors received us with good grace on board . . . this is the true story of the capture of the Dutch fleet, devised and executed by a twenty-three-year-old Chef de Bataillion.

Lahure does not say any fighting took place, and the truth seems to lie somewhere between the two versions, perhaps in the scenario advanced by Erik Durschmeid in his book *The Weather Factor*. There he suggests that Lahure rode up to *Admiraal Piet Heyn*, where Captain Reyntjes[11] stood on the quarterdeck, looking down on a young officer, backed up by little more than the French revolutionary flag, but confidently yelling 'I demand your immediate surrender'.

Knowing about the ceasefire, the captain calmly replied, 'Why don't we discuss such serious matters over dinner aboard my ship?' There, they reached an oral agreement to maintain the status quo until clear orders arrived from both sides. Five days later, the Dutch crews swore an oath to comply with French orders and maintain naval discipline, but were allowed to remain under the Dutch flag.

AUGUST 1798 –
INADEQUATE PRECAUTIONS AT ABOUKIR BAY

The French naval and military armament converging on Mediterranean ports of embarkation was too large to be kept secret. British Intelligence advised that rumours of a descent on Egypt by Général Napoléon Bonaparte need not be taken seriously, but Admiral Lord Saint Vincent was not so sure.

He sent Rear Admiral Horatio Nelson to see if he could find out what was going on. Nelson determined that French *Vice-Amiral* François Paul Brueys d'Aigaïlliers had assembled an armada of warships and troop transports at five or more ports, but as for their destination, he reported, 'They order their matters so well in France that all is secret'.

Nelson Plays Hide-and-Seek

The British Admiral was about to endure the most frustrating period of his career. In mid-May, a storm drove his squadron away from its patrol area. After repairing serious storm damage, he returned to find empty harbours. By a freak of nature, the gale had missed the embarkation ports, and Brueys had taken advantage of the situation to leave. It seems impossible that a large, unwieldy, slow-moving force could have avoided detection and destruction, but Nelson followed actual and rumoured sightings of the French fleet for eleven weeks.

He was sailing at almost twice the speed of the lumbering transports and following a shorter course. As a result, the two fleets crossed during the night, without sighting one another, although French lookouts reported hearing strange ships' bells in the darkness. Reaching Alexandria, Nelson found another empty harbour.

Not realizing he had made faster passage, he assumed Brueys must have diverted to the Adriatic or the Aegean, or perhaps landed troops in Syria. So he set off along the coast, hoping to intercept. Once again, the fleets almost met. Brueys' leading frigate *La Junon* reached Alexandria barely two hours after Nelson's last ship, the brig *Mutine*, sailed away.

Finding nothing off the Syrian and Anatolian coasts, and with water and supplies running dangerously low, Nelson reprovisioned at Syracuse.

Then a merchant captain reported having sighted the French four weeks earlier, heading for Egypt. Nelson set a southerly course again, sending *Alexander* and *Swiftsure* ahead to reconnoitre. When they reached Alexandria, the Tricolore was waving over the domes and minarets of the city, but spirits sank when lookouts reported only transports and merchantmen in the anchorage.

Sir John Ross, one of *Orion*'s officers, wrote, 'I do not recollect to have felt so utterly helpless, or out of spirits, as when we sat down to dinner.' Then *Zealous*, cruising along the coast, reported sighting warship topmasts across the low sandbars of Aboukir Bay. Ross continues, 'All sprang from their seats, and only staying to drink a bumper to our success, we were in a moment on deck.' Aboard *Vanguard*, Nelson signalled 'Prepare for Battle' and, with improved appetite, sat down to finish his own meal.

French Dispositions and Nelson's Plans

Throughout the eighteenth century, and especially during the American War of Independence, French naval commanders had often anchored their capital ships close to the shore, in line-ahead with their extremities protected by gun batteries on shore. This disposition was virtually unassailable, since it presented a solid wall of guns to any enemy approaching from its seaward side. Moreover, being at moorings they needed no men for sail-handling, and could assign all the crew to combat.

Nelson saw that Brueys had adopted this defensive formation, but noted the French Admiral had made four serious and ultimately fatal omissions:

1   He had not detached guard frigates to patrol offshore and warn of an approaching enemy.

2   He had not anchored within range of friendly shore batteries.

3   He had failed to stretch cables between each ship, and from the end ships to the shore, thus preventing an enemy passing through or around the line.

4   He was not close enough to shoal water to prevent an enemy sailing inshore of the line.

Also, thinking themselves safe on the landward side, the French had cluttered their larboard batteries with stores and other paraphernalia which could not be cleared rapidly for action. Nelson may have anticipated this because the French Royal Navy had made the same mistake off Dominica in 1782, and the Revolutionary Navy was less efficient. Moreover, although Nelson had no way of knowing it, almost half the French crews were enjoying a 'run ashore'.

The sea was calm and a favourable breeze was blowing so, despite approaching darkness, Nelson decided to speed in before the French had time to prepare. He had rehearsed this tactical situation over and over again with his captains. The line would divide, some of them sailing around the head of the line to attack from landward (where the guns were unmanned and unloaded) while others closed in from seaward to engage them two-on-one from opposite sides, gradually moving along the line and blasting each ship in sequence.

As they moved in, seventy-four-gun *Culloden* humiliatingly perched herself on a sandbar. Fifty-gun *Leander* paused to offer assistance, further reducing the already inferior British firepower. Brueys then had 1,178 guns to Nelson's 888 – almost a thirty-three per cent advantage in fire-power – but the disparity in weight of metal was even greater, because French main batteries fired 40-pound balls, while the British guns were 32-pounders.

The Battle of Aboukir Bay (The Nile)

The speed and ferocity of the attack took the French by surprise, as did its timing, with barely two hours of daylight left. All night long the slaughter went on, with 2,000 guns flashing and roaring away in a narrow strip little more than a kilometre long. It was hot work on the gun decks, and John Nicol, one of *Goliath*'s seamen, reported he was 'much indebted to the gunner's wife, who gave her husband and me a drink of wine every now and then which lessened our fatigue much'.

By about 8:30 p.m., the five leading French ships had been over-whelmed. Half an hour later, Admiral Brueys suffered a ghastly wound, but refused to be carried below, saying, 'A French Admiral should die on his quarterdeck'. At almost the same moment, Nelson was struck by a piece of langridge and temporarily blinded by the flow of blood from a scalp wound. Shortly after midnight, the gunfire began to slacken as French ships were progressively knocked out.

Aftermath

When dawn broke, John Nicol reports: 'I went on deck to view the state of the Fleets, and what an awful sight it was. The whole Bay was covered with dead bodies, mangled, wounded and scorched, not a bit of clothes on them except their trousers'.

On the French side, six ships had surrendered and were wearing the Union Flag above the Tricolore; four others had burned, sunk, or blown up; three had been disabled and run aground. Due to the French practice of firing high, most of the British had suffered rigging-damage, but only three had been hull-damaged.

Contre-Amiral (Rear Admiral) Villeneuve managed to slip away with two 40-gun frigates, plus 74-gun *Généreux* and 80-gun *Guillaume Tell*. These were the only capital ships left to France in the entire Mediterranean, giving Britain absolute mastery of the sea. Nelson himself said, 'Victory is not a name strong enough for such a scene . . . it was a conquest.' However, it would not have been so easy if Brueys had taken a few simple precautions.

OCTOBER 1803 –
UNCHARTED WATERS OFF TRIPOLI

Piracy and the slave trade had long been major sources of revenue for states on the Barbary Coast. The trade was considered a respectable profession, and the rulers of coastal towns and villages – variously titled Dey or Bey, and Bashaw or Pasha – sponsored local pirates, known as Corsairs, under a licensing system which gave them a fixed percentage of prizes, loot and ransom money.

During the sixteenth and seventeenth centuries, Corsair galleys and sailing ships ranged far afield, terrorizing shipping in the Mediterranean and along the Atlantic seaboard of Europe. Between 1569 and 1616 they took 466 ships off the British Isles alone, and in 1631 they sacked Baltimore in Ireland, taking its entire population away. Only a lucky few were ransomed – 20,000 Christians were sold in Algiers' slave bazaar during the first half of the seventeenth century, and there were many other markets.

American Shipping Attacked
By the late eighteenth century, most of the war-torn European nations found it easier to pay 'tribute' (protection money) than to try to stamp out the trade. Only the French and British Mediterranean fleets were powerful enough to win their merchants a degree of immunity. However, with its Declaration of Independence, not only did the fledgling American Republic lose the protection of the Royal Navy, but Britain actively encouraged Corsair attacks on vessels wearing the rebel Stars and Stripes.

After suffering substantial losses off the coasts of Portugal, Spain and North Africa, Congress reluctantly decided to purchase immunity. Even then, American shippers soon discovered Corsairs had no compunction about breaking treaties and capturing ships whenever they felt like it. In September 1800, US Navy Captain William Bainbridge said, bitterly,

'Had we but ten or twelve frigates and sloops in these seas, we should not experience these mortifying degradations.'

Shortly afterward, the Bashaw of Tripoli demanded increased tribute. By this time, the United States was already paying one-fifth of its annual revenue as gifts, ransom and tribute to the four Barbary States. Enough was enough, and the increase was refused, leading the indignant Bashaw to declare war, but the Americans were no longer toothless. In 1794, Congress had passed a 'Bill to Provide a Naval Armament'. Half a dozen powerful frigates had been commissioned, and their crews had been 'blooded' during an undeclared naval war with France.

The United States Strikes Back

President Thomas Jefferson responded to the Bashaw's declaration by dispatching Commodore Richard Dale with orders to protect American shipping and compel the Barbary States to observe existing treaties. The mission started well enough, but an attempt to blockade Tripoli harbour failed. After six months, Dale sailed away with little accomplished. Congress then resolved 'More effectually to protect the commerce of the United States against the Barbary Powers' and sent a second force under Commodore Richard Morris, who only mounted a lackadaisical and ineffectual blockade of Tripoli. He was recalled, court-martialled for dereliction of duty, and dismissed.

Jefferson then dispatched a third and more powerful squadron, under Commodore Edward Preble, flying his command pendant on the 44-gun frigate *Constitution*. Preble sent Captain William Bainbridge, with the 35-gun frigate *Philadelphia*, ahead of his main force to resume the blockade of Tripoli.

Decoyed onto the Rocks

On 31 October 1803, Bainbridge sighted an inward-bound blockade runner and set off in hot pursuit. Exploiting home waters, the Tripolitanian skipper scooted around numerous uncharted rocks, luring his deeper-draughted pursuer to follow. Under full sail, *Philadelphia* wedged herself onto a reef with bows raised two metres (six feet) into the air.

The *Philadelphia*'s crew did everything possible to refloat their ship. Guns, ammunition, anchors and stores were hurled overboard. The foremast was jettisoned. Even part of the stern was hacked off. But the frigate held stubbornly to her perch.

When Tripolitanian gunboats swarmed out for the *coup de grâce*, Bainbridge tried to disable his ship by flooding the magazines and drilling holes in the hull. Then he struck his colours and went into captivity accompanied by 314 officers and crew.[12]

February 1813 –
Impetuosity in Chesapeake Bay

During the war of 1812, superiority of the British Royal Navy forced the United States into a policy of commerce raiding, its few naval ships being reinforced by numerous privateers. However, Britain was preoccupied by its war with Napoleonic France and tended to send second rate units to the Americas. This allowed the generally well designed, stoutly built, and expertly crewed American ships to win a few startling victories against overconfident and complacent British vessels.

One such event occurred in February 1813. During a chance encounter between two sloops-of-war off the Brazilian coast, USS *Hornet* sank HMS *Peacock* after a mere eleven minutes of combat. *Hornet*'s commander, James Lawrence, was rewarded with promotion to command the 38-gun frigate USS *Chesapeake* being refitted at Boston, where she took aboard a green and untried crew.

Lying outside Boston Harbour as part of the British blockade, was HMS *Shannon*. Her commander, Philip Brooke, was so intent on gaining honour and prestige through a single-ship action that he had even forsworn prize money, refusing to capture merchant ships, because sending off prize crews would reduce his fighting strength. On 1 June 1813, he issued a challenge to *Chesapeake*. Convinced of American moral superiority, and wanting to add to the lustre of his victory off Brazil, Lawrence agreed to a frigate-to-frigate, gun-to-gun meeting.

The two ships had identical firepower, each being armed with thirty-eight 18-pounder guns, but the American was slightly larger and had a crew of 379 versus *Shannon*'s 329. In contrast to Lawrence's recently recruited crew, most of Brooke's men had served with him for seven years.

The Frigate Duel

As soon as he saw *Chesapeake* coming out, Brooke moved out of sight of land and took in sail to wait for the American to approach. He told his gunners to load with double charges of either two balls, or a single ball with grapeshot, and to aim for the hull rather than try to bring down masts and rigging. He had also mounted 9-pounder carronades on his quarter-deck, from where they could destroy the opponent's wheel.

Lawrence knew the veteran British crew could probably outmanoeuvre his people, so he impetuously drove downwind directly at *Shannon*. He was moving too quickly to pull up alongside and sailed past his enemy. With most ships this would not have mattered, as little damage was usually done by the first broadside of ranging shots. However, Brooke had devoted his command to preparing for this moment, training his gun captains to lay their weapons accurately and fire rapidly in total silence so that orders could be clearly heard.

He waited until *Chesapeake* was so close that a miss would be impossible, then ordered each gun to fire at the American's foremost gunport as soon as it came to bear. Every shot struck home, raking the American from stem to stern.

Thanks to their windward position, the sharpshooters in *Chesapeake*'s fighting tops could not see the British due to smoke from their own artillery drifting towards *Shannon*. The latter's marines, however, had a clear field of fire on the enemy decks, killing or wounding two-thirds of the deck personnel, including Lawrence who was struck in the hip. Then the quarterdeck carronades destroyed the American's helm and, at about the same time, her forestays were cut away, causing her headsails to collapse. Out of control, she exposed her stern to British fire.

Badly wounded, she drifted stern first into *Shannon*, about fifteen metres (fifty feet) abaft the bow. Brooke immediately leapt aboard, followed by a fifty-strong boarding party. As deck fighting began, Lawrence was struck in the groin by a musket ball and was carried below. Lying there in agony he called out 'Leave me. Go on deck. Tell the men to fire faster and not give up the ship. While I live the colours shall wave.'

By this time the two ships had worked apart, but about sixty British held the upper deck and the fight was effectively over. Suddenly, three Americans rushed at Brooke. He ran his sword through the first, but the second clubbed him with a musket butt, while the third split his skull open to the brains with the slash of a cutlass. Both remaining Americans were promptly killed by furious British sailors.

Thirteen minutes after the first shot was fired, *Chesapeake* struck. A small British Union Flag was raised, and the firing ended. But then *Shannon*'s First Lieutenant started to replace it with a larger ensign. A carronade gunner saw the first flag going down, assumed the Americans had retaken their ship, and shot, killing the officer and three British seamen with 'friendly fire'. Altogether, eighty-three Britons and 148 Americans had been killed or wounded in thirteen minutes of battle, a toll higher than Nelson's *Victory* suffered in six hours at Trafalgar.

Aftermath

Chesapeake was taken to Halifax as a prize. Incredibly, Brooke recovered from his horrendous injury, although his naval career was over. Lawrence died of his wound and was buried at Halifax, disinterred, reburied at Boston, dug up again, and finally laid to rest in New York. However, he had achieved immortality because his phrase 'Don't give up the ship' became the rallying cry of the United States Navy.

JULY 1816 –
CALLOUS INHUMANITY OFF SENEGAL

A huge canvas by French master painter Theodore Géricault created a storm of controversy at the 1819 Paris Exhibition. Not only did *The Raft of the Medusa* depict an actual event with scandalous political implications, but many regarded the painting as a subversive attack on the much-cherished 'honour' of the newly reconstituted Royal French Navy.

Three years earlier, four of its ships had left for West Africa, planning to re-establish control over Senegal and the important trading base of Saint Louis, which had been under British occupation since the Napoleonic Wars. The flagship, the 44-gun frigate *Méduse (Medusa)*, was commanded by *Capitaine de Frégate* Hugues Duroy de Chaumareys – a political appointee, who had never captained a ship and had not been to sea at all for twenty-five years.

Grounding
Being the fastest ship in the convoy, *Méduse* soon outdistanced *Argus* and *Loire*. Little *Echo* managed to keep up during the first day, but disappeared overnight leaving the frigate alone. Since de Chaumareys was an incompetent seaman, he delegated a passenger named Richefort (Harbour Master-designate of Saint Louis) to take over navigation on his behalf. Richefort does not seem to have been very good at these duties either. The ship almost ran aground while crossing the Bay of Biscay, and missed its landfall at Madeira by 160 kilometres (100 miles).

Governor-elect Colonel Julien-Desiré Schmaltz then ordered de Chaumareys to head for Saint Louis by the shortest possible route, even though this meant hugging a dangerous shoreline normally avoided by mariners. By 2 July, the water around the ship was becoming muddy, but Richefort reassured a worried passenger saying, 'My dear sir, we know our business. Attend to yours and be quiet. I have twice passed the Arguin Bank. I have sailed upon the Red Sea, and as you can see I am not drowned.'

Shortly afterward, *Méduse* shuddered, listed to port, and came to an abrupt stop. In spite of his boast, Richefort had run her onto the notorious but well charted Arguin Bank, which lies north of Cap Blanc (modern Ras Nouadhibou), and was only about 100 kilometres (sixty miles) from Saint Louis. The grounding was not serious, but both governor and captain refused to jettison any guns or cargo in order to float *Méduse* off. At one point she drifted away on her own, but the inept captain promptly sailed her back, this time damaging her rudder.

Setting off for Saint Louis

The sea was calm, and de Chaumareys decided to leave a fifteen-man anchor watch on board while the rest rowed to Saint Louis, coming back later to lift off the men and cargo. Passengers and crew totalled 400, including administrative personnel, soldiers for the occupation force, merchants, adventurers and prostitutes. After the boats were filled to capacity, the surplus would board a raft to be towed behind them.

Proper execution of de Chaumareys' plan could have preserved the lives of all. The ship was in no immediate danger. There was plenty of time to draw up a roster for the boats, and for shipwrights and carpenters to build a large and seaworthy raft. Instead, there was a complete breakdown of naval, military and civil discipline. It became a matter of every man for himself. Captain and Governor were among the first of 250 passengers to fight their way onto one of *Méduse*'s six boats. They then pushed off from the frigate's sides with considerably less than their full capacity, refusing to return for more.

The hastily-constructed raft of masts, spars and timbers was lashed together in a crude unseamanlike manner. Its planking was insecure and there was no protection from sun or waves. With an area of about seventy square metres (750 square feet), it could reasonably accommodate twenty to twenty-five people, but was crammed to overflowing with 149. De Chaumareys had squeezed on six barrels of wine and two casks of water, but only enough food for one meal. He had provided no charts, instruments, spars or sails.

On 5 July they set off. Two men were too intoxicated to board the raft and were left behind with the anchor watch. At first, all went according to plan but, before they had gone fifteen kilometres (ten miles) the overloaded raft sank below the surface and became almost impossible to tow.

Rafters Abandoned

With the Governor's consent, de Chaumareys ordered the tow ropes cut, stranding the rafters some eighty-five kilometres (fifty-three miles) from shore. Not one officer or man protested this inhumane betrayal of their shipmates and fellow countrymen. On the contrary, survivors report that the cry '*Nous les abandonnons*' (We're abandoning them) was obeyed with alacrity as it passed from boat to boat.

The rush and scramble to desert the ship had been accomplished with so little forethought or discipline that the only mariners on the raft were a young midshipman and ten seamen. Between them they rigged a crude mast and tried to sail the clumsy vessel shoreward.

When dawn broke, a dozen passengers were found trapped between the loose timbers, crushed and mangled to death. Several more had been suffocated in the press of bodies, and others had disappeared, presumably fallen overboard and drowned. But worse was to come. Next night the wine barrels were raided and another sixty were killed in a drunken brawl.

A day later – horribly burned by the African sun, bruised and battered by the raft's shifting timbers, lips split and bleeding for lack of moisture, and stomachs aching for lack of food – they resorted to cannibalizing the overnight dead, mixing human flesh with that of flying fish which had landed on board.

By the morning of the fourth day, only forty-eight remained alive. One of them discovered a still-unbroached wine cask and they had another donnybrook in which eighteen were killed. Three more died during the following night, leaving twenty-seven to greet the dawn.

After surviving another day and night, the fifteen strongest deemed the other twelve too weak to survive and threw them overboard in order to lighten the load and conserve drinking water. Six days later the raft was sighted by British brig HMS *Argus*. The fifteen murderers were weak but alive. However, five of them died shortly after being landed at Saint Louis.

Aftermath
By the time *Méduse*'s boats reached the safety of Saint Louis, Governor and Captain had simply assumed the rafters would have died, and did nothing to arrange their rescue. They seem to have forgotten all about the anchor watch. Weeks went by before anyone thought of organizing a rescue mission to lift them off. When it finally reached *Méduse*, fifty-three days after she was abandoned, fourteen of the seamen were dead, and the remaining three were crazed by hunger and thirst. Before they could be shipped home, two of them died and the third was murdered. Returning to France, de Chaumareys was court-martialled but, thanks to his royal connections, acquitted.

NOVEMBER 1820 –
CETACEAN REPRISAL IN MID-PACIFIC

Two beaver hats and thirty pounds was the price demanded for Nantucket Island by its indigenous inhabitants when they sold it to a consortium of Massachusetts men in 1659. Thirteen years later, looking for a profitable source of revenue, the islanders brought in whalers to teach them how to catch and process the huge marine mammals. Each cadaver yielded lamp oils, lubricants, candles, pharmaceuticals, perfumes and corset staves, making this one of the world's most important and profitable industries.

By 1800, Nantucket was one of the richest enclaves in the United States and proudly proclaimed itself 'Whaling Capital of the World', although the title was hotly contested by New Bedford on the nearby mainland. Eventually, over-exploitation depleted the local population and hunters had to venture deeper into the oceans to find whale pods.

In 1820, Captain George Pollard took the 238-ton *Essex* around Cape Horn and further into the Pacific Ocean than any Nantucket whaler had previously ventured. By November, the crew had caught several whales and processed them to fill more than 1,000 oil barrels. Under their profit-sharing articles, each looked forward to a short voyage and a relatively wealthy return.

Encounter With a Whale[13]

Early on the morning of Monday 20 November 1820, spouts were sighted and Pollard set a course to intercept. Nearing the pod, he heaved-to and launched three dories with six-man crews. Only the steward and cabin boy remained on board. First mate Owen Chase harpooned one of the females, but her thrashing tail damaged his boat, forcing him to return to the ship. Meanwhile, Captain Pollard and second mate Mathew Joy chased after other females.

Shortly after Chase came aboard, a huge male suddenly breached, spouted and swam at high speed directly towards the ship. The cabin boy, who had the helm, tried to steer off, but the eighty-ton monster rammed *Essex* at the waterline just abaft the bow. Owen Chase reports: 'The ship brought up as suddenly and violently as if she had struck a rock and trembled for a few seconds like a leaf. We looked at each other with perfect amazement, deprived of the power of speech.'

The whale surfaced beside the ship, shook himself and dived again, making the whole ship shudder as he passed under and knocked off its twelve-inch false keel. Then he swam off and thrashed around on the surface for a while, before turning to charge again, this time with his head well above water. As he neared, the crew noticed his skull bore many battle scars.[14] Owen Chase says, 'He was approaching with twice his ordinary speed. . . . The surf flew in all directions about him, and his course was marked by a white foam of a rod in width (five metres or sixteen feet), which he made with the continual violent thrashing of his tail.' The force of his attack threw everyone on board to the deck.

Perhaps sounding, but probably mortally wounded, the whale then disappeared below the surface. Chase signalled Pollard and Joy to return but, before they arrived, *Essex* rolled over onto her beam-ends. As his dory drew alongside the stricken vessel the captain hailed, 'My God Mr Chase, what is the matter?', to which the mate replied, 'We've been stove by a whale!' Pollard ordered the masts cut away, after which *Essex* rode upright and higher in the water.

She stayed afloat for two days, during which the crew gathered all the water and supplies they could, along with navigational instruments and tables. Using planks cut from *Essex*'s deck, they heightened the gunwales of the dories by eighteen inches (forty-six centimetres), and they adapted spars to form schooner-type masts for each dory.

Small Boat Odyssey

When the ship finally foundered, Pollard wanted to head for Tahiti, a mere two weeks' sail away, but stronger-willed Chase persuaded the crew it was inhabited by cannibals. In fear of being eaten, they insisted on heading for Easter Island, some 3,500 kilometres (2,100 miles) away. To reach there they would have to find the trade winds, which should be blowing somewhere south and east of their position.

After twenty-two gruelling days, with food supplies exhausted, they made landfall on uninhabited Henderson Island. There they found water, and feasted on a limited supply of sea-birds and eggs. There was not enough to sustain twenty hungry males for more than a few days so, leaving behind three men who wanted to take the chance of being picked up, the three boats set off again.

A series of storms blew them too far south and, rather than beat into contrary winds, they decided to pass by Easter Island and continue another 4,000 kms (2,500 miles) to mainland South America. A few days later, Chase's dory disappeared during a gale and, a week after that, another storm separated the remaining boats, one of which was never seen again.

In Chase's boat, they were all on the brink of starvation, and too weak to hold a stable course. The first crewman to die was thrown overboard. But when a second expired the crew elected to feed themselves rather than toss another meal to the sharks. Chase reports: 'We separated his limbs from his body, and cut all the flesh from the bones; after which we opened the body, took out the heart, and then closed it again – sewed it up as decently as we could, and committed it to the sea.'

The meat lasted them ten days, but did them little good. Because its source had died of starvation, it lacked the fat which is essential for human digestion and nutrition. Chase and two other survivors were finally rescued by *Indian*, an English brig. After eighty-nine days at sea in an open boat, they were dehydrated, starving, burned by sun and sea salt, beards caked with dried human blood, and close to insanity.

Aboard Pollard's boat, some crewmen proposed cannibalism but were violently opposed by the Captain. However, unlike Chase's boat, there were no natural deaths and eventually it became apparent they would all die unless they ate someone to sustain the others. Pollard reluctantly agreed to draw lots, to choose the order in which sacrificial victims would successively be shot.

Five days after Chase's rescue, Pollard and one other were found by a fellow Nantucket whaler. They were sitting on the floor of their dory, surrounded by human meat and bones, sucking the ribs of a shipmate. Both violently resisted giving up these marrow bones until long after being fed and comforted by the whaler's crew. Pollard had stuffed the chewed bones of his young cousin Owen into his pockets for proper burial at home.

Aftermath
Their journey of almost 4,500 nautical miles (8,400 kms; 5,200 miles) had been longer than Captain Bligh's famous voyage in 1789, and five times that of Shackleton's 1916 epic passage. After the five survivors reached Valparaiso, a ship was sent to Henderson Island to rescue the three sailors left there. They were still alive, but only just. Years later, according to Nantucket legend, George Pollard was asked if he had known a man called Owen Coffin. Instead of saying he had been his cousin and shipmate, the captain gave the macabre reply 'Know 'im? Why bless you I ate 'im!'

OCTOBER 1827 –
MISUNDERSTANDINGS AT NAVARINO BAY

In 1822, Greek patriots renounced Turkish rule. In response, Sultan Mahmud II occupied Chios and killed or enslaved its entire population. However, the Greeks were not intimidated, and liberal-minded volunteers from across Europe flocked to fight with them. Early in 1825, the Sultan called for help from quasi-independent Egypt. In response, Governor Muhammad Ali sent his son, Ibrahim *Reis-Pasha*[15], with a fleet and 5,000 crack troops. After quelling the rebels on Crete and Cyprus, Ibrahim invaded Morea.

European Intervention
In July 1827, Britain, France and Russia demanded an armistice and Turco-Egyptian withdrawal. When they were rejected, the three governments sent naval squadrons to the region. Early in September, the senior Allied commander, British Admiral Sir Edward Codrington, accompanied by French Admiral Comte Henri de Rigny, sailed into the Bay of Navarino for a meeting with Ibrahim. Their orders were to enforce the armistice, but avoid hostilities, except in self-defence. Although the talks were friendly, Ibrahim insisted he must obey the Sultan's order to invade the rebel stronghold on Hydra.

Codrington said the Allies would sink the Egyptian fleet if it attempted to leave, and Ibrahim asked for time to consult the Sultan. The admirals gave him three weeks, and de Rigny sailed off to patrol the Aegean, leaving Codrington to maintain the blockade. Then Ibrahim learned of an attack by an independent mercenary in the Corinthian Gulf and mistakenly assumed the Allies had violated the truce. After attempting to break out, but being turned back by Codrington, he landed his troops and began 'ethnic cleansing' Morea. This was the first of two misunderstandings.

Shortly afterward, the Russian squadron arrived and the French returned, bringing the Allied fleet to full strength. Hoping their presence would be enough to stop the carnage, the admirals decided to enter the harbour for further negotiations. A frigate was sent, under flag of truce, to advise Ibrahim of their peaceful intent.

The Situation in the Bay

On returning, it reported that eighty or so armed Ottoman transports lay at the back of the Bay of Navarino, protected by the powerful Turco-Egyptian fleet of three line-of-battle ships, four double-banked 64-gun frigates, and fifteen 48-gun frigates. These vessels were defensively deployed in a long horseshoe formation, with a second line of about fifty smaller warships behind. Their flanks were protected by shore batteries and fire-ships, and their broadsides covered the Narrows at the harbour entrance.

The Allies had twenty-seven vessels and, although eleven of these were ships-of-the-line, their 1300 guns were outnumbered by the 2,000 guns of the Ottoman fleet, not to mention the shore batteries. However, they expected to negotiate rather than fight so, although the frigate reported Ibrahim's artillery run out and ready for action, they decided to emphasize their non-belligerent stance by exposing themselves to the Ottoman broadsides.

Unintended Battle

Codrington ordered his Marine Band to play cheerful music as they sailed in to anchor in the middle of the Egyptian horseshoe. As a precaution, they cleared for action, but guns were kept inboard with ports in the half-open fine-weather cruising position. Then came the second misunderstanding, followed by rapid escalation.

A British frigate sent its cutter to ask one of the Turkish ships to make space by moving its anchorage. The boat was unarmed, but a trigger-happy Turkish marine decided it was hostile and fired a single musket shot. His aim was good and he hit the boat's officer. In return the frigate's marines gave covering musket fire and, on hearing their fusillade, an overexcited Egyptian cannoneer fired at the French flagship, which replied with a full broadside.

Like Nelson's engagement at Aboukir Bay, this was a duel between anchored gun batteries, rather than a conventional fleet action. Muzzle-to-muzzle, the two sides blazed away at each other with heavy guns and carronades. When the smoke cleared, the Anglo-Franco-Russian Alliance – with fewer, but larger and more heavily-gunned ships – had sunk or destroyed more than three-quarters of the Turco-Egyptians, inflicting tremendous loss of life, but suffering fewer than 700 casualties themselves.

Aftermath

The Battle of Navarino Bay was the Ottoman Empire's worst maritime defeat since Lepanto in 1571. In a stationary fight that involved neither tactics nor sailing skill, nominally friendly powers had destroyed, or damaged beyond repair, more than sixty warships. One of the bloodiest naval encounters ever, it ensured Greek independence and left Russia with absolute naval supremacy in the Black Sea. It was also the last major battle fought exclusively by wooden-hulled sailing vessels with smooth-bore cannon – for the age of steam-driven iron ships with rifled guns was dawning.

For their part in humiliating the Turks and liberating Greece, Admirals de Rigny and de Heyden were fêted and honoured by their respective governments, but the unfortunate Codrington had forfeited his career. His victory was diplomatically inexpedient for Britain, whose policy was to support Turkey as a bulwark against Russian expansion.

FEBRUARY 1847 –
NO CELESTIAL OBSERVATION (1)

A hundred and forty years after Shovell's disaster, mariners were still having problems with dead reckoning. One of these was Captain Parsons of the steamer *Tweed*, which left Havana, Cuba on 9 February 1847 bound for Vera Cruz, Mexico. She carried a large cargo of quicksilver, a supply of coals for the bunkers of British warship HMS *Hermes*, and 151 passengers and crew.

Throughout the 10th and 11th, it blew heavily from the north, the weather being so thick that no observations could be taken. At 3:30 a.m. on the 12th, the forecastle lookout screamed 'Breakers ahead!' Captain Parsons, who was on deck, immediately ordered helm hard-a-starboard and engines full-astern, but to no avail. Not only were wind and sea moving onshore, but *Tweed* was carrying foresail, fore-trysail, and fore-topsail which overpowered the engines and drove her forward.

She hit the reef with such force that her engines broke off their mountings and were unable to back her off. For thirty-five minutes, while she rolled and struck, several passengers and crewmen were washed overboard. Then they managed to launch two cutters on the lee side, but so many crowded on board that they foundered.

Minutes later, *Tweed* broke into two parts which drifted into smooth water inside the reef. Some managed to stay on board until the sections sank, others floated by clinging to spars and flotsam. When dawn broke, it was discovered that a strong current had taken the ship some fifty kilometres (thirty miles) off course to strike one of the Alcranes. This group of rocky islets are the summits of a reef or spit twenty-four kilometres (fifteen miles) long and nineteen kilometres (twelve miles) wide; lying about 115 kilometres (seventy-one miles) off the Yucatan coast.

Navigators consider the spit the most dangerous in the Gulf of Mexico, especially since the nearby currents are so powerful and capricious that they can carry vessels up to sixty-five kilometres (forty miles) off course in a single day. *Tweed* was fortunate to have struck at low tide. At high water, that section of the reef would had been totally submerged, leaving no foothold for survivors.

Aftermath

Seventy-two people had perished, but an equal number were still alive, most of them in their night clothes. As the tide rose, they moved to higher ground. They had several casks of wine and brandy, but no drinking water, and barely managed to survive for three days on raw fish and lobsters. Then they found a box of Lucifer matches and, after drying them out, were able to light fires for warmth and cooking.

The ship's engineers contrived an apparatus to distil sea water, after which they were able to make biscuits using a barrel of oatmeal and three casks of flour recovered from the wreck. They managed to patch up a small boat, and the Chief Officer set off to seek rescue. The frail craft might never have made it to the mainland, but had the good fortune to fall in with the Spanish brig *Emilio*, which alerted British steamship *Avon*. Between them the two ships picked up all survivors.

AUGUST 1847 –
NO CELESTIAL OBSERVATION (2)

Just after dawn on 28 October 1847, three half-naked and exhausted seamen stumbled into an Irish farmhouse. Before being fed and put to bed, they told the hospitable farmer they were William Coulthard, George Lightford and John Stevens, survivors from the 320-ton sailing ship *Exmouth*. They had spent the night in a crevice on the rock which wrecked their ship, and with daylight discovered a way to scramble up the cliff and reach the farm.

Three days earlier, *Exmouth* had left Londonderry, Ireland, for Québec, Canada, with a light south-west breeze. She carried a crew of eleven, including the master, Isaac Booth, and some 240 passengers. About half were farmers and tradesmen emigrating with their families, the rest being women and children going to join their husbands or fathers.

During the day, the wind increased to gale force, and continued to blow for forty-eight hours. Several sets of sails were ripped to shreds, and both ship's boats were stove in and washed overboard. Rather than stand to westward, where he would have had ample sea room, Captain Booth headed south-eastward, hoping to find a safe harbour to repair damage and replace torn sails.

About 11 p.m. on the 27th, a light was sighted on the starboard quarter and tentatively identified as that on the Isle of Tory. As it became clearer, it was seen to be flashing rather than stationary, and Booth realized it must have been the lighthouse on the Rhinns of Orsay. After almost three days without a sun or star sight, he was nearly 160 kilometres (100) miles out in his reckoning, and in a very dangerous situation. All attempts to claw off were ineffectual and, about half past midnight, *Exmouth* was dashed upon the cliffs.

Hoping to find a way ashore for the passengers, the captain and four seamen climbed to the maintop, while five more crewmen went up the foremast. They had trouble holding on as *Exmouth* was thrown broadside on to the rocks and bounced off again three times. Then on the fourth impact, the mainmast broke and fell into a crack in the rock. Coulthard, followed by Lightford and Stevens, climbed up the rigging into their crevice. Then a fifth wave splintered the mainmast, and its recoil dragged the ship out to sea where she disappeared beneath the surface, taking captain, crew and passengers with her.

FEBRUARY 1852 – WOMEN AND CHILDREN FIRST

The sea was calm, the skies were clear, and the captain had plotted a course to avoid the treacherous offshore rocks, but no one had realized that her iron hull (a rarity at the time) would cause a compass deviation. With a terrible crunch, HMS *Birkenhead*, a brigantine-rigged sailing ship, impaled herself on Pinnacle Rock, just off Danger Point on the South African coast.

The serious rent in her hull was worsened when Captain Robert Salmond put her auxiliary paddle-wheels full astern in an attempt to back off the rocks. Then she flooded quickly because the bulkheads of her watertight compartments had been pierced to increase dormitory space for embarked troops. A hundred or more passengers drowned in their sleep, but the remainder rushed on deck where their sergeants formed the soldiers in parade order.

Captain Salmond shouted, 'Abandon ship! Every man for himself!', but Lieutenant Colonel Alexander Seaton, bellowed, 'Stand fast the ranks – women and children first!' This is the first time the latter phrase, later to become a maritime tradition, is known to have been used.

All but three of the eight lifeboats stowed on her paddle-boxes were stuck there by multiple coats of paint, and one of these was crushed when the funnel collapsed. Seven of the twenty-five women passengers took to the two remaining boats, together with thirteen of thirty-one children.

Next day, the schooner *Lioness* rescued them along with fifty-four seamen, 113 soldiers, and six marines, who had been clinging to flotsam or hanging in the rigging of topmasts projecting above the water. An estimated 445 had drowned or been eaten by sharks, including Captain Salmond and Colonel Seaton who, with most of the troops, had steadfastly obeyed his order to stay in their ranks.

PART FOUR

The Late Nineteenth Century

MAY 1855 – THE VERDICT WAS MANSLAUGHTER

A chattering crowd gathered on Plymouth docks, waiting for permission to board the sailing ship *John*. Most were families, such as those of labourer James Eastcott, travelling with his wife and eleven children, and miner William Walters, with his wife and six children. There were also single women, such as Mary Ann Penman and Elisabeth Pearce, going to join husbands, fathers or fiancés in Canada.

As they waited amid piles of carpetbags, cardboard suitcases and boxes of household goods, they took a good look at their home for the next several weeks. Even a refit two years earlier could not hide the fact that forty-five-year-old *John* had seen better days. Her master, Captain Rawle, did not inspire them with much confidence either.

Late on the afternoon of Thursday 24 May 1855, the last of 287 emigrants came on board and Captain Rawle cast off. Sometime during that evening, he strayed off course and, at about 10:30 p.m., ran his elderly ship onto the Manacles, a dangerous set of rocks off the western coast of Cornwall.

The wind was blowing heavily and tremendous seas were lashing the coast, but *John* was taking water fast so Rawle decided to beach her. She grounded about sixty metres (200 feet) offshore with her deck well above water. Three passengers managed to get off in one of the boats, and seven embarked on a raft quickly knocked together by the ship's carpenter. All made it safely ashore. However the tide was rapidly running-in and, at the flood, reached almost to her maintop. Most of the crew and a few passengers took to the masts, but the rest were swept overboard by the fierce waves.

Aftermath

Early next morning, coastguard lookouts sighted the wreck, with dozens of people clinging to the rigging. Rushing to the spot, they succeeded in plucking off Captain Rawle and almost all his crew, plus ninety-three passengers, including two young women. By coincidence, fifty-one of the survivors were taken back to Plymouth aboard the *Avon*, the ship which had rescued passengers from *Tweed* eight years earlier.

A coroner's jury investigated the 194 drowning deaths. They returned a verdict of manslaughter against Captain Rawle, and expressed 'extreme disapprobation' of the manner in which the crew had saved themselves, though making an exception in the case of Andrew Eider who, the jurors noted, had done his best to save passengers. They also strongly disapproved of the vessel having been taken to sea without signal gun, muskets, rockets or blue night signals. Finally, they recommended building a lighthouse on the Manacles.

SEPTEMBER 1858 –
EXCESS VENTILATION IN MID-ATLANTIC

The German steamer *Austria* was one of a new generation of trans-Atlantic liners which broke with tradition by trying to make life reasonably comfortable for their passengers. Public areas sparkled with varnished bulkheads and mahogany veneers, and one of her advertised features was the large number of hatches and ports which circulated air to keep her cabins fresh and cool. Following the sailing ship tradition she had a figurehead – a gilded Austrian eagle – gracing her overhanging yacht-like bow.

On the afternoon of Monday 13 September 1858, *Austria* was nine days out of Southampton and about 1600 kilometres (1,000 miles) east of Nova Scotia, barrelling along at eleven knots and hoping to reach New York within five days. While some passengers lay back to digest a sumptuous luncheon, and the more energetic played games on deck, Captain Fredrich Heydtmann decided to take advantage of the 'genial' weather to fumigate his ship.

In accordance with accepted practice, the fourth mate and boatswain would go down to the steerage deck with a pot of pitch, into which they would dip a red-hot iron chain. The resultant clouds of smoke would work their way upwards, not only fumigating the ship, but leaving the pleasant odour of tar throughout.

On this particular day, they left the chain in their portable furnace for longer than usual, so its entire length became heated. When the boatswain picked up its 'cool end', he gave a scream of pain and dropped it again. The tar pot overturned, and its contents spread over the white-hot chain to ignite. All of the vaunted hatches and ports were wide open to disperse the fumigating smoke throughout the ship. Acting like a series of bellows, they performed the same service for the fire.

Seeing flames spreading along the deck, amateur yachtsman Charles Brew rushed to the steersman and told him to turn *Austria* abeam to the wind, but the seaman understood no English, and the blaze rapidly raced from stem to stern. Music professor Theodore Glaubenskee was one of many passengers enjoying the sunshine when he saw fire erupting through the middle deck, and 'noticed men, women and children running to-and-fro in despair and uttering the most heart-rending cries'.

Panic took over. Captain, crew and passengers raced for the lifeboats, pushing, shoving, yelling, fighting and capsizing most of those they did manage to launch. Charles Brew reported: 'The scene on the quarter deck was indescribable. . . . Passengers were rushing frantically to and fro . . . some wholly paralyzed by fear, others madly crying to be saved, but a few perfectly calm. . . . Flames pressed in so closely upon them that many jumped into the sea.'

Meanwhile *Austria* steamed ahead, out-of-command, following a long circular course with no-one on the bridge or in the engine room. The whole ship was an inferno, with flames streaming behind. Amazingly, there were still living souls on board, including Professor Glaubenskee who had joined another passenger next to the eagle figurehead. Shortly before sunset, French barque *Maurice* heaved to nearby and sent off rescue boats. *Austria* was still afloat, burning brightly, but with no way on since her engines had finally stopped.

Maurice picked up seventy survivors, including Charles Brew and Professor Glaubenskee. In the morning, she was joined by Norwegian barque *Catarina* who lifted another twenty-one from floating wreckage. These ninety-one included seventeen crew, but only six women. Five hundred and nine had perished in the fire or by drowning.

SEPTEMBER 1860 – INADEQUATE NAVIGATION RULES ON LAKE MICHIGAN

At 2:30 in the morning of 8 September 1860, excursion steamer *Lady Elgin*[16] was in the middle of Lake Michigan, headed from Chicago to Milwaukee, when those passengers who happened to be awake saw lights rapidly approaching on the port side. Seconds later, there was a tremendous crash, which knocked over and extinguished almost all the ship's oil lamps, creating confusion for the crew and panic among her passengers.

Political Background

Throughout the previous decade there had been, in the words of Republican Presidential candidate William Seward, 'an irrepressible conflict . . . which means that the United States must and will, sooner or later, become entirely a slaveholding nation or entirely a free-labour nation.' By 1860 this controversy had developed into a heated debate over States' Rights in which the State of Wisconsin had become deeply embroiled.

As feelings became more impassioned, one State Senator went so far as to introduce a motion declaring war on the Federal Government unless it abolished slavery. More moderately, Governor Alexander Randall suggested secession. However, one of Wisconsin's premier militia units was the Milwaukee Union Guard, whose commander, Captain Garrett Barry, stated that, although personally opposed to slavery, he would consider secession to be treason. The State promptly disarmed and disbanded the entire unit, and revoked Barry's commission.

A Fund-Raising Excursion

Infuriated, Barry's men decided to re-constitute themselves as the 'Independent Union Guard' and, in order to raise money for replacement weapons, sold tickets for an excursion to Chicago on *Lady Elgin* – one of the largest, fastest, and most luxurious paddlewheel steamers on the Great Lakes. The itinerary included a drill exhibition by the Guards, a speech by Democratic presidential candidate Stephen Douglas, and a dinner-dance, after which militiamen and their guests returned to the ship.

Lady Elgin's Captain, Jack Wilson, did not like the look of the weather, and suggested waiting for it to clear, but the Guards insisted on leaving, and were backed up by the U.S. Postal Service which was anxious to maintain its delivery schedule.

At 11:30 p.m., *Lady Elgin* cleared Chicago with some 300 excursionists and about 150 regular travellers on board. This was a fifty per cent overload, since she was only designed to carry 300 passengers. Some went to bed, while others planned to dance and play cards in the salons throughout the night. Captain Wilson's fears were soon justified. High seas and gale force winds came up, but *Lady Elgin* rode the storm well.

Aboard *Augusta*

Meanwhile, two-masted schooner *Augusta* was on a reciprocal course, bound for Chicago with a deck load of heavy lumber. Unlike Captain Wilson, her skipper, Captain Darius Malott, had been caught unawares by the gale. His ship was out of control, and still wearing a full suit of unreefed canvas. Her cargo had shifted and she was almost on her beam ends.

Shortly after 2:00 a.m., First Mate John Vorce sighted *Lady Elgin*'s lights and reported to the captain who – deeply involved with reducing sail and preventing his vessel from capsizing – ignored the warning. He continued on a course which would pass the steamer to starboard, instead of on the port side as required under the Rules of Lake Navigation. For ten minutes he did not even order his own navigation lights to be lit.

Twenty minutes later, he looked up, saw the paddlewheeler dead head, and screamed at the helmsman, 'Hard up, man! For God's sake, hard up.' It was too late. *Augusta*'s bowsprit and stem drove themselves deep into the steamboat's side, just abaft her port paddlewheel.

Lady Elgin was moving fast, and the schooner was dragged for some distance, until her headgear and the steamship's paddlewheel broke off and floated away together, leaving gaping holes in both vessels. Captain Malott could no longer see the other ship and remarked, 'Well, that steamer sure got away in a hurry.'

Believing *Augusta* had only caused superficial harm, but had herself received underwater damage which might cause her to founder, he continued on to Chicago as fast as possible. On arrival, he reported the collision but, because he said the other vessel was not badly damaged, no rescue ships were dispatched.

Aboard *Lady Elgin*

Captain Wilson and First Mate George Davis were both in bed at the time of the collision. The former rushed to the pilot house and ordered an immediate turn towards the nearest land, while the latter went below and found water flooding into the engine room. He realized that *Lady Elgin* would probably never reach the shore, so took all possible emergency action. A cargo of heavy cast-iron stoves was moved to starboard in order to raise the yawning hole above the port waterline. Fifty head of cattle were released from below-deck pens and driven overboard to take their chance of swimming to shore.

Four lifeboats were lowered. The first leaked and sank, the second was not secured and had no oars, so it drifted out of control, with only the First Mate and a few crewmen on board, the other two took on a mere eighteen people before setting out for the shore. As *Lady Elgin* began to founder, a rogue wave carried away large sections of her upper-works. Almost simultaneously, a large crack appeared in her hull, preventing passengers from accessing the life preserver storage.

Some Milwaukee fire-fighters were among the passengers, and they grabbed axes to cut away part of the hurricane deck as a makeshift raft. Just as fourteen embarked on this frail craft, a thunderstorm brought pouring rain, and lightening flashes to illuminate the otherwise dark night. A survivor called Bellman recalled that he and the captain were among those who clambered onto another large section of hull, going on to say:

> On this extempore raft not less than 300 people were collected . . . (it) was mostly under water from the weight of its living burden, and very few who clung to it but were above the waist in the turbulent sea. . . . They clung to their places in silent terror, and neither groans nor prayers were audible; no voice, save that of the captain raised aloud in encouragement and good cheer, being heard amidst the roar of the wind and the ceaseless splash of the combing waves.

Finally, constant working in the water broke their conveyance into several large pieces and a number of smaller ones, which drifted apart and mostly sank. When dawn broke, about 100 survivors could be seen perched on each of two large hull sections which were still floating. Another 150 or so were bobbing in the water, a few with life preservers, but most hanging-on to bits of flotsam or wreckage.

One was riding the carcass of a dead cow, another clung to the Union Guards' big bass drum, a third sat on a steamer trunk.[17] Fortunately it was early September, and the lake was still quite warm. It took about five hours for them to float fourteen kilometres (nine miles) to the shallows. The Mate's boat was the first to drift ashore, and he scaled the steep, high cliffs to report the disaster.

By 8:00 a.m. hundreds of volunteers had gathered to greet the rafts and wreckage drifting inshore with about 380 passengers still clinging to them. But the gale had generated massive surf and a powerful undertow and between them they drowned or pounded to death two out of every three survivors.

Captain Wilson was dashed against the rocks while trying to save two women. His body drifted almost 100 kilometres (sixty miles) before coming ashore in Indiana. Captain Barry of the Union Guards also saved many victims, but finally collapsed from exhaustion and drowned only thirty metres (ninety-eight feet) from safety. Ninety-eight survived the Great Lakes' worst disaster, leaving 387 unaccounted for. Bodies continued to wash up until just before Christmas, but more than half were never found.

Aftermath

As soon as he learned the other ship had sunk, Captain Malott tried to justify his actions, claiming *Lady Elgin*'s navigation lights were incorrectly placed, and this had led him to misjudge her course and distance. But the popular press and public pilloried him. They even suggested he was a pro-slavery agent who had tried to eliminate the Union Guard by deliberately ramming their vessel.

Angry mobs gathered and threatened to burn *Augusta* or lynch her crew, but the latter managed to escape and quietly changed her name to *Colonel Cook*. A Court of Inquiry eventually exonerated both captains, blaming inadequate and badly drafted Rules of Lake Navigation for the disaster.

APRIL 1865 – OVERWORKED AND OVERBURDENED ON THE MISSISSIPPI

Amazingly, the worst maritime disaster in American history was riverine and occurred within sight of shore on both sides. The Civil War had just ended, Abraham Lincoln had been assassinated, and thousands of released Union prisoners of war were gathered at Vicksburg, Mississippi, waiting for transport to take them home. At the dock, river steamers were vying for the lucrative shipping contract, which paid $5 per enlisted man and $10 per officer.

A Corrupt Union Officer

According to the *Wheeling Register* of 23 May 1865, the Transportation Quartermaster at Vicksburg openly boasted he had negotiated a fare of $3.15 per man with the captain of *Sultana* and expected to make at least $3,700 out of the differential. Presumably this was why he ignored other waiting ships and crammed everyone aboard the two-year-old freighter which had a cabin accommodation for 376 passengers. These were filled by Union Army officers and 236 civilians paying full fare.

Decks and holds were then cleared to take at least 2,300 tired, weary and emaciated Union enlisted men, many of them wounded (no-one knows the exact number, because the Quartermaster stopped counting at 1,866). An unrecorded number of Confederate prisoners was also boarded, guarded by two companies of infantry. Finally, Captain Cass Mason found space for twelve ladies of the Christian Commission who had been serving as nurses. To stabilize the top-heavy ship, 150 livestock and 100 hogsheads of sugar were stowed in the lowest holds.

Catastrophe

Sultana left Vicksburg so heavily laden that it took almost twice as long as usual to reach Helena, Arkansas, where she discharged some of her cargo. Then she steamed on to Memphis, Tennessee, where she took on more freight. Just before midnight on 26 April, she pulled away from the dock and headed north, engines straining to force her heavy load against the current.

Two hours later, her number three boiler, having operated at full pressure for over twenty hours, gave up and exploded. Shards of metal, bits of broken steam pipe and fragments of grating sprayed out in all directions, bursting though bulkheads into the troop decks, killing and maiming hundreds of sleeping soldiers. Splinters also pierced the other two boilers, which themselves blew up, creating a huge hole and setting *Sultana* afire.

Eyewitness Accounts

Senator W.D. Snow of Arkansas told the *Wheeling Register* of 2 May that he had heard no explosion, and only felt the boat shudder, but this was enough to make him get out of bed and put his clothes on. He continues:

> Just before finishing dressing I became aware of a large volume of steam being driven through the cabin by the wind. I opened the door of my state room, and in an instant realised the horror . . . with a fresh breeze carrying the flames with lightning-like rapidity . . . towards the ladies salon.

Private Chester Berry of Wooster, Ohio, who was sleeping on deck, described the scene as he saw it: 'The upper decks of the boat were a complete wreck and the dry casings of the cabins, falling in upon the hot bed of coal were burning like tinder.' Another Ohioan, Private Otto Barden, added:

> Hot steam, smoke, pieces of brickbats, and chunks of coal came thick and fast. I gasped for breath. A fire broke out that lighted up the whole river. I stood at this hatch-hole to keep comrades from falling in . . . stood there until the fire compelled me to leave.

Despite Barden's efforts, many men fell into the gaping hole amidships; many of those already below were kicked or trampled by maddened horses and mules. Hundreds were trapped to be consumed by flames, while hundreds more jumped overboard into the fast-flowing chilly water. Lieutenant Joseph Elliott of Indiana, who had been asleep in his cabin, reported:

> The thought came to me that I had had a nightmare, and in that condition of mind I . . . made for the stern of the boat, hardly knowing what I was doing. . . . Looking down into the river, I saw that the men were jumping from all parts of the boat. . . . Such screams I never heard – twenty or thirty men jumping off at a time – many lighting on those already in the water – until the river became black with men, their heads bobbing up and down like corks, and many disappearing never to appear again.

Elliot later came upon a man who was bouncing like a ball, with his head and shoulders above water. He asked him how he did it and the man replied, 'Don't touch me; I'm riding a barrel!' An unnamed private soldier said he had stumbled over the crate containing a ten-foot 'man-eating' alligator. He claimed to have killed it with his bayonet and then used its crate, with the dead beast still inside, as a raft to float to shore.

Rescue Attempts
The explosions were clearly heard in Memphis, and rescue ships set out immediately. First to arrive was a cutter from USS *Essex,* which was

anchored near the Hen and Chicken Islands about five kilometres (three miles) above the city. It picked up a number of survivors, but the sentries at Fort Pickering refused to let them ashore, because guerrillas were active and their orders were to shoot anyone attempting to land.

The only woman known to survive was Mrs Harvey Ennis, wife of a lieutenant in the Union Navy, who rode to shore on the back of a plunging mule, having lost husband, child and a sister. More survivors were picked up by the steamer *Pocahontas* and a flotilla of local sailing and rowing boats and canoeists.

The rescuers worked by the flickering flames of *Sultana*, which had drifted downstream and settled on the bottom with her blazing super-structure above water. But soon their task became grisly. Over the next few days 1,438 bodies were recovered, but almost as many had died in the blaze. The exact number would never be known.

JULY 1871 –
MENTAL ABERRATION IN GIBRALTAR BAY

The British Channel Squadron made a fine sight as it steamed across Gibraltar Bay heading for the Atlantic Ocean. It was formed in two divisions abeam of each other in line ahead. HMS *Minotaur*, wearing the flag of Vice Admiral George Wellesley, a nephew of the Duke of Wellington, headed the port (seaward) column. The starboard (inshore) column was led by HMS *Agincourt*, carrying Rear Admiral Wilmot. These broadside ironclads were sister ships, three and four years old respectively. At 10,690 tons they were the largest fighting ships afloat, powered by steam engines driving single screws, but still carrying full sets of sail on five masts.

At this time, British warship captains and other seaman officers had no accountability for navigation. This was the sole responsibility of special-ists whose rank was preceded by the title 'Staff'. On Admiral Wellesley's orders, Staff Commander Kiddle laid off a course to take the *Minotaur* division safely clear of the only offshore hazards on the route, Carnero Point and Pearl Rock. By a mental quirk or oversight, he completely forgot the presence of the second division, leaving insufficient sea-room for it. In consequence, Captain Beamish ran *Agincourt* directly onto Pearl Rock.

Aftermath
Staff Commander Kiddle's contribution to the accident seems to have been ignored by the subsequent court martial, which reprimanded Captain Beamish and his navigator, Staff Commander Knight, and

ordered both Vice Admiral Wellesley and Rear Admiral Wilmot to haul down their flags, the former for failing to ensure a safe course had been set for the entire fleet, and the latter for maintaining station when his primary duty was to keep clear of danger.

Wellesley later bounced back to be promoted to Admiral in 1875, and First Sea Lord two years later. As for *Agincourt,* although badly damaged, she survived to become flagship of the 1878 Dardanelles Expedition. In 1908 she was converted to a coal hulk, and served in that capacity until 1960.

SEPTEMBER 1871 – OVERRIGGED AND UNSTABLE IN THE BAY OF BISCAY

During the late 1850s, it slowly became apparent, even to the most hide-bound naval establishments[18], that steam-powered vessels could manoeuvre in weather which would becalm wind-driven ships. Moreover, they remained reasonably stable gunnery platforms in seas which would force sailing ships to close their gunports.

In 1859, France launched the partially-ironclad wooden frigate *Gloire,* panicking Britain's Royal Navy into building the steel-framed, iron-armoured *Warrior* in response. Still fully-rigged, but with a steam-powered single screw, she was twice the size of the French vessel, faster and vastly superior to all previous line-of-battle ships. However, it was during the American Civil War that steam-driven ironclads began to prove their worth.

In 1861, John Ericsson designed and built USS *Monitor.* She was small, makeshift and experimental, with none of *Warrior*'s sophistication or seagoing qualities, being essentially a semi-submerged, steam-powered, ironclad raft, surmounted by an armoured rotating turret which carried two powerful eleven-inch Dahlgren guns, able to engage from any angle, not merely on the beam.

A Revolutionary Private Design
Ten years later, a young naval architect, Cowper Phipps Coles, proposed a turreted ocean-going design to the British Admiralty. When it was rejected by Controller of the Navy Sir E. J. Reed, he decided to go ahead and build it himself. Thanks to support from Albert, the Prince Consort, he managed to secure the only private battleship contract ever issued by the British Royal Navy.

Christened HMS *Captain,* she carried four 25-ton rifled guns in two rotating turrets, and could be propelled by either steam or sail. The low freeboard, which gave her such an attractive profile, was actually a mistake.

The design specification of 8 feet 6 inches had somehow been transposed by the builders, who gave her a freeboard of 6 feet 8 inches instead.

The combined weight of guns, funnel and three tall masts carrying an incredible 50,000 square feet of sail, combined with a narrower hull than any other ironclad, led Reed to prophesy, 'She will capsize due to instability'. Coles countered by boasting, 'She walks the water like a thing of life'. Despite Reed's objections, *Captain* passed stability tests, was taken into naval service, and successfully test-fired her heavy guns during a gale.

Disaster

Coles himself came on board for her third sea trip in September. Towards midnight on the night of 6th-7th, the barometer began to drop sharply. Soon, the wind rose to near gale force, with heavy rain squalls, and *Captain* heeled hard to starboard. Mounted on sturdy tripod masts her mass of sail held firm and acted as an immense windbreak.

Under a sudden gust, she lurched further to starboard. Captain Hugh Burgoyne asked the angle of heel, and the lieutenant of the watch reported in quick succession, 'eighteen degrees – twenty – twenty-six – twenty-eight – she's going over!' On her beam ends, the water poured in and she went down in seconds, taking Coles, Burgoyne and 481 others with her.

Aftermath

When daylight came and *Captain* was missing, Admiral Milne turned his flagship, *Lord Warden,* around and went back along their course. He found only floating wreckage, but later discovered that eighteen seamen had managed to launch a small boat and make their way safely to Finisterre. Later, an Admiralty Court ruled that *Captain* was over-rigged with excessive top-hamper, making her too unstable for use at sea. The Court concluded, 'It was a mistake to purchase the ship in opposition to the views and opinions of the Controller of the Navy.'

Next year, two ships to Reed's own design were launched. They were the world's first armoured capital ships relying entirely on steam propulsion, with no sails and a single military mast for signalling. The hulls of *Devastation* and her sister ship *Thunderer* were not unlike *Captain,* but they had higher superstructures. They turned out to be good steady seaboats, stable even in the heaviest seas. Coles' patented turrets were installed in both, and royalties on them kept his widow in comfort for the rest of her life.

July 1873 –
Compass Deviation on the Atlantic

'Ninety-eight – ninety-nine – three hundred – that's the lot!' *City of Washington*'s Chief Mate heaved a sigh of relief as the last heavy steel rail was winched into the cargo hold to lie alongside 700 previously loaded metal drums. Shortly afterward, the 2,000-ton steamship left Liverpool for New York, with ninety-six crew and 271 passengers.

On 27 June, after three days at sea, dead reckoning placed the ship sixty-four kilometers (forty miles) south of the position shown by an actual noon observation. None of the ship's officers seems to have found this variation significant, or considered it might have been because the compass was affected by the magnetic field of her cargo. From that day on, no observations could be made due to thick fog, so navigation had to be based entirely on dead reckoning.

On 2 – 3 July, *City of Washington* passed over the Grand Banks of Newfoundland. However, because dead reckoning showed her to be far to the south and over deep water, Captain William Phillips did not order soundings to be taken. The ship continued to make a fast run for two more days without once casting the lead until, at 1:15 p.m. on 5 July she ran ashore on reefs off Little Point Ebert in Nova Scotia. The weather was calm, boats were speedily lowered, and all 567 people on board were landed safely.

Aftermath
A Court of Inquiry was convened by the Governor General in Council as required under Canadian law. Presided over by Royal Navy Captain P.A. Scott, assisted by retired shipmaster, Captain George Mackenzie, and Royal Navy navigating officer, Staff Lieutenant D. M. Browne, it reached the following conclusions.

> It was imprudent to ignore the dead reckoning between the 25th and 27th June . . . which must have shewn that the compass had a large amount of easterly deviation. It was also imprudent to pass the Grand Banks of Newfoundland, without trying for soundings to correct the reckoning . . . and as thick weather prevailed for two days after passing the Banks, it was highly imprudent to continue at full speed without taking a cast of the lead . . . particularly so, when it ought to have been known by the master that so much more iron and steel had been placed on board since compass corrections had been obtained. . . . The Master's Certificate of Service held by William Robert Phillips, the master, shall be suspended for the

space of one year from the date of the loss of the steamship *City of Washington*, and this certificate is hereby suspended accordingly.

These findings were endorsed by P. Mitchell, the Canadian Minister of Marine & Fisheries. However, since the verdict was not brought down until 17 July 1874, the suspension had already expired and amounted to little more than a reprimand, although it remained as a blot on Captain Phillips' record.

AUGUST 1888 –
INATTENTION ON THE ATLANTIC

Second Officer Jörgensen of the Danish steamship *Geiser* was asleep in his bunk when a terrible grinding crash abruptly woke him. Starting up in terror, he was astounded to see the stem of a ship looming inches from his head. Water poured over him as it began to recede. Instinctively, he grabbed the anchor chain hanging from the strange bow, and was carried back with it. Hauling himself to the deck, and running to the bridge, he recognised Captain Laub, and realized he was aboard *Geiser*'s sister ship *Thingvalla*.

The time was 3:35 a.m. on 14 August 1888 and, minutes earlier, *Geiser* had been steaming eastward from New York to Copenhagen, lightly laden with 107 passengers and a crew of nearly fifty. *Thingvalla* was on a reciprocal course with 455 passengers and a slightly smaller crew. The night was dark, with light rain and haze, but no fog. Neither ship had posted lookouts.

Captain Laub later told reporters that, on hearing the *Thingvalla*'s engines go into reverse, he had rushed to the bridge in his night clothes, but the crash had occurred before he got there. Hence he could not tell them what caused the collision, and was unaware of how far away *Geiser* had been when first sighted, or how long it was before the impact. *Geiser*'s Captain, William Möller, recalled that Chief Officer Brown had called from the bridge and excitedly told him a strange vessel was bearing down on them:

> I instantly jumped off the sofa, and taking my trousers in my hand, I ran up to the bridge. I saw the lights of a big steamer on our starboard bow. . . . We blew two blasts of the steam whistle as a warning. ... She instantly crashed into our starboard side amidships, opposite the main rigging. On sighting her, the Chief Officer had promptly ordered the engines reversed, and by the time I reached the bridge our vessel was going full speed astern. She struck us with

such force as to cut through half the breadth of our ship. I saw at once that *Geiser* would go down, and shouted to the men on deck to call all hands and get out the boats.

With both ships going full-astern, they separated. *Geiser* 'rocked like a cradle', heeled over onto her side, and foundered, only seven minutes after the collision. Most passengers died in their bunks. Perhaps thirty or forty managed to reach open air. Some rushed blindly along the deck, only to fall into the gaping hole made by *Thingvalla*. Others milled around, unaware of 700 lifebelts within easy reach.

The crew managed to launch three boats, one of which capsized; another floated away empty, and the third, badly overloaded, was sucked down when *Geiser* sank. It surfaced moments later, but without its occupants. Surviving passengers and crew slid off the side as *Geiser* heeled over. Captain Möller stayed on his bridge until:

> The ship gave a plunge and I felt her go from under me into the whirlpool created by her displacement of the water. I felt myself drawn down by the suction and I was whirled around in the eddy but did not lose consciousness. I was fully a minute under the water and when I came to the surface, there were numbers of people and a large quantity of wreckage floating on the water. I got hold of a floating oar (and) swam for about thirty-five minutes when I was picked up by one of *Thingvalla*'s boats. When all our people who were saved got on board, I mustered my men and with the passengers we helped *Thingvalla*'s crew to support her forward bulkhead which was in danger of being stove in by the pressure of water.

Thingvalla's boats rescued fourteen passengers[19] and seventeen crew, leaving about 126 unaccounted for. This tragedy on a reasonably clear night was almost certainly because the watch officers on both ships had failed to keep a good lookout.

MARCH 1889 – NATIONAL PRIDE AT APIA

As trade with Asia grew, European and American diplomatic policies focused on securing commercial access to Chinese ports and the many islands of the Pacific, preferably to the exclusion of rival trading nations. Although the Samoan Archipelago was off the major trade routes, Britain, Germany and the United States each developed commercial interests and negotiated treaties during the 1870s.

In the late 1880s, a Samoan Civil War broke out and Germany, which had colonized part of the archipelago, intervened by stationing a corvette and two gunboats in Apia harbour. The United States which had a naval base at Pago Pago, was enraged and countered by sending three of its warships to Apia. Britain, with its own colonial possessions nearby, sent a ship to keep an eye on the others, who seemed to be on the brink of war.

The German and American vessels were relics of the age of wooden ships, equipped with muzzle-loading guns and moderate steam power to supplement their sails; but British corvette *Calliope* was a more modern iron ship with relatively powerful engines. Apia usually provides a secure reef-bound anchorage between March and November, but is exposed to heavy seas during the December to February hurricane season.

Typhoon Strikes

A number of civilian vessels and these seven warships were lying in the cramped anchorage, when gathering clouds forecast the arrival of a late-season typhoon. The ships were dangerously close together, but they were there to project national power, and none of their captains wanted to 'lose face' by being the first to withdraw to safer open water.

The storm struck with the awesome force of 150 km/h (95 mph) winds. German gunboat *Eber*, the smallest warship present, was blown onto the reef and totally destroyed with the loss of all her crew. American sloop *Vandalia* and German gunboat *Adler* also suffered heavy personnel losses and were wrecked beyond repair.

American frigate *Trenton*, whose boilers were extinguished by water entering through hawse-pipes, dragged her anchors, whirled helplessly and sank, but casualties were light. German corvette *Olga* and American gunboat *Nipsic* also dragged their anchors and were driven ashore, later to be hauled off and repaired.

Only British Captain Kane had the presence of mind to up anchor and steam into the wind. Even at full-ahead, *Calliope*'s powerful engines could only give her one knot of headway but, slowly, she struggled into open water and was the only ship to survive. The other ships – together with 146 German and fifty-one American seamen – were victims of hubris and a misplaced sense of honour.

Aftermath

The shared disaster eased tension, and diplomatic negotiation super-seded naval confrontation. A decade later, the Berlin Conference created a German protectorate over the Western Samoan islands of Savaii and Upolu, while giving the United States hegemony over the Manua Islands and Tutuila to the east. Needless to say, the inhabitants were not consulted about their loss of independence.

June 1893 – Miscalculation off Syria

In 1891, Vice Admiral Sir George Tryon was appointed Commander-in-Chief in the Mediterranean, with Britain's newest battleship, HMS *Victoria*, as his flagship. During a long and distinguished career he had become so irascible, demanding and forceful that few subordinates dared question his orders, and even his peers often found it easier to agree than to argue. But he had also gained the reputation of being innovative and forward-looking, and under his command the eleven-battleship Mediterranean fleet became an evolutionary, almost experimental squadron.

Constant exercises, involving unexpected and complicated manoeuvres, proved difficult and trying for Rear Admiral Sir Hastings Markham, who was described by a contemporary as being an 'Anxious, conforming, hidebound, conventionalist; dedicated to staying out of trouble and not displeasing his superiors.' Inevitably, such a milksop was despised and ridiculed by innovative Tryon who, in spite of an overbearing personality, tried to encourage initiative among subordinates. His frequently public criticism further undermined Markham's fragile confidence, creating the dangerous situation of a second-in-command who never dared to question a decision.

Tryon versus Nelson

Tryon firmly believed that too much time was lost by signalling, whether in combat or while exercising, saying, 'It is apparent to me that a fleet can be rapidly manoeuvred without having to wait for a series of signal repetitions'. A century earlier, Horatio Nelson had come to the same conclusion, his solution being to hold regular conferences with his captains, during which they discussed every conceivable combination of tactical situations until, as described by his flag-captain, Edward Berry:

> There was no possible position in which they could be found that he did not take into his calculation, and for the most advantageous attack of which he had not digested and arranged the best possible disposition of the force which he commanded.

As a result, Nelson's captains always knew what their admiral expected and was likely to do, minimizing the need for signals. Tryon's solution was almost the exact opposite. He seldom explained his plans, simply ordering that whenever the flagship hoisted the signal 'TA', the rest of the fleet should conform to its movements without further instruction.

Recipe for Disaster

On 22 June 1893, the fleet was steaming off the Syrian coast. The sea was calm and visibility was excellent. Taking advantage of the ideal weather, Sir George planned a new manoeuvre to test his captains and crews. He would form them into parallel columns, then reverse course by turning inward and passing side-to-side, somewhat like a military band counter-marching. In discussion with his chief-of-staff, he said he would form the columns six cables apart.[20]

Tryon could be devastatingly sarcastic in response to stupid questions, but was usually ready to listen to sensible ones, so Commander Thomas Hawkins-Smith did not hesitate to suggest that the combined turning circles of *Victoria* and Markham's *Camperdown* demanded at least eight cables spacing. Tryon testily replied, 'Very well, eight it shall be.' Later, however, he seemed to have forgotten this conversation, and told his Flag Lieutenant, Lord Guilford, to signal, 'Fleet to form columns of divisions in line ahead, disposed abeam to port of the flag.' Then he added, 'and make the columns six cables apart'.

When Hawkins-Smith saw the signal at the masthead, he asked Guilford, 'Haven't you made a mistake?', but Guilford showed him the memo form on which the Admiral had written the single digit '6'. Instead of going to Tryon to remind him of their previous conversation, he ordered Guilford to ask if the Admiral had meant to say eight. Annoyed at being questioned by a junior officer, Tryon irascibly snorted, 'leave it as it is'.

Collision

When the columns had formed and were steaming in parallel, Tryon made the signal, 'Invert course, turning inward in succession'. He intended the columns to turn in unison, but Rear Admiral Markham, remembering the combined turning circles, reasonably assumed 'in succession' meant that the Admiral's division would turn first, leaving sea room for his column to turn astern of it.

Tryon was furious at the Rear Admiral's delay, especially since the fleet was now in danger of running onto the coast near Tripoli. He signalled Markham 'What are you waiting for?' A more self-confident subordinate would then have pointed out the danger of collision. But Markham, humiliated by the public rebuke, replied 'Because I did not quite under-stand your signal.' Then he began the turn, and Tryon told his Flag Captain, Archibald Bourke, to turn in unison.

Bourke began the turn, then protested, 'Sir, we shall be too close to *Camperdown*.' Tryon did not reply, probably because he was reviewing the geometry of the manoeuvre in his mind. After several more minutes, Bourke almost shouted, 'We must do something Sir! May I go astern?'

Tryon assented, but by then it was too late. *Camperdown*'s massive armoured ram sliced into *Victoria*'s side penetrating almost three metres (9.5 feet), and thrusting her some twenty metres (sixty-six feet) to starboard.

Aftermath

The other battleships lowered boats which rowed towards the stricken flagship, but Tryon refused rescue and signalled them off, saying *Victoria* was not mortally wounded. In fact she was, and went under in less than fifteen minutes, taking 358 officers and men including the Admiral with her.

Markham held a solemn funeral service at sea and then took the fleet back to Malta. But as *Camperdown* steamed into Grand Harbour, her Marine Band stood on the quarterdeck playing lively tunes, leading Admiral Sir Charles Dundas to comment, 'On such a pathetic occasion it would have shown better taste to have had less demonstration.'

February 1898 –
Blown-Up in Havana Harbour

By purchase and by conquest, the United States had established an immense land empire in North America, but naval strategists argued that overseas expansion was also essential in order to secure fuelling and maintenance bases for its rapidly expanding fleet. Their lobbying had already resulted in a Treaty for Annexation of the Hawaiian Islands, and an incident in Cuba, fanned by an inflammatory press, was to provide the catalyst for other acquisitions on both the Atlantic and Pacific sea frontiers.

Cuban rebels against Spanish colonial rule hoped to incite United States intervention by burning American-owned sugar plantations and mills. On 25 January 1898, USS *Maine* (an armoured cruiser, reclassified as a 'second-class' battleship, to give her greater prestige) was sent to Cuba, ostensibly to protect American property and citizens, but covertly to show support for the revolutionaries. Apprentice First-Class Charles Hamilton wrote to his father saying:

> We were out to sea when the orders came for us to proceed at once to Havana. We are the first American ship that has been here in six years. We are now cleared for action with every gun in the ship loaded and men stationed around the ship all night. . . . By the look of things now I think we will have some trouble before we leave.

Explosion

For three weeks the shiny white ship with mustard funnels lay at anchor, entertaining and being entertained by the Spaniards, who seemed confident of crushing the three-year-old rebellion. Then, on 15 February, as Captain Charles Sigsbee, *Maine*'s Commanding Officer, later recounted:

> I was just closing a letter to my family when I felt the crash of an explosion. It was a bursting, rending, and crashing sound, or roar of immense volume, largely metallic in character. It was succeeded by a metallic sound – probably of falling debris – a trembling and lurching motion of the vessel, then an impression of subsidence, attended by an eclipse of the electric lights and intense darkness within the cabin. I knew immediately that the *Maine* had been blown up and that she was sinking.

Aftermath

Rescue boats came alongside from Spanish cruiser *Alfonso XII,* and Ward Line steamship *City of Washington* but, sadly, only ninety-two crewmen were saved. Eight later died of their wounds, bringing the death toll to 266 or three-quarters of the crew.

Among many newspaper reporters and illustrators covering the revolution was Frederick Remington, who cabled his publisher, William Randolph Hearst, saying, 'There is no war', to which Hearst famously replied, 'You furnish the pictures, I'll furnish the war'. On 25 March, a Court of Inquiry determined *Maine* had been sunk by 'a mine planted by persons unknown'.[21] True to his word, Hearst ignored this verdict, declared the Spaniards culpable, and bombarded the public with the rallying cry 'Remember the *Maine*! To Hell with Spain!' Within a month, the United States and Spain were at war.

MAY 1898 – DEFEATISM AT MANILA BAY

As soon as war was declared, *Contra-Almirante* (Rear Admiral) Patricio Montojo y Pasarón anticipated an American attack on his base at Manila in the Philippines. He intended to fight, but knew the seven elderly wooden ships in his line-of-battle would be hopelessly outclassed by Commodore George Dewey's five armoured cruisers and two gunboats.

Anticipating defeat, he took two humanitarian measures. To avoid civilian 'collateral damage' he moved his fleet from Manila to Cavite, although it would only be protected by eight shore-based guns instead of thirty-nine. Then, to save the crews of his twenty-five ships from drowning, he anchored the antiquated vessels in shallow water, where they would ground when inevitably sunk.

Dewey, who had repainted his bright white ships a dull wartime grey, decided on a night attack, hoping to pass the formidable Manila shore-batteries unobserved. He was, naturally, unaware that no-one had thought to authorize them to shoot. As soon as dawn broke on a calm and lightly-misted Manila Bay, the Spanish ships, followed by some of the Cavite shore batteries opened fire but, never having had enough ammunition for target practice, they only made thirteen hits.

The Americans had had copious supplies of practice ammunition, but their gunnery proved little better. They steamed back and forth across the Spanish fleet five times, firing 5,859 shells but only scoring with 142 (an abysmal 2.4 per cent). Before turning for a sixth run, Dewey was informed that only 15 per cent of the fleet's ammunition remained and prudently decided to withdraw for a council of war with his captains. By this time, the bay was so obscured by smoke that neither side really knew what was going on.

At the conference, Dewey learned he had destroyed Montojo's flag-ship *Reina Christina*, and the old wooden cruiser *Castilla*, and set fire to three others, while his own ships were virtually unscathed, and the only casualty was an engineer officer who had had a heart attack. He also discovered that the earlier report should have said that 15 per cent of ammunition had been expended.

After sending the crews to breakfast, he planned to resume the one-sided battle, but Montojo had ordered his remaining ships to scuttle themselves and the fight was over. By August, the war was also over, and the American Empire had expanded to include the Philippines, Hawaii, Guam, Wake, Midway and Puerto Rico, plus a commanding presence in Cuba. The naval lobby had secured its overseas bases far sooner than expected.

PART FIVE

Recent Times

JUNE 1904 –
CRIMINAL NEGLIGENCE ON THE EAST RIVER

'Flags were flying, the band was playing a lively air, and all three decks were crowded to capacity with a happy throng that looked for a pleasant day's outing.' So wrote a *New York Times* reporter describing holiday passengers boarding the steam paddlewheeler *General Slocum* at a pier on New York's East River.

This excursion boat, named after a Civil War hero, was twenty-six years old and had an unhappy record, having run aground on six occasions, and collided with other vessels on four. Except for her captain and chief engineer, all thirty-five crew members were recently hired and inexperienced.

The passengers – 1,310 women and children and fifty men – were going to the annual picnic of St Mark's Evangelical Lutheran Church on Long Island. They were led by their pastor, Rev. George Haas, who was accompanied by his wife and daughter. The day before the trip, the Church delivered three barrels of glasses. After the stewards had unpacked them, a deckhand illegally stored the barrels, still packed with hay, in a forward cabin.

Conflagration

At about 10 a.m., while some 500 children were dancing on deck to the band, twelve-year-old Frank Perditsky ran to the pilot house and yelled, 'The ship's on fire'. Captain van Shaick dismissed the warning as yet another childish prank. At about the same time, people were seen waving wildly from the shore. Some of the passengers waved back, interpreting the gestures as friendly greetings rather than an alert that smoke was coming out of the forward ports.

Within minutes, the forward section of the boat had become a mass of flames, which rapidly moved aft, fanned by the ship's full-speed forward motion. Cabin walls became so hot that contact with bubbling paint seared the skin. Crewmen rushed to fire hoses, but when the water was turned on the rotten canvas burst. Then they tried to launch *Slocum*'s six lifeboats, only to find them stuck to the deck by twenty-six years' accumulation of paint. They burned before they could be freed.

Escape & Rescue

Passengers, most of whom could not swim, desperately tried to pull life jackets from overhead wire-mesh containers but many could not be opened. When they could be unsealed, a lot of jackets turned out to be rotten. They disintegrated into crumbs of cork, while others dragged their wearers under, because iron bars had been inserted by an unscrupulous contractor to give them the prescribed weight.

With his own clothes already smouldering, Captain van Shaick decided to run aground. Later he said: 'I started to head for 134th Street, but was warned off by the captain of a tugboat, who shouted to me that the boat would set fire to the lumber yards and oil tanks there. . . . I then fixed upon North Brother Island.'

Why he made this decision remains a mystery. If he had turned toward the nearest point on the Bronx shore, *Slocum* would have beached gently in less than a minute and there would have been a fair chance of disembarking passengers. Instead he took a much longer route, to crash into a steep-sloped rocky coast with deep water below the keel.

Shortly after she struck, the entire upper works crashed down on the lower decks, crushing some passengers, and throwing others overboard or into the inferno. Those still surviving slid over the side on ropes, or jumped into the fast-flowing water to be swept away or crushed by still-turning paddlewheels. Others tried to lower themselves from the rails and lost the skin of their palms, which stuck to the hot metal.

Aftermath

1,020 passengers perished by fire or drowning, while many of the 340 survivors told ghoulish tales of rescue boats demanding money or jewellery before accepting them on board. In contrast, Captain van Shaick and the harbour pilots stepped onto the deck of tug *Jack Wade*, without even getting their feet wet. The chief engineer died at his post, but every other crew member survived.

An inquest determined the conflagration was started by a cigarette or match, tossed carelessly into one of the hay barrels. The jury indicted the captain, mate and owners of *General Slocum*; employees of the Nonpareil Cork Works, who had stuffed life jackets with iron bars; and the inspector, who had certified fire and lifesaving equipment a mere five weeks earlier. Remarkably, only Captain van Shaick was convicted. Four years into a ten-year sentence, he was pardoned by President Taft in response to a petition signed by a quarter of a million supporters.

OCTOBER 1904 –
PANIC REACTION ON THE NORTH SEA

A noble and resplendent audience was enjoying an opera at the Mariinsky Theatre in St Petersburg, when a breathless messenger delivered an urgent telegram to Tsar Nicholas II: 'Humbly reporting to Your Imperial Majesty . . . Japanese torpedo boats undertook a sudden attack on our squadron stationed in . . . the Port Arthur base.'

This attack, made in February 1904 without Declaration of War, was followed by a blockade and siege of Port Arthur, Russia's only ice-free port in the east. Six months of land warfare ensued, accompanied by spasmodic naval skirmishing. Then the Tsar ordered Admiral Wilgelm Witgeft to take the Pacific Squadron from Port Arthur to the relative safety of Vladivostok.

He was intercepted in the Yellow Sea by Admiral Heihachiro Togo and, during a fierce exchange of gunfire, Witgeft was killed. The Russian ships scattered and made their way individually back to Port Arthur. A few days later, Russia's Vladivostok squadron was decimated in a fight in the Korea Strait, leaving Japan in absolute control of the Sea of Japan, and much of the Yellow and East China Seas.

The Tsar then ordered a Second Pacific Squadron to be hastily assembled at Baltic ports. Some crew members were ill-trained and inexperienced, and the ships had not worked-up together, but Admiral Zinovy Rozhestvensky was not allowed time to turn them into a co-ordinated fighting fleet.

Two huge problems were fuel and ammunition. Almost all the world's bunkering facilities were controlled by Britain, which was friendly to Japan, so the Squadron would have to rely on a German steamship line to bring coal to ports along their route. Sufficient shells were available for a battle, but there were none to spare for target practice. As for morale, Captain Bukhvostov of battleship *Alexander III* told a friend:

> I am afraid we will lose half the squadron on our way to the Far East. If this does not happen, the Japanese will annihilate us. Their ships are better, and they are real sailors. (However) I can promise you one thing; we shall all die, but never surrender.

Early in October, Russia's secret agents in Norway reported rumours that Japanese torpedo boats were operating out of English ports. A few days later Russian freighter *Bakan* said she had sighted four torpedo boats in the North Sea, adding that, in the dark, she almost mistook them for fishing boats. Rozhestvensky's squadron received both warnings and was placed on alert.

'Battle' on the Dogger Bank

On 19 October, the squadron entered the North Sea. It was split into four divisions, each under separate command and about eighty kilometres (fifty miles) apart. Next night, at 8:45 p.m., repair ship *Kamchatka* urgently signalled, 'Being . . . attacked from all directions . . . steering in different directions to avoid torpedo boats'. Then she was silent until 11:20 p.m., when Admiral Rozhestvensky asked if the torpedo boats were still in sight, and received a negative reply.

At 12:55 a.m. on the 21st, several small ships without lights were spotted converging rapidly on the flag battleship *Knyaz Suvorov*. Rozhestvensky immediately ordered evasive action, and flooded the oncoming craft with searchlights. They were identified as torpedo boats, and *Knyaz Suvorov* opened fire. The rest of the division joined in. Later, an eyewitness described the scene:

> Bugles blared; drums rumbled; rails rattled under the weight of handtrucks laden with shells; heavy guns were fired . . . lighting the darkness with flashes . . . and stirring the night with echoing thunder . . .

Knyaz Suvorov fired a salvo at flashes to port, then realized that they were not enemy gunfire, but recognition signals from cruisers *Aurora* and *Donskoi*. Random shooting continued at other shadowy targets for another ten minutes. When 'cease fire' was finally sounded, officers had to drag panicked gunners from the controls to stop them shooting.

Aftermath

In his report, Rozhestvensky admitted they had caused collateral damage to civilian fishing vessels, going on to explain why he had not stopped to rescue survivors: 'Since the fishing trawlers' behaviour looked suspicious, and since I was not sure all the torpedo boats . . . had been disabled, I left the injured to the care of their comrades.' In fact, there had never been a Japanese presence, and the only target had been an English fishing fleet.

London, already pro-Japanese, was furious and Russia seemed on the brink of war with Britain as well as Japan. All through the Bay of Biscay, the Russians were shadowed by British warships, which then blockaded them in Spanish Tangier. Across the Strait, at Gibraltar, Admiral Lord Beresford ordered eleven battleships, eight cruisers, seven torpedo boats and three destroyers to combat readiness, but diplomacy took over. After ten tense days, Beresford was advised 'Government considers crisis past'. The blockade was lifted and Rozhestvensky was free to continue towards the Far East and devastating defeat at Tsushima as predicted by Captain Bukhvostov.

MAY 1914 –
FOGGY CONFUSION ON THE SAINT LAWRENCE

Every spring, even before the last ice floe drifts out to sea, the St Lawrence estuary wakes from winter dormancy and traffic begins to flow. Trans-Atlantic liners can then dock at the river ports of Montréal and Québec, saving passengers the long and tiresome train journeys they had had to take all winter to and from harbours on the Atlantic seaboard.

Converging Courses

At 1:30 a.m. on 29 May, the Canadian Pacific liner *Empress of Ireland*, outward-bound from Québec and just downstream of Rimouski, drew close to the shore and slowed down to drop river pilot Adelard Laurier at Father Point, where the river widens and pilotage is no longer needed. The 14,000-ton vessel was carrying 1,057 passengers and 420 crew.

At the same time, Norwegian collier *Storstad* was a short distance downriver, inward-bound with a cargo of coal from the mines of Cape Breton Island. She too was hugging the coastline, heading for Father Point to pick up her pilot for the voyage to Montréal. *Storstad* was a powerful 6,000-ton ship, built on the Isherwood system, an immensely strong type of construction, designed to withstand head-on collision with ice floes off the Norwegian coast. Instead of ribs running vertically from deck to keel, her main frames were horizontal from stem to stern.

When the ships sighted one another at around 2:00 a.m., the night was cold, but calm and clear with good visibility. They were about thirteen kilometres (eight miles) apart. Aboard *Empress*, Captain Henry Kendall crossed ahead of *Storstad* and turned onto his downriver course. If both vessels continued as they were, they would pass starboard side to starboard side with room to spare.[22]

As the liner approached, First Mate Alfred Toftenes saw her green light slightly to the left of *Storstad*'s bow. He assumed she was going to hold her course and pass green-to-green. Then, as they later testified, all five crewmen on watch saw *Empress'* range lights moving closer together, until they were dead in line and both red and green navigation lights were visible. The liner's swing seemed to continue, since her range lights separated and only her red light was still visible. It seemed to Toftenes she was now planning to pass red-to-red. At this moment, a creeping bank of fog enveloped *Storstad*, and the liner's lights faded from view.

Collision

When *Empress* entered the fog bank, Captain Kendall ordered full astern and gave three blasts on the whistle. Hearing a single long blast in reply, he assumed *Storstad* was both acknowledging his signal and indicating she was holding course. When he judged *Empress* had no more way on he ordered 'stop engines' and gave two blasts which were again acknowledged by one long one. He remained motionless, waiting for the other ship to pass by.

Toftenes had also stopped engines as a safety precaution, but had not called sleeping Captain Thomas Andersen to tell him they were in fog. Then, because he feared the current would carry *Storstad* into *Empress'* path, he started up again. Fog distorts the direction of sound but, judging that the blast of the liner's whistle was coming from port, he ordered a turn to starboard and finally called the master.

No sooner did Andersen reach the bridge than he saw a bright white masthead light about thirty degrees off the port bow. Below it and to the right, a green light shone hazily through the fog. He rushed to the telegraph and slammed it to 'full astern', simultaneously yelling for Toftenes to give the appropriate three short blasts of the whistle, but it was too late.

There was a bright shower of sparks, but no jarring impact because *Storstad*'s ice-breaking stem, pushed by the momentum of 6,000 tons of ship and 11,000 tons of coal, sliced smoothly into the liner's side, penetrating some eight metres (twenty-six feet), like a steel chisel. The shock was greater aboard *Empress*, which was momentarily pushed onto her beam ends.

The impact threw Kendall off the bridge, but he got to his feet, grabbed a megaphone and screamed 'Keep your engines full ahead' to the unknown assailant. Andersen complied. He feared his own bulkheads might have crumpled under the shock, and realized the best chance for both vessels was to keep the one's bows jammed in the side of the other like a cork.

However, thanks to the fast-flowing current, *Empress* still had way on. Slowly and inexorably, her movement dragged the collier backwards and sideways, opening up a huge five metre (sixteen foot) wide gash in the liner's hull, halfway between her twin funnels, and extending some six metres (twenty feet) below the waterline. Water began to flood both boiler rooms at about 273,000 litres (60,000 gallons) a second.

Escape and Rescue

As the boiler rooms filled up, the liner listed sharply to starboard, submerging more of the gash, together with the open ports of passenger cabins. Those on the starboard side were probably flooded while their occupants were still asleep, giving them only seconds to avoid drowning. The few who did get away, found themselves disorientated in the strange alleyways of a ship they had only boarded a few hours earlier. Then the lights went out. Few if any of 800 people below decks managed to escape.

The list made it impossible to launch more than five (or six) lifeboats, but there were more than enough cork lifejackets aboard. Unfortunately, there had been no drill and most passengers did not know where to find them, or how to put them on. Ten minutes after impact, the ship tilted until her funnels hit the water, and many passengers were tossed into the ice-cold river.

Others perched on the side of the hull where, according to a survivor from Winnipeg, named Mr Cunningham, 'It was like sitting on a beach, watching the tide come in.' Four minutes later, *Empress of Ireland* raised her shapely stern to the sky and slid under. It was only nine hours and forty-two minutes since she had left Québec.

Perhaps 200 were in the lifeboats. Another 500 or so were floating in water which was just a few degrees above freezing. Those who had donned Board of Trade lifejackets discovered they were so badly-designed that they tended to push their wearer's heads underwater and drown them. Soon the living were surrounded by the dead and dying.

Then the fog rolled away as suddenly as it had come in, and *Storstad* moved in to the rescue. Despite valiant efforts, her crew only managed to pull aboard 485 dazed and hypothermic survivors, many with broken limbs. Some twenty later died aboard the collier, bringing total losses to 840 passengers and 172 crew.

Aftermath

A Canadian Court of Inquiry found the evidence as foggy as that night on the river, and reached no firm conclusion. There was a bizarre moment when the Court-appointed interpreter turned out to be a Russian, who spoke limited Swedish and was unable to communicate effectively with *Storstad*'s Norwegian-speaking crew.

Reports of times, distances and bearings were ambiguous and irreconcilable. The Court heard conflicting stories of altered courses, confused signals and red running lights which should had been green. Captain Holtung of *Alden,* another Norwegian collier, testified he passed *Empress* steering a very erratic course some forty-eight kilometres (thirty miles) upstream from the collision. His testimony was confirmed by *Alden*'s Canadian pilot, Lapierre.

In the end, the only blame apportioned by the Court concerned the Norwegian mate; 'We are of the opinion that Mr Toftenes, the officer in charge of the *Storstad*, was negligent in omitting to tell the captain when the fog was coming in.' Even this gentle reprimand was reversed by a Norwegian Maritime Inquiry, held in the Montréal Consulate, which absolved *Storstad*'s officers of any responsibility for the accident. Too many questions remained unanswered, although both Inquiries agreed that if the ships had held to their original courses, they would have crossed without incident.

SEPTEMBER 1914 – THE PRICE OF GIVING AID ON THE NORTH SEA

At the beginning of the First World War, the British Royal Navy assigned four elderly armoured cruisers, crewed by reservists and cadets, to patrol an area of the North Sea known as Hoofden Shallows or the 'Broad Fourteens'. On 20 September, three of them sortied without the normal escort, because the weather was deemed too rough for destroyers. Two days later, they were steaming at ten knots without zigzagging when they were sighted by *Leutnant* Otto Weddigen, commanding German submarine *U-9*, who later reported:

> I had been . . . partly submerged with about five feet of my periscope showing. Immediately I caught sight of the first cruiser and two others I submerged completely and laid my course so as to bring up in the centre of the trio, which held a sort of triangular formation. . . . I soon reached what I regarded as a good shooting point. . . . I loosed one of my torpedoes at the middle ship. . . . There was a fountain of water, a burst of smoke, a flash of fire, and part of the cruiser rose in the air.

Weddigen's torpedo had struck *Aboukir* on her port side just under one of her magazines, which exploded, blasting a huge hole in her hull. She lost power, and developed a twenty-degree list, causing Captain Drummond to order 'abandon ship'. All but one of her boats had been destroyed in the explosion, so most of the crew had to jump into the sea.

Thinking *Aboukir* had struck a mine, the other cruisers closed in to pick up swimming survivors. Drummond, who had realized it was a torpedo, signalled them off, but Captain Nicholson of *Hogue* heaved to and lowered rescue boats. He believed the hull of foundering *Aboukir* would screen his ship from the submarine. However, *Aboukir* rolled over and sank, exposing *Hogue* and leading Weddigen to say, 'The English were playing my game, for I scarcely had to move out of my position.'

He fired two torpedoes, which struck *Hogue* amidships and flooded her engine room. The firing affected *U-9*'s trim; she briefly broke the surface and was fired upon by the sinking ship's gunners. Weddigen said: 'Her crew were brave, and even with death staring them in the face kept to their posts, ready to handle their guns, which were useless for I submerged at once.' Meanwhile, Captain Johnson of *Cressy* had also stopped to lower boats but, as soon as he realized there was a submarine present, he got underway. Weddigen continues:

> By this time the third cruiser knew of course that the enemy was upon her and she sought as best she could to defend herself. She

loosed her torpedo defence batteries . . . she steamed in a zigzag course, and this made it necessary to hold my torpedoes until I could lay a true course for them. . . . I had to come to the surface for a view and saw how wildly the fire was being sent from the ship. Small wonder when they did not know where to shoot, although one shot went unpleasantly near.

U-9's torpedo struck *Cressy* on her starboard side. Later, Dr Gerald Martin, the ship's surgeon, told the *Morning Post* newspaper, 'The effect was similar to that which would have been produced by the vessel running against a huge rock.' The blow was not fatal, and a second missile was launched. This time *Cressy* suffered a boiler explosion, turned turtle, and slowly subsided. The entire affair had taken less than an hour.

Aftermath

Harwich's force of light cruisers and destroyers rushed out in response to the distress signals but, before they arrived, survivors were rescued by nearby fishing trawlers and merchant ships, one of which, Netherlands ship *Flora*, took 286 to neutral Holland. Under the rules of war, they should have been interned, but the Dutch quickly returned them. In total, 837 were saved, but 1,459 perished, most of them elderly reservists or youthful cadets.

October 1914 – The Price of Withholding Aid on the North Sea

Less than a month later, there was a sequel. On 14 October, *U-9* encountered elements of the 10th cruiser squadron. This time it was one of her officers, rather than Weddigen, who reported:

> Three cruisers . . . were converging, and steering for . . . the vicinity where we lay. . . . The cruisers, big armoured fellows, came zigzagging. We picked one which afterward turned out to be HMS *Hawke,* and manoeuvred for a shot. It was tricky work . . . we were in position for a stern shot at an angle, but she turned. It was a fatal turning, for it gave us an opportunity to swing around for a clear bow shot at 400 metres. 'Second bow tube – fire!' Weddigen snapped out the order.

Hawke sank in less than eight minutes, with only enough time to launch one small six-man dory but, in the aftermath of the *Aboukir-Hogue-Cressy* incident, strict orders had been issued banning major warships from stopping in dangerous waters. As result, the other cruisers steamed away leaving 573 crewmen in the water, 524 of whom drowned.

Aftermath

As reward for sinking four heavy cruisers, Weddigen was promoted to *Kapitänleutnant* (Lieutenant Commander), awarded the Iron Cross, and given *U-29*, a more modern submarine. With her he sank four merchantmen. Then, on 18 March 1915, returning from an attack on the British battle fleet in the Orkneys, *U-29* was rammed and sunk with all hands by HMS *Dreadnought* – the only time that famous vessel was in action.

JANUARY 1915 –
SIGNAL CONFUSION AT DOGGER BANK

David Beatty, his handsome profile topped – contrary to naval regulations – by a rakishly askew admiral's cap, was lionized by the British press and public as 'our second Nelson'. Having joined the Navy in 1884, he served with distinction in the Sudan Campaign of 1896, and was promoted to captain for courageous leadership ashore during the China War of 1900. In 1910, like Nelson before him, he was made up to flag rank at the early age of thirty-nine. Two years later he was given command of the Fast Battle-Cruiser Squadron.

German Offensive Strategy

When the First World War began, the British Royal Navy enjoyed effective control of the North Sea, having twenty-eight dreadnoughts and battle cruisers to oppose eighteen in the Imperial German Navy. Barely three weeks into the war, Beatty's squadron sank a destroyer and three cruisers in the Battle of Heligoland Bight. Then, with the High Seas Fleet effectively bottled-up in its home ports by the British Grand Fleet, Germany decided to employ its fast cruisers and battle cruisers in hit-and-run raids on English coastal towns.

During 1914, Scarborough and Hartlepool were bombarded, killing many civilians. Beatty sortied to intercept but, as one officer described the pre-radar problem, 'they simply come out of one rainstorm and disappear into the next'. Then the Allies had a stroke of luck. The Imperial Russian Navy captured the German cruiser *Magdeburg* with all code books intact. Copies were provided to British Naval Intelligence, enabling it to decipher German signals.

On 23 January 1915, Admiral von Ingenohl, Commander-in-Chief of the German Navy, signalled Rear Admiral Franz Hipper to sail from his base in the Jade Estuary and scout the Dogger Bank region of the North

Sea. With three battle cruisers, one heavy- and four light cruisers, he was to attack the British fishing fleet and any light forces in the region or, if neither was encountered, bombard coastal towns again. The fleet would be supported by Zeppelin *L-5*.

This signal was intercepted and decoded by the British Admiralty's secret deciphering service, known as *Room Forty*. Commodore Tyrwhitt's Harwich-based force of light cruisers and destroyers was ordered to rendezvous at Dogger Bank with Beatty's Rosyth-based force of five battle cruisers and Commodore Goodenough's squadron of four light cruisers. The British left their home ports within minutes of the German departure.

An Imprecise Communication

Just before dawn on 24 January, German light cruiser *Kolberg*, on the left of Hipper's fleet, sighted light cruiser *Aurora* of Tyrwhitt's force. They opened fire, and each scored two hits on the other. Hipper immediately turned his heavy units towards the gunfire, expecting to overwhelm inferior enemy forces.

Soon, light cruisers *Southampton* and *Birmingham* made contact with light cruisers *Stralsund* and *Graudenz*, who were screening the German heavy ships. Goodenough promptly engaged and signalled *Nottingham* and *Lowestoft* to join him. Beatty thought the first two could deal with the Germans, and told his flag lieutenant to order the others to stay in their scouting positions.

Lieutenant Commander Seymour signalled *Nottingham*, 'Light Cruisers resume position for look-out. Take station ahead five miles.' Since he had not named specific ships, *Nottingham* forwarded the signal to his commodore, who naturally assumed it meant all four of them and broke off the action, losing the chance of destroying the German cruisers before they sighted Beatty's battle cruisers.

The Fleets Engage

Shortly afterward, *Stralsund* <u>did</u> sight the smoke of Beatty's force and alerted Hipper who, finally realizing he was outgunned, turned to head for the German Bight. However, assuming the British force consisted of battleships, which he could easily outrun, he did not go to full speed, but conformed to his slowest ship, 23-knot heavy cruiser *Blücher*. By the time he realized Beatty's faster battle cruisers were overhauling him, the range had dropped to 23,000 metres (25,000 yards).

The German battle line consisted of *Seydlitz* (flag), followed by *Möltke* and *Derfflinger*, with *Blücher* trailing behind. Barrelling ahead at 27 knots with *Lion* (flag), *Tiger* and *Princess Royal*, Beatty left slower *New Zealand* and *Indomitable* struggling to keep up. At 8:52 *Lion* opened fire, but the range was too great and visibility was poor due to smoke being put up by the light forces. Beatty ordered them out of the way and closed the range.

At 9:40 *Lion* scored a hit on *Seydlitz,* penetrating the barbette of one rear turret and igniting reserve shell propellant. Flames passed through a connecting door, which should have been sealed, and killed the crews of both turrets. The magazines were flooded just in time to prevent them blowing up.[23] In an ongoing exchange of gunfire, *Lion* and *Blücher* each suffered repeated hits and were forced to slow down.

Another Misleading Signal

Always seeking personal publicity, Beatty planned to repeat Nelson's famous signal 'Engage the enemy more closely', but Seymour told him that phrase was no longer in the signal book, so a substitute was chosen. Shortly afterward, the Admiral ordered a change of course to better inter- cept Hipper. Due to battle damage, *Lion* had no power for her signal lamps, and most of her signal halyards had been shot away, so Seymour decided to combine the two orders and signalled, 'Attack the rear of the enemy – bearing north-east.'

The ship to the north-east was *Blücher,* lying to the rear of the other Germans. As a result of this second confusing signal, Beatty, in crippled *Lion,* had to watch helplessly as his second-in-command, Rear Admiral Archibald Moore in *New Zealand,* led the rest of the British force against already-doomed *Blücher,* while Hipper steamed south-west to make good his escape from potential annihilation.

Aftermath

The British guns finished off *Blücher* and moved in to pick up survivors, but rescue attempts had to be abandoned when Zeppelin *L-5* bombed the operation. German casualties were 954 killed, eighty wounded and 189 captured. The British had had fifteen killed and thirty-two wounded.

At the subsequent inquiry, Beatty stood by Commander Seymour, but meanly tried to pin blame on Commodore Goodenough and Rear-Admiral Moore, disregarding the fact that they had merely been following Seymour's imprecise signals. He did not succeed.

February 1915 – Timidity at the Dardanelles

When the First World War broke out in 1914, the Russian army enjoyed virtually unlimited manpower, but suffered severe shortages of matériel and munitions. Thanks to faulty intelligence, poor communications and incompetent leadership, it suffered a series of devastating defeats and asked the Allies to relieve the pressure by attacking Turkey. With all available land forces earmarked for the Western Front, the British proposed a purely naval venture with five key objectives:

1   Draw Turkish troops away from the Russian Front.

2   Sever communications between Turkey and the Central Powers.

3   Discourage Bulgaria from joining the enemy.

4   Open an ice-free route for military aid to, and wheat from, Russia.

5   Most importantly, force the Sultan into an early peace.

Plan of Attack

The Allied C.-in-C., British Vice Admiral Sackville Carden, planned the assault in six sequential phases. First, the large forts on Cape Hellas and at Kum Kale (guarding the entrance to the Straits) would be bombarded into silence. Second, the minefields below the Narrows would be swept. Third, twenty forts commanding the Narrows would be bombarded into impotence. Fourth, the main minefield off Kephez Point would be cleared. Fifth, forts above the Narrows would be silenced. Finally, the fleet would cross the Sea of Marmara to bombard Constantinople.

Originally, the battleships assigned to this task were only those the French and British considered too old for fleet action but, at the last moment, the British committed *Queen Elizabeth*, the biggest, fastest and most heavily-armed ship in the Royal Navy, together with the modern battle cruiser *Inflexible*.

The assault began on 19 February 1915, when the largest and most powerful fleet ever to steam across the Aegean – twenty-two capital ships, supported by cruisers, destroyers, minesweepers and a float plane carrier – swept into the Straits. But the plan was too ambitious, and its execution too timid.

Bombardment & Minesweeping

Flat-trajectory naval shells, designed to penetrate heavy armour and explode deep in a battleship's vitals, were unsuitable for the destruction of earthworks, a task requiring the plunging fire of mortars or howitzers. Nevertheless, by a combination of naval shellfire and landings by demolition parties of Royal Marines, all guns in the outer forts were destroyed, completing the first phase of the plan.

The second phase was also satisfactorily completed, although underpowered minesweeping trawlers had great difficulty pulling their sweeps against the current, and were constantly attacked by mobile field artillery.

Before the assault could be resumed, weather conditions forced post-ponement, and ill-health forced Admiral Carden to resign. On 18 March, his replacement, Rear Admiral John de Robeck, initiated phase three of the attack with a fleet of sixteen battleships in three lines abreast, supported by cruisers, destroyers and naval spotting aircraft.

As the battleships advanced, they came under fire from heavy guns in the inner Turkish forts, most of which bounced harmlessly off their thick side armour. Then, more dangerously, explosive shells from mobile howitzers began to plunge through their lightly-armoured decks, forcing them to wheel and retreat in line ahead.

As they went, several were hit by mysterious underwater explosions, believed at the time to be mines floating down with the current, or torpedoes fired from shore bases. In fact, after the Strait had been swept, the minelayer *Nousret* had crept in, under cover of darkness, to anchor twenty new mines – in a line parallel with the Strait rather than across it in the normal pattern. Of eight British capital ships, two were sunk and two seriously damaged. Of eight French, one was sunk and another severely crippled.

Retreat from the Brink of Success

Heavy gales prevented renewed action for several days and, while the fleet lay idle, de Robeck convened a strategy conference. His senior officers insisted the Straits could still be forced by naval action, but the Admiral told London he could not proceed unless Allied ground troops first occupied the Peninsula. First Lord Winston Churchill replied 'Naval operations in the Dardanelles cannot be delayed by troop movements', while War Minister Kitchener cabled 'If the Fleet gets through . . . you will have won, not a battle but the war'.

In truth, the initial bombardment had achieved far more than de Robeck believed. Many Turkish batteries had been destroyed, and the fire-control systems of almost all the rest had been knocked out. Moreover, their ammunition supplies were virtually exhausted. The Sultan prepared to evacuate his court, and United States Ambassador Henry Morganthau told Washington that Constantinople was in a state of panic.

Even without that knowledge, a sea soldier of the calibre of British Horatio Nelson, Japanese Heihachiro Togo or American David Farragut would have pressed on. If but a single capital ship had survived to put Constantinople under its guns, Turkey would almost certainly have been knocked out of the war, while Russia might have been kept in. The post-war analysis of the Turkish General Staff agreed, saying:

A naval attack executed with rapidity and vigour at the outbreak of the war might have been successful. . . . If the Entente Fleets had appeared before Constantinople the eight divisions retained there would had been impotent to defend it.

However, by the time the weather cleared, the timid admiral on the spot had prevailed over hawkish cabinet ministers at home, and the enterprise was abandoned. The only tangible result of this aborted naval attack was the trebling of the Dardanelles defences in time to meet a hurriedly assembled (and ultimately disastrous) Anglo-French amphibious operation.

May 1915 –
Atlantic Travel Warning Ignored

The First World War was nine months old and, while immense land armies were bogged down in trench warfare, Britain had imposed a blockade which seemed to contravene the spirit of 'Traditional Rules of War', even though it did not actually breach any treaties or agreements. As a result, German commerce virtually vanished from the seas.

Travel Advisory
In retaliation, Germany announced a counter-blockade, which also violated 'Traditional Rules'. The British did not take it seriously, because her High Seas Fleet – still trapped in the Baltic by the British Grand Fleet – was unable to sortie into the Atlantic, while her U-boat fleet seemed too small to pose a serious threat to commerce. Nevertheless, on 1 May 1915, the German Embassy posted an advisory notice in American newspapers:

> Travellers intending to embark on the Atlantic voyage are reminded that a State of War exists between Germany and her allies and Great Britain and her allies; that the zone of war includes the waters adjacent to the British Isles; that, in accordance with formal notice given by the Imperial German Government, vessels flying the flag of Great Britain, or of any of her allies, are liable to destruction in those waters and that travellers sailing in the war zone on ships of Great Britain or her allies do so at their own risk.

Due to sail from New York on the day of this warning was RMS *Lusitania*, one of the world's largest, fastest and most luxurious liners. She had been officially requisitioned for war duties by the British Admiralty, but none had been assigned and she continued to offer regular transatlantic passenger services. Submarine warfare was a new and little understood phenomenon so – seeing the German warning as a toothless bullying threat – not one of 218 previously-booked American travellers cancelled their reservation.

U-Boats Deploy

Five days earlier, *Fregattenkapitän* (Commander) Herman Bauer of the Third Submarine flotilla had issued a deployment order to three of his U-boats, telling them to 'Head via most rapid route around Scotland (and) await large English troop transports. . . . Attack transports, merchant vessels, warships . . . as long as supplies allow.'

While *U-30* patrolled in front of Dartmouth and *U-27* lurked in the Bristol Channel, *U-20*, commanded by *Kapitänleutnant* (Lieutenant Commander) Walther Schwieger, passed around the west coast of Ireland, and turned east to linger off the southern Irish coast. On the way she sank a small schooner and two merchantmen, but several other torpedoings were unsuccessful.

At 1:20 p.m. on 7 May, Schwieger was running low on fuel and considering a return to base when he sighted a large liner approaching, and wrote in the U-boat's log: 'Starboard ahead four funnels and two masts of a steamer at right angles.' He was pleased to see she had no destroyer escort, and surprised she was moving straight ahead without the normal precaution of steering a zigzag course. As a result, he barely had to manoeuvre to reach a favourable attack angle.

The Attack

U-27 had only three torpedoes left, and Standing Orders required two to be kept in reserve at all times so, in spite of the importance of the target, Schwieger fired a single missile rather than a spread. On board *Lusitania,* lookout Leslie Morton reported 'Torpedo coming in from starboard'. Seconds later, another seaman, Thomas Quinn, sounded the alarm, but the bridge was slow to react and the torpedo struck just abaft the bridge. Electrical power was lost immediately and, a few seconds later, there was a powerful secondary explosion.[24]

Panic set in among the passengers, most of whom were just finishing their luncheon. The explosions had damaged the engine controls, and for ten interminable minutes the ship ploughed ahead at 20 knots (37 km/h; 23 mph). As she went she listed to starboard, first fifteen degrees, then lurching to seventeen, and finally twenty-five degrees.

Her twenty-two lifeboats had been secured to the deck by double chains, and precious minutes were lost releasing them. By then the list was so severe that it was impossible to swing many of them clear of the ship, and only eight were successfully launched. She also carried forty-eight collapsible boats, but there was not enough time to assemble any of them.

Aftermath

Some passengers jumped over the side to escape the sinking ship, but others such as Lady Mackworth stood quietly on deck until she went down, a mere eighteen minutes after the torpedo strike. Later she wrote:

> I suddenly felt the water all about me . . . I went right under – a long way – and when I came to the surface I had swallowed a lot of water. . . . I managed to seize a boat which I saw in front of me, and hang on to it. The water was crowded with wreckage . . . and people swimming. . . . I became unconscious, and the next thing I remember was lying on the deck of the *Bluebell*, with a sailor bending over me saying, 'You are better now'.

The attack could be seen from the Irish coast, and dozens of fishing boats and small craft rushed to the rescue but, in spite of their best efforts, only 764 people survived, while 1,195 lives were lost – 123 of them American. Although the United States did not enter the war for two more years, this incident did much to swing the tide of public opinion against Germany.

DECEMBER 1917 –
PASSING ON THE WRONG SIDE AT HALIFAX

The First World War had been raging for over three years, when a neutral ship, Norwegian whaler *Imo,* steamed out of Halifax, Nova Scotia, heading for New York where she was to pick up relief supplies for Belgium. Incoming at the same time was *Mont Blanc*, a French munitions ship which had been sent to Halifax from New York, because she was not fast enough for an American convoy – indeed, she might even have been too sluggish to keep up with a 'slow' convoy out of Halifax.

She was laden with thirty-five tons of benzol, ten tons of guncotton, 2,300 tons of picric acid (for making explosives), and 400,000 pounds of TNT – all destined for the French war effort. Inexcusably she was not wearing a red flag – the international signal for hazardous cargo.

Enormous Halifax Harbour is entered through a channel called 'The Narrows'. The rule of the road is that ships going through this channel should slow down and pass each other 'red-to-red' or 'port-to-port' – meaning that each captain should keep to his right, so that the left side of each ship passes the other. However, *Mont Blanc* saw that *Imo* was bearing down fast and had strayed too far to the left, encroaching on *Mont Blanc*'s channel and threatening to force her dangerously close to the eastern shore.

Mont Blanc signalled 'I am in my correct channel', but *Imo* moved even further to port. To avoid a head-on collision, *Mont Blanc*'s captain, Aimé le Medec, ordered 'dead slow' and 'hard aport', intending to cross *Imo*'s bow and pass starboard-to-starboard. He might have made it, except that Norwegian skipper Haakon Fron suddenly realized the danger, and made a simultaneous emergency turn to starboard.

Imo's bow struck deep into the French ship's side, missing the high-explosives, but sending sparks into the picric acid, which was stored directly below the highly inflammable benzol. Knowing their cargo, *Mont Blanc*'s crew took to the lifeboats and rowed furiously for Dartmouth on the eastern shore, leaving the abandoned ship to drift towards Halifax town on the opposite side.

The burning ship was a spectacular sight as she drifted past a pier, setting it on fire. The Halifax Fire Department responded but, at 9:05 a.m., just as they were connecting to a hydrant, a brilliant flash and wind-storm engulfed the entire city in what has been called 'The largest man-made explosion before the nuclear age'. Windows were shattered eighty kilometres (fifty miles) away, and the shock wave travelled 430 kilometres (270 miles) to be felt in Cape Breton. One of *Mont Blanc*'s anchor shanks, weighing more than half a tonne (1,105 lbs), was thrown almost four kilometres (2.5 miles) inland.

Thousands of spectators had gathered at the waterfront and in the windows of buildings overlooking the harbour. More than 1,600 were instantly killed, and the number of dead and injured eventually reached 11,000 – many of them blinded by flying window glass. Much of Halifax was levelled, and fire spread rapidly, consuming most of the wooden downtown buildings.

MARCH 1918 –
FRIENDLY FIRE OVER THE ENGLISH CHANNEL

Lieutenant de la Marine Sainte-Remy, commander of *Dirigeable AT-0* (a French naval airship), came out of his quarters at Le Havre, and was pleased to see the weather was fine for his upcoming anti-submarine patrol. After he had taken off and climbed to 490 metres (1600 feet) he found good visibility, except for a light surface mist.

Through the haze, he spotted something moving on the water ahead. He couldn't be sure what it was, but speeded up and dropped a bit of altitude to investigate. Soon he realized it was a submarine cruising on the surface. Even though it was probably a U-boat, he decided to make sure it was not one of his own. Dropping even lower, he passed over the boat. It had identification markings on its casing, but nothing he recognized, so he decided it must be German.

At that moment, the boat fired rockets from her stern, obviously trying to ignite the highly-flammable gas in the airship's fabric hull. His air gunners responded with a volley of machine-gun fire, which stopped the rocket-launching, and caused the submarine to crash dive. This seemed to confirm its hostile identity, so he dropped two 32-kilogram (70-pound) bombs, both of which missed. Circling for a second bombing run, he dropped four more, one of which struck the still-visible conning tower and forced the boat to re-surface.

Almost as soon as she came up, crewmen started jumping overboard, but only four escaped before the vessel foundered. Even in the fourth year of the First World War, there was still a residue of humanitarian concern for survivors, so Sainte Remy descended to eighteen metres (sixty feet) and threw lifejackets to the swimmers. They shouted back and, to his horror, he heard not German but English.

The French airship had sunk British submarine *D-3*, commanded by Lieutenant Maitland-Dougall of the Royal Canadian Navy. Returning from a week-long patrol, she had painted the correct British recognition markings for the first half of March on her casing, but for some reason these had not been reported to the French naval airship command. As for the 'attack' on the dirigible, *D-3*'s rockets were signal flares intended to confirm the boat's friendly identity. Sadly, by the time Sainte-Remy had reported the tragedy, and French destroyer *Typhone* had rushed to the scene from Le Havre, all four survivors had drowned.

September 1923 –
Follow the Leader to Honda Point

Speeding along the California coast at 20 knots (37 km/h; 23 mph), the fourteen 'four-stackers', of United States Navy Destroyer Squadron Eleven, encountered heavy seas, which lifted their sterns and left propellers spinning. They were on a 24-hour exercise run from San Francisco to San Diego, led in line-ahead (column) by Captain Edward Watson in flagship USS *Delphy (DD261)*, closely followed by Destroyer Divisions 33, 31 and 32 in that order.

At 9:00 p.m., intending to pass through the Santa Barbara Channel, Watson turned eastward. The light on Point Arguello had not been seen, but visibility was poor and he assumed they had passed it. In fact, due to navigational errors, compounded by unusual counter-currents created by an earthquake off Japan, they had not yet reached it. Navigators on some of the following ships calculated the turn as premature, but dared not challenge the flagship.

Headlong onto the Rocks

Immediately after the change of course the Squadron entered a heavy fogbank. It was heading directly for the sharp lava rocks and shallows off Honda Point but, confident of his position, Watson did not slow down. Five minutes after the turn, there was a tremendous scraping noise as *Delphy* ran along a gravel bank at full speed, followed by a huge thump as she hit the rocks known as 'The Devil's Jaw'. Watson immediately ordered full astern to try and drag her off, but she remained firmly impaled.

Coming up close behind, *S.P. Lee (DD310)* made an emergency turn to port and came to rest broadside-on to the cliffs, north of *Delphy*. Next in line was *Young (DD312)*. After her keel was ripped open by the jagged rocks, she was caught in the flagship's propeller wash which rolled her onto her side. Almost simultaneously, *Delphy* capsized.

The two remaining ships of Division 33 barrelled ahead in the fog. *Woodbury (DD309)* was wrecked on another group of offshore rocks, while *Nicholas (DD311)* struck a reef to seaward of *Lee* and her bow broke off. The screams of scraping metal, and *Delphy*'s wailing siren warned Division 31 in time to slow down, but not to avoid disaster.

Fuller (DD297) struck the rocks just past *Woodbury*, while *Chauncey (DD296)* grounded herself inshore of *Young*. Shortly afterward, *Farragut (DD300)* ran onto a gravel bank, and *Somers (DD301)* grounded along-side her, both lightly enough to back off with only minor damage. The last ship in Division 31, *Percival (DD298)*, and all four in Division 32 managed to stop before striking.

Aftermath

Rescue attempts began immediately. Local ranchers, alerted by the noise, rigged breeches buoys from the clifftops down to the wrecked ships. *Chauncey* threw a lifeline to nearby *Young*, and survivors from the capsized vessel scrambled aboard. Fishing boats picked up the crews of *Fuller* and *Woodbury*. Survivors of other ships managed to wade ashore over the rocks.

The seven grounded destroyers were total losses. No salvage work was even attempted, and removable equipment was sold to a scrap merchant for $1,035. Only twenty-three men were lost, almost all of them from *Young*. Eleven officers were court-martialled, the largest single group in US Navy history, but it was another whitewash. Watson suffered loss of seniority, three others were admonished and the rest acquitted. *Chauncey*'s skeletal remains can still be seen on the rocks off Honda Point.

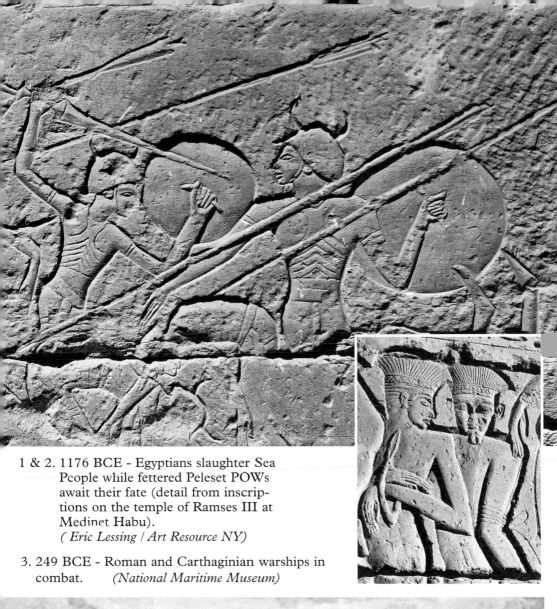

1 & 2. 1176 BCE - Egyptians slaughter Sea
People while fettered Peleset POWs
await their fate (detail from inscrip-
tions on the temple of Ramses III at
Medinet Habu).
(Eric Lessing / Art Resource NY)

3. 249 BCE - Roman and Carthaginian warships in
combat.   *(National Maritime Museum)*

4. 1120 - *White Ship* founders on Barfleur Rocks (from an illuminated manuscript, ca 1321, in the British Museum). *(The British Library; Cotton Claudius D.ii.f.45b)*

5. 1274 - Before the first kamikaze wind destroys the invading Mongol fleet, Samurai
   Suenaga is wounded by Mongol arrows and a grenade fragment.
                                    (International Society for Educational Information)

6. 1281 - Before the second kamikaze destroys another Mongol fleet, Suenaga leads a
   boarding party aboard one of the Mongol ships.
                                    (International Society for Educational Information)

7. 1667 - A Dutch boarding party approaches HMS *Royal Charles*.
(National Maritime Museum)

8. 1782 - HMS *Royal George* heels onto the schooner *Lark*. *(National Maritime Museum)*

9. 1813 - USS *Chesapeake* sorties to engage HMS *Shannon*.

(*Kellscraft Studio*)

10. 1816 - Raft of the *Medusa* (original painting by Theodore Géricault).

(Eric Lessing / Art Resource NY)

11. 1820 - A sperm whale rams the whaler *Essex* (from the frontispiece of the book by Thomas Nickerson). *(Nantucket Historical Association)*

12. 1827 - Russian warships *Hanhoute* and *Azov* silhouetted by an exploding Turco-Egyptian frigate. *(National Maritime Museum)*

13. 1855 - Emigrants gather on the quay awaiting embarkation.
(Website www.vasson.vassar.edu)

14. 1865 - *Sultana* leaves Vicksburg overloaded with Union soldiers.
(US Library of Congress)

15. 1904 - *General Slocum* smoulders on North Brother Island.
(Mariners' Museum Newport News)

16. 1914 - *Storstad*'s icebreaking prow is barely damaged by her collision.
(National Archives of Canada)

17. 1915 - A U-boat crew watches a torpedoed British vessel sink (from a watercolour painted during the action by Claus Bergen). *(Eric Lessing / Art Resource NY)*

18. 1923 - Seven ships of US Destroyer Squadron 11 wrecked on Honda Point.

(US Naval Historical Center)

19 & 20. 1939 - Günther Prien leaves Kiel for Scapa Flow ... and returns to dine with the Führer. *(Website www2.hgo.se)*

21. 1942 - *Scharnhorst* seen from *Prinz Eugen* during their Channel Dash.
(Website www.scharnhorst-class.dk)

. 1942 - *Queen Mary*'s prow after her collision with *Curacoa* (note that only about a third of the damage is visible). (*Queen Mary*, Long Beach, California)

. 1945 - *Cap Arcona* ablaze after the air attack. (*Public domain websites*)

24. 1948 - *Kiangya* sitting on the Wangpoo (Huangpu) river mud (taken on or about 3 December). (*Unknown Chinese newspaper*)

25. 1949 - *Noronic* ablaze at her berth in Toronto harbour. (*Toronto Star*)

26. 1950 - USS *Missouri* being hauled off her ignominious perch on the Norfolk mud-banks. (*Timberland Equipment Limited*)

27. 1956 - Eleven hours after the collision, *Andrea Doria* heels over and sinks with port lifeboats still aboard ... *(Mariners' Museum Newport News)*

28 ... meanwhile, injured *Stockholm* limps into the Hudson River with 15 metres (50 feet) of her bow missing or crushed. *(Illustrated London News)*

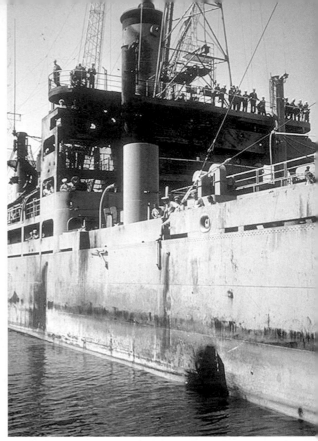

29 & 30. 1967 - USS *Liberty*
shows little damage above the
waterline, but a 9x12 metre
(30x40 foot) hole in dry dock.
(Website www.ussliberty.com)

31. 1969 - USS *Pueblo*. (US Navy)

32. 1987 - Salvage vessel *Norma* nears *Herald of Free Enterprise*. (SMIT Salvage)

33. 2003 - Hoisting a 3,000-tonne section of *Tricolor* from the floor of the English Channel.   (*Combinatie Berging* Tricolor)

34. 2003 - A section of *Tricolor*, neatly sliced through the engine room.
(*Combinatie Berging* Tricolor)

PART SIX

The Second World War
– The Axis Ascendant

JULY 1937 – THE CONFLICT BEGINS

Contrary to the Eurocentric viewpoint, which dates the war from Hitler's invasion of Poland in September 1939, a global perspective sees it as beginning in July 1937, when the Japanese invaded China, and ending in September 1945, when they surrendered aboard USS *Missouri* in Tokyo Bay.

Taken as a whole, it was a blunder of monumental proportions and a maritime catastrophe of unprecedented magnitude – an eight-year killing spree which sank many thousands of ships and took hundreds of thousands of seafarers' lives.

Many of those killed were innocent civilians, while others were prisoners of war. This was because – except for well identified hospital ships in clear weather – belligerents firing from submerged submarines or high-speed aircraft had no means of determining what passengers or cargo their target might be carrying. It would be impossible to describe all the war's maritime incidents in a book of this size, but twenty-one have been selected for discussion.[25]

OCTOBER 1939 –
SUBMARINE INFILTRATION OF SCAPA FLOW

No sooner had Britain declared war than *Kommodore* Karl Dönitz, head of the German submarine service, began to consider an audacious and hazardous plan to attack the Royal Navy's base at Scapa Flow in the Orkney Islands, north of Scotland. This was a huge anchorage, twenty-four kilometres (fifteen miles) long and thirteen kilometres (eight miles) wide; bounded by five main islands and a number of smaller islets.

In 1939 it was believed impregnable, thanks to heavy defences and narrow entrance channels, three closed by booms and two by sunken blockships with anti-submarine cables stretched between them. Moreover, unpredictable currents and riptides were considered powerful enough to carry a submarine off course. Nevertheless, intelligence and reconnaissance reports led Dönitz to select one of these five channels as possibly feasible for a raid. He wrote:

Holm Sound is protected exclusively by two apparently sunken ships lying obliquely in the navigable water of Kirk Sound, together with one ship lying on the north side. South of these obstructions . . . there is a gap, 170 metres wide, 7 metres in depth. . . . Also north of the sunken ships there is a small gap. The shore on both sides is practically uninhabited. I hold that a penetration at this

point on the surface at the turn of the tide would be possible. . . .
The main difficulty concerns navigation. [Cited in British Admiralty
NID.24T 16/45.]

Dönitz asked recently-promoted *Kapitänleutnant* (Lieutenant
Commander) Günther Prien to volunteer for this daring mission, which
had been given the mundane title *Operationsbefehl Nordsee 16* (North Sea
Operations Order 16). Prien had had combat submarine experience
during the Spanish Civil War and had been the most junior officer ever
to be given command of one of the advanced Type VIIB U-boats. Within
four days of Britain's declaration of war, he had sunk three British
freighters and been awarded the first naval Iron Cross of the Second
World War.

Dönitz gave Prien forty-eight hours to decide whether to accept the
assignment. He did, and the raid was scheduled for the night of 13–14
October 1939, when both periods of slack water would occur during
darkness. Security was so tight that details were transmitted only by
word of mouth and only within the submarine service. Staff in other
branches of the *Kriegsmarine* (German Navy) knew nothing of the plan –
an omission which was to backfire later.

Prien's Raid Begins

Early in October, all U-boats were withdrawn from Scottish waters.
Dönitz did not want a chance sighting or sonar contact to put the Home
Fleet on submarine alert. Shortly afterward, *U-47* slipped quietly away
from depot ship *Weichsel* at Kiel. On her conning tower, the conventional
skull-and-crossbones emblem was supplemented by a top hat and
umbrella – symbols deriding British Prime Minister Neville Chamberlain,
the appeaser of Munich. At 0400 hours (4:00 a.m.), she arrived off Scapa
Flow and submerged for a fifteen-hour wait on the bottom. Ship's cook
Walz prepared a 'hangman's dinner' of soup, veal cutlets, pork ribs, pota-
toes and cabbage.

At 1915 hours (7:15 p.m.) on Friday 13th, *U-47* surfaced and crept
along Holm Sound, making her way towards smaller and more-heavily
defended Kirk Sound. Amid the swirling waters of a fast inward-flowing
tide, Prien zigzagged through the narrow gaps between blockships
Thames, Soriano and *Minich*, scraping *U-47*'s keel over the anti-
submarine cables stretched across them. Suddenly, the boat slewed hard
astarboard and grounded on a sandbank. He ordered all tanks blown and
eased her back into deeper water. At 0027 (12:27 a.m.), the boat exited
the turbulent channel into the calm waters of the Flow itself, where Prien
had an unpleasant surprise.

Missing Battle Fleet

The huge anchorage was empty, with not a single battleship, battle-cruiser or aircraft carrier to be seen, not even a cruiser or destroyer. This lack of targets was due to poor coordination between the *Kriegsmarine*'s surface and submarine branches. Coincidentally with Prien's raid, and thanks to Dönitz's obsession with secrecy, battle cruiser *Gneisenau*, cruiser *Köln* and nine destroyers had been ordered to sortie with the specific and successful objective of luring the Home Fleet away from Scapa Flow and within range of German bombers.

The submariners remained despondent for twenty-eight long minutes. Then, *Oberleutnant-zur-See* Englebert von Varendorff, scanning with night glasses, spotted a capital ship tucked away in the north-east corner of the Flow. It was veteran battle cruiser *Royal Oak*, which had been one of the fastest ships at the Battle of Jutland in 1916, but was too slow to keep up with the fleet of 1939. She had been left behind as anti-aircraft guardship for nearby Kirkwall.

Attack

The bow of another ship could be seen beyond the battle cruiser, and Prien chose that as the target for his first torpedo, aiming two more at *Royal Oak*. One hit *Royal Oak*'s anchor chain, severing it so that it thundered noisily into the water. The others missed or misfired, as did a fourth torpedo fired from the stern tube. With all tubes empty and the enemy alerted, a lesser captain would have headed for the exit as quickly as possible. But Prien ordered the forward torpedo-room to reload – a twenty-minute job. Then, he reports:

> At 0113 (1:13 a.m.), the bow tubes fired another three-torpedo salvo. Three minutes later, they all struck *Royal Oak*'s starboard side.

Prien's report describes the scene:

> Flames shot skyward, blue . . . yellow . . . red. Like huge birds, black shadows soared through the flames, and fell hissing and splashing into the water . . . huge fragments of mast and funnels. . . . The bay awoke to feverish activity. Searchlights flashed and probed with their long white fingers . . . small swift lights low over the water, the lights of destroyers and U-boat chasers.

By 0215 hours (2:15 a.m.), Prien had skilfully navigated the outward passage, and set course for home. Meanwhile the great ship had heeled over, her huge 15-inch guns swivelling in their turrets to increase the momentum. In less than ten minutes, she sank. Eight hundred and thirty-three seamen and officers, including visiting Admiral H.E.C. Blagrove, died with the ship or in hospital from their wounds, but there were 386 survivors. One of them, Able Seaman Stanley Cole, recalled his harrowing escape in an interview published in *The Orcadian* newspaper on the sixty-third anniversary of the sinking in 2001:

> I pulled myself through the lower gap of the guard-rail and launched myself in a half dive, half slithering movement down the ship's side . . . my right foot was jammed in the guttering of the 'blister', the anti-torpedo bulge. . . . I stayed trapped, head down, for several seconds before I was able to free myself. . . . Coughing and spluttering, I became aware that my right foot and leg seemed to be hanging in the water. . . . It was like trying to swim through liquid tar, and I was convinced I wasn't going to make it. . . . Kicking out as best I could with my good leg . . . I could feel bodies of drowned shipmates under my foot. . . . Then, just as I had all but given up the struggle, along came a ship's whaler and I felt myself hauled over the boat's side.

Aftermath

Returning to Wilhelmshaven, *U-47* was met by *Grossadmiral* Raeder, who invested the entire crew with the Iron Cross, and promoted Dönitz to Rear Admiral. Hitler's personal aircraft then flew them to Berlin, where the Führer hung the coveted *Ritterkreuz* (Knight's Cross) round Prien's neck, calling the raid 'The proudest deed that a German U-boat could possibly carry out.'[26] His sentiments were echoed by Winston Churchill, who called it ' . . . a remarkable exploit of professional skill and daring'. The loss of one antiquated battleship had not been a serious blow to the Royal Navy's combat capability, but the damage to its prestige was immense.[27]

JUNE 1940 –
AIRBORNE DEATH AT SAINT-NAZAIRE

In September 1939, Cunard cruise liner *Lancastria* sailed from the Bahamas to the United States on her last peacetime voyage. In New York she was painted battleship grey, her ports were blacked-out, and she began service as a troopship. Over the next eight months, German armies overran Poland, Denmark, Norway, Holland and Belgium, and drove the British Expeditionary Force back to Dunkirk, from where 226,000 British and 112,000 Allied troops were evacuated by the Royal Navy.

On 5 June 1940, having regrouped with professional speed and precision, Hitler's armies began the Battle of France, breaking through valiant resistance and occupying Paris on the 14th. Arrangements were hastily made to evacuate as many British citizens as possible. Prophetically code-named *Operation Aerial*, a steady stream of ships ferried troops and civilians across the Channel from a number of ports.

When France asked for an armistice, it became obvious the evacuation would have to end, even though large numbers of people would be left behind. One of the last pick-ups from Saint-Nazaire was made by *Lancastria*, which began loading evacuees at 4:00 a.m. on 17 June, the day of the French surrender.

On previous trips, Captain Rudolph Sharp had limited passengers to 3,000 – already several times her normal capacity – but, with so many waiting and so little time left, he allowed as many as could board to board. Counting ceased at 4,000, but loading continued unabated. Civilian evacuees jostled for space with British and Polish soldiers and airmen. Soon every square inch of deck, alleyway and compartment was occupied by at least 7,500, and possibly as many as 9,000 souls.

In the early afternoon, overloaded *Lancastria* pulled away from Saint-Nazaire docks and anchored in the Loire Estuary alongside other evacuation ships awaiting permission to leave. Shortly after 2:00 p.m., the first of a steady stream of German Dornier 17 bombers flew over the virtually undefended sitting targets.

In two hours of spasmodic bombing, only three bombs actually hit the liner, but at 4:15 p.m. a fourth bomb was dropped straight down her funnel to explode inside the engine room. This was a death stroke. Just over fifteen minutes later, the liner rolled onto her port side and sank in fourteen fathoms (25.6 metres; eighty-four feet) of water. Only two lifeboats had been deployed.

Aftermath

Nearby HMS *Highlander*, herself crammed with evacuees, attempted rescue operations, along with several other ships. They were badly hampered by ongoing German air raids and by fuel oil from ruptured bunkers, which made their boats slippery and difficult for survivors to scramble aboard. Survivors speak of soldiers drowning under the weight of weapons and equipment they had been ordered not to abandon. Then another German bomb ignited the oily waters creating an inferno around the ship.

Eventually, some 2,500 *Lancastria* passengers were saved, but between 5,000 and 6,500 men, women and children had died – no-one will ever know the correct number, but even the lowest estimate makes it Britain's worst ever maritime disaster.

FEBRUARY 1940 –
FRIENDLY FIRE OVER THE NORTH SEA

It was a clear, almost cloudless, moonlit night as the First German Destroyer Flotilla sped along *Weg-Ein,* a ten-kilometre- (six-mile) wide lane through the defensive minefield guarding the German Bight. In line ahead and travelling at almost 26 knots, they were on their way to Dogger Bank to identify and attack suspicious craft reported by aerial reconnaissance. Their mission was code-named *Unternehmen Wikinger* (Operation Viking). At about the same time, two squadrons of Heinkel 111 bombers were on the runway at Neumünster airfield, warming up for a sortie over the North Sea.

The *Luftwaffe* (German Air Force) had developed highly effective integration with army ground forces, but had done almost nothing to coordinate with maritime operations. The *Kriegsmarine* (German Navy) had to rely on whatever aircraft Marshal Goering was prepared to release for each specific enterprise. Moreover, requests for naval/air cooperation had to follow such long and tortuous chains of command through both services that approval sometimes arrived after an operation had been completed. Such was the case with fighter cover for *Wikinger.*

At 12:00 noon on 22 February, *Fliegerkorps X* (Air Corps 10) alerted *Marinegruppe West* it had tasked bombers to attack Allied merchant shipping in the area between the Thames Estuary to the south and the Humber River in the north. Because they were strictly forbidden to attack outside that area, naval HQ assumed it was unnecessary to advise *Fregattenkapitän* (Commander) Berger of the *Fliegerkorps'* plans, or to tell the *Luftwaffe* that its flotilla was outward-bound.

At 5:35 p.m., *Major* Martin Harlinghausen, Chief of Staff of *Fliegerkorps X,* learned of the request for fighter cover and telephoned *Marinegruppe West* to ask where its ships would be operating. At this point it should have been obvious to all participants that a serious situation could arise if destroyers and bombers met in the dark of night. However, neither naval nor air authorities made any attempt to advise their people in the field. It did not seem to occur to them that the paths of destroyers and aircraft would cross on the way to their respective target areas.

Mistaken Identities
At 5:45 p.m., *Oberfeldweldwebel* (Sergeant Major) Jäger took off from Neumünster, headed north until he reached the Island of Sylt, and then turned west over the North Sea. Shortly after 7:00 p.m. his observer, *Feldwebel* Schräpler, sighted the luminous wake of a ship. Although outside the prescribed attack zone, Jäger circled to investigate this potential 'target of opportunity'.

They had had no training in ship recognition, but he and Schräpler tentatively identified it as a freighter. When the Heinkel passed over the ship, anti-aircraft fire opened up from below. With its hostile nature seemingly confirmed, they raked it with machine-gun fire, and then climbed to 1500 metres (4900 feet) for a bombing run.

The flak had come from destroyers *Richard Beitzen (Z4)* and *Erich Koellner (Z13)* both of which had misidentified the aircraft as hostile. However, as it passed over the last destroyer in line, *Max Schultz (Z3)*, one of the bridge crew reported seeing German insignia. At that moment Jäger's machine-guns opened up and the report was discounted. The flotilla forged ahead, at high speed and on maximum anti-aircraft alert.

As they heard the Heinkel returning on its bombing run, all six destroyers opened up their full barrage, but could not see what they were shooting at since it was coming directly from a black cloud in front of the moon. Jäger swooped in and dropped a string of bombs on *Lebercht Maas (Z1)*. Two missed astern, but the third struck between the bridge and forward funnel. The ship slowed down and signalled '*Habe treffer. Brauche hilfe*' (Been hit. Need help).

The other destroyers turned to the rescue, but were ordered back on course by Berger in flotilla leader *Friedrich Eckoldt (Z16)*. He himself then moved in to help. At 7:56 p.m., when he was within 500 metres (1600 feet) of the stricken vessel, two more bombs fell. The first raised a huge water fountain between the two ships, while the second sent up a fireball to almost twice mast-height. When the smoke cleared *Lebercht Maas* was seen to have broken in two. Both bow and stern were visible above the water, but their habitable parts were submerged with men trapped inside.

Chaos on the Surface

When the second attack was over, Jäger headed west towards the original target area, but his crew reported more dark shadows and wakes on the sea beneath them. These came from *Erich Koellner, Friedrich Eckoldt, Max Schultz* and *Richard Beitzen*, rushing to rescue survivors swimming in ice-cold water. They had picked up sixty of them when the Heinkel returned and another huge explosion ripped the night sky. This time *Max Schultz* was the victim.

Theodore Riedel (Z6) was going to the rescue when her sonar reported a submarine contact. She headed for the contact and dropped four depth-charges, two of which exploded too close to her own rudder and jammed it so she could only steam in circles. Then a panicked lookout on *Erich Koellner* reported a visual submarine sighting (there were actually no submarines in the vicinity), and Commander Berger ordered all ships to stop rescue operations and concentrate on the submarine hunt. *Kriegsmarine* historian Michael Emmerich reports:

The next twenty-five minutes could only be described as pure chaos. A periscope or submarine sail was 'seen' almost every minute; even the wrecks of the sinking destroyers were identified as submarines. Countless torpedoes were 'spotted' by the lookouts when the four destroyers were racing between the two sunken ships. When the *Erich Koellner* accelerated to top speed one of its boats was still towed beside it and capsized while the destroyer got faster and faster, all survivors in it being lost.

Aftermath

At 8:36 p.m., flotilla commander Berger ordered the remaining four destroyers back to base. First, they returned to the sinking ships to take on board survivors and pick up their boats which had been left there. However, during the hunt for a non-existent British submarine, all but sixty of the crew of *Lebercht Maas* and the entire ship's company of *Max Schultz* had died in the cold North Sea water. Due to administrative inefficiency, poor inter-service cooperation, misidentification and local confusion, the death toll from friendly-fire totalled 578.

SEPTEMBER 1941 –
SUBMARINE ACTION IN THE SICILY STRAIT

Bright cobalt-blue paint was the trademark of the 10th British Submarine Flotilla whose boats, operating out of Malta, destroyed one-quarter of all German and Italian shipments to the battlefields of North Africa. On 17 September 1941, intelligence reported three Italian liners scheduled to ferry a German army division from Taranto to Tripoli. Ace submariner Lieutenant Commander David Wanklyn was tasked to intercept, and he deployed the four boats under his command in a line along the convoy's anticipated course.

At about 3:00 a.m. on the 18th, the northernmost submarine, *Unbeaten*, sighted the convoy. It was too far away to attack and, due to communication difficulties, thirty minutes passed before she could alert Wanklyn in *Upholder*. By then, the convoy was already looming, silhouetted against a low moon.

The transports were steaming too fast for Wanklyn to reach optimal firing position, so he decided to risk an opportunistic shot from about 5,000 yards (4600 metres). The compass was swinging madly as *Upholder* yawed from side to side in a cross swell but, sighting by eye and mentally compensating for movement of the boat, he fired a spread of four torpedoes before diving to evade counter-attack.

One of these torpedoes sank 19,507-ton *Neptunia*, while another blew the propellers off her sister ship *Oceania*. Both *Unbeaten* and *Upholder* closed in for the finishing blow, but Wanklyn shot first. Two of his 'fish' struck the crippled ship which went down in eight minutes. Further west, *Ursula* fired at fast-retreating *Vulcania*, but missed astern.

This action in Sicily Strait cost the Axis two irreplaceable Italian transports and 5,000 German troops, making it one of the most costly maritime disasters of the Second World War.

DECEMBER 1941 – LACK OF AIR COVER IN THE GULF OF SIAM

During the first twenty-five months of the Second World War, Admiral Sir Tom Phillips had sat behind a desk as Vice Chief of Naval Staff. This had denied him first-hand experience of the fierce air-sea battles in the Channel and the Mediterranean and, being a 'battleship admiral' of the old school, he still insisted that any aircraft rash enough to approach a major warship would be destroyed long before it could release its weapon. In this, he vastly underestimated the enormous quantity of anti-aircraft artillery needed to fend off simultaneous assaults by high-level bombers, torpedo aircraft and dive bombers,

Late in 1941, he was appointed to command the first instalment of a powerful British Far Eastern Fleet, being assembled – despite the demands of the war against Nazi Germany and Fascist Italy – to counter a mounting Japanese naval threat. Fleet aircraft carrier *Indomitable* was intended to accompany the initial component, but ran aground in the West Indies, leaving new battleship *Prince of Wales*, venerable battle cruiser *Repulse*, and four escorting destroyers without naval air cover.

On 6 December, just four days after they arrived at Singapore, a large Japanese seaborne expedition was reported to have entered the Gulf of Siam. Two days after that (7 December at Hawaii on the other side of the International Date Line) the Japanese struck Pearl Harbor, Hong Kong and the Philippines. Shortly after midnight, they started landing troops on the Malayan Peninsula, and Phillips deemed it his duty to strike them.

Royal Air Force officers warned the admiral they could provide little air cover over the southern landing beaches, and none at all in the north. He ignored their advice, partly because of his fundamental belief in the superiority of gunnery over aircraft, partly because frequent rain squalls and low cloud cover were expected to inhibit air operations, and partly because he thought he would catch the enemy unprepared. None of these factors worked out as he anticipated.

Interception Attempts

Phillips' force was sighted by submarine pickets, which alerted Admiral Kondo, who set out to intercept, with two battleships, six cruisers and destroyer escorts. Then the cloud cover dispersed exposing the force to reconnaissance aircraft, which alerted 22nd Naval Air Flotilla at Saigon. This promptly unloaded bombs intended for a raid on Singapore, re-armed with torpedoes, and set out for a night attack on the British ships. Finding nothing, it returned to base.

Phillips was aware of being shadowed by Japanese aircraft and, having lost the element of surprise, turned homeward. On the way, he wasted time by investigating a false report of another landing. Then he heard that a chain of invasion barges had been sighted and, instead of sending a single destroyer to deal with them, lost his last chance of a high-speed retreat to Singapore by diverting his entire force.

Meanwhile, the Japanese 22nd Naval Air Flotilla had dispatched search aircraft, followed an hour later by nine waves of bombers and torpedo-bombers with nine aircraft in each. Thanks to Phillips' diversions, both surface and air searches missed his force completely. However, after ranging as far south as Singapore, the bombers set out for home and, purely by chance, their northerly return course led them directly over the British force.

Attack

The first wave of high-level bombers swept in just after 11:00 a.m. *Repulse* was straddled, but only one bomb hit, causing a fire which was quickly extinguished. The next wave dropped torpedoes, two of which struck *Prince of Wales*. The combined effect of their 1200-pound warheads blasted a huge hole in her hull, causing extensive flooding. Worse, they put both port propellers out of action, making the ship hard to steer.

The third wave turned back to *Repulse,* but she escaped damage. The fourth wave also attacked the battle cruiser, dropping nine torpedoes which quick-thinking Captain Tennant successfully 'combed'. Then *Repulse*'s luck ran out. The fifth and sixth waves came in simultaneously from opposite sides, and one of their torpedoes struck amidships. Although wounded, she could still make 25 knots, and her artillery kept throwing up an anti-aircraft barrage.

Yet another torpedo destroyed *Repulse*'s steering gear, and this was quickly followed by a seventh attack in which three torpedoes scored hits. Captain Tennant ordered 'all hands on deck' just before his ship heeled over and sank. The time was 12:33 p.m., barely an hour and a half since the attack began.

Meanwhile, *Prince of Wales* had been hit by two more torpedoes, and a fifth struck moments before *Repulse* went down. Stoutly-built, she could still crawl along at eight knots but, at 1:20 p.m. another bombing attack completed the job and she foundered. Shortly afterward, a flight of RAF Buffalo fighters finally arrived and drove off the Japanese, who were ready to leave anyway.

Aftermath
Admiral Phillips and his flag captain, John Leach, both went down with *Prince of Wales,* but destroyers managed to save some 2,000 officers and men out of almost 3,000 on board the two ships. Thanks to Captain Tennant's timely order, this proportion was much higher than it might otherwise have been.

The sinkings left three American aircraft carriers as the only Allied capital ships between East Africa and the North American seaboard, and gave the Japanese effective control of 238,865,000 square kilometres (92,202,000 square miles) of Indian and Pacific Ocean.

JANUARY 1942 –
ANGLOPHOBIA ON THE EASTERN SEA FRONTIER

Shortly after its entry into the Second World War, the United States suffered a little-known but crippling military setback, which almost brought the Allied war effort to a grinding halt and might have starved Britain out of the conflict altogther. No sooner had Hitler declared war on the United States, than Admiral Karl Dönitz, head of the German submarine service, mounted an all-out assault on the Maine-Florida coast (known to the US Navy as the Eastern Sea Frontier). The campaign, code-named *Unternehmen Paukenschlag* (Operation Drumbeat), had an impact far greater than the more-famous debacle at Pearl Harbor.

Dönitz's U-boats could remain on station for long periods, thanks to re-supply by large cargo- and fuel-carrying submarines, known as '*Milch Cows*'. Their tactic was to lie submerged on the bottom during daylight and come up at night. Once on the surface they were speedy enough to catch any unescorted merchant ship and sink it by gunfire or torpedo.

American Unpreparedness
They found rich pickings. The US Navy had virtually no coastal defence vessels, and was neither geared for, nor willing to accept, the convoy system which had proved so successful in two world wars. Moreover, American merchantmen were careless, providing vital information by radioing course and position to each other. They were also gullible. One U-boat set up a freighter by signalling 'This is the lightship. You are standing into danger, alter course to pass near me.'

In addition, the American people could not believe there was any danger close to home. War to them was something which only happened in foreign parts – somewhere in Europe or the Pacific. There was no blackout, so at night ships were silhouetted against the glare of onshore lights. Miami alone had a ten-kilometre (six-mile) neon strip along its waterfront, but the Chamber of Commerce refused even to tone it down, arguing that that would drive away tourists.

In fact tourists did come – in droves – not to see the neon lights so much as to watch the offshore spectacle of brilliantly burning tankers. The fuel supply situation became so critical that General George Marshall, Chairman of the Joint Chiefs of Staff, wrote to Admiral Ernest King, Chief of Naval Operations, saying:

> I am fearful that another month or two will so cripple our means of transport that we will be unable to bring sufficient men and planes to bear against the enemy in critical theatres to exercise a deter-mining influence on the war.

But King's intransigence was Dönitz's best friend. Stern, irascible and undiplomatic, his daughter summed up his nature when she wrote, 'He is the most even-tempered man in the Navy – always in a rage.' At some time during his career, he had acquired an immense mistrust and dislike of the British Royal Navy, and a profound belief that its officers were pompous and arrogant know-it-alls.

This was unfortunate because, by this time, the hated British and their Canadian Allies had had thirty months of anti-submarine warfare in which to develop and fine-tune the tactics and technology which would eventually win the long drawn-out Battle of the Atlantic.

British Dismay

Their naval intelligence and convoy experts rushed to offer assistance to the new Ally, only to be roundly (and rudely) rebuffed by King who, as one British officer commented, 'Seems to prefer U-boat sinkings to accepting our help'. Prime Minister Winston Churchill picked up the story in *The Second World War*:

> For six or seven months the U-boats ravaged American waters almost uncontrolled, and in fact almost brought us to the disaster of an indef-inite prolongation of the war. . . . Only six U-boats of the larger 750-ton type were at first despatched. . . . Their success was imme-diate. By the end of January (1942) thirty-one ships of nearly 200,000 tons had been sunk. . . . This great sea highway teemed with defence-

less American and Allied shipping. Along it the precious tanker fleet moved in unbroken procession to and from the oil ports. . . .

In February, U-boat losses in the Atlantic rose to seventy-one ships, of 384,000 tons, all but two of which were sunk in the American zone. This was the highest rate of loss we had so far suffered throughout the war. . . It was soon to be surpassed. . . The protection offered by the United States Navy was for several months hopelessly inadequate. . . Neither had the Coastal Air Defence been developed . . . U-boats prowled . . . with a freedom and insolence which was hard to bear.

On 10 February, Britain sent (unasked) ten corvettes and twenty-four of its best-equipped anti-submarine trawlers, complete with fully-trained and experienced crews. They were reluctantly accepted, but were too few to make a significant difference anyway. By the latter part of March, British patience was becoming exhausted. First Sea Lord, Admiral of the Fleet Sir Dudley Pound, complained it was pointless for the Royal Navy to escort ships safely across the Atlantic, only to have them destroyed as soon as they entered American waters.

Angrily, King mounted a propaganda counter-offensive. Although aware that no existing munition was powerful enough to penetrate the U-boats' hardened concrete bunkers, he persuaded President Roosevelt that the problem lay in Britain's failure to attack and destroy submarine bases and repair yards.

The desperate US Navy even lied to conceal the truth from the American public, issuing a Press Release announcing the destruction of twenty-eight U-boats when, in fact, there were less than half as many in the region, and not a single one of them had been sunk.

Aftermath

The breakthrough came when Britain sent its top anti-submarine expert to Washington. Commander Roger Winn met King's Deputy Chief of Staff, Admiral Edwards, who rudely told him that the US Navy could solve its own problems and had plenty of resources with which to do it. Winn was so exasperated that he forgot the huge difference in rank and replied, 'The trouble is, Admiral, it's not only your own bloody ships you're losing, a lot of them are ours'. Anger got through where politeness had not. America reluctantly accepted the British submarine tracking system, and introduced coastal convoys.

But it was Adolf Hitler who finally reduced the menace. He had become obsessed with the prospect of an Allied invasion of Nazi-occupied Norway, and ordered Dönitz to withdraw a substantial portion of the U-boat fleet for its protection.

FEBRUARY 1942 – FIRE IN NEW YORK HARBOUR

French liner *Normandie* was one of the greatest in an era of great trans-Atlantic liners. When she entered service in 1935, she was the longest, largest, fastest and most beautiful thing afloat, with a revolutionary hull designed by a Russian naval architect and interiors decorated by designers of the Paris Exposition.

Four years later, the Second World War broke out and, rather than risk their pride and joy in U-boat-infested waters, the French left her in New York Harbour. When the United States entered the war, the Navy requisitioned the ship, re-named her USS *Lafayette* and started to convert her into a high-speed troop transport. She was scheduled to make her maiden voyage with 15,000 troops on 14 February 1942.

Five days before then, she was lying at Pier 88 on the Hudson River with 2,500 dockyard workers and 500 crew members on board. Most were strangers to the ship with little idea of her layout. At 2:30 p.m., a crew of welders was working in the main saloon when a spark set fire to a pile of 1,140 kapok life jackets, which had been moved into their proximity to make room for another crew laying linoleum flooring.

Fire extinguishers failed to work, alarms had been temporarily disconnected, the ship's own fire department had not yet got a telephone, and none of the other people aboard had been assigned emergency duties or given fire instructions. For a full fourteen minutes, nobody thought of calling the New York Fire Department, by which time the blaze had a firm grip.

Workmen tried to isolate individual bales of burning kapok by hauling them away from the fringes of the inferno, but only succeeded in spreading the fire. Soon they gave up. Those who could began streaming down the gangways, while flames forced others to congregate forward. They were rescued by NYFD Ladder Company 4, which lifted an 85-foot aerial ladder to the bow. By this time, fireboat *James Duane* had reached the ship from her berth at 35th Street and started spraying from the seaward side.

Meanwhile four pumpers, two more ladder companies, another fireboat and two battalion chiefs had raced to the scene. They soon discovered that the French couplings of *Normandie*'s 504 onboard hydrants had not been converted to American standard fittings. As a result, hoses had to be unrolled from the pumpers, stretched along the length of the pier, up gangways down which panicked workers were still streaming, hauled along 300-metre (1,000-foot) long decks, and hoisted up stairways through eye-smarting dense black smoke. Naval signalmen teamed up with the firefighters, using semaphore signals to direct the placement of hoses, call for increased water pressure, and convey other vital information.

By 3:00 p.m., some forty land hoses, three fire boats and a number of tugs were pouring water into the burning hull. But at about 3:15, *Normandie*'s boilers ran out of steam and were no longer able to power her drainage pumps. Soon the weight of some 15 million litres (4 million gallons) of water created a pronounced list to port. Extra shore lines were added in an attempt to hold her upright, and Admiral Andrews of the Third Naval District asked Fire Commissioner Walsh to stop pumping in water lest she capsize.

The ship's designer, Vladmir Yourkeviych, offered his advice, but was rebuffed by naval authorities, who decided the only way to both douse the fire and prevent *Normandie* from rolling over was to scuttle her. But navy engineers found it impossible to open all twenty-nine sea cocks simultaneously, or to reach the engine room to pull condenser plates, which would have had the same effect.

Members of the Fire Department Rescue Squad were then lowered over the side in bosun's chairs to cut drainage holes, but as soon as their acetylene torches penetrated the steel plates, water gushed out and extinguished them. A larger hole was cut above the waterline and a pumper tried to suck water out, but with little success.

At 12:20 a.m., the list increased to fifteen degrees and it was decided to abandon ship. It was too dangerous to recover the fire hoses, so they were cut with axes and left behind. Twenty-five minutes later *Normandie* rolled gently over and settled on her side in the mud amid floating debris, oil, and grime.[28]

FEBRUARY 1942 –
A PYRAMID OF BLUNDERS IN THE CHANNEL

When the Second World War began, pocket battleships *Deutschland* and *Graf Spee* were already at sea. Like huge pirates, they ranged the oceans preying on unprotected merchant vessels and cutting supply lines to the United Kingdom, which was totally dependent on sea transport for food and war matériel. *Graf Spee* was scuttled after the Battle of the River Plate in 1939, and next year *Deutschland* had to head home with engine trouble. They were replaced by the larger, faster, more-heavily gunned battle cruisers *Scharnhorst* and *Gneisenau,* and heavy cruiser *Hipper.*

In March 1941, *Hipper* returned to Germany, while the battle cruisers fled to the French port of Brest to escape a converging British fleet. In May, attempting to sortie via the Denmark Strait, battleship *Bismark* was attacked and sunk by the Royal Navy. Her consort, heavy cruiser *Prinz Eugen*, escaped and also took refuge at Brest. The three ships constituted a minor 'fleet in being', capable of creating havoc if they managed to escape into the open sea. British and German planners each considered three possibilities:

1   A sortie into the Atlantic to resume commerce raiding.

2   An attempt to reach a Norwegian or German port via the Iceland Channel.

3   An attempt to force passage through the Strait of Dover.

The Home Fleet was tasked to counter the first two but, with regard to the third, First Sea Lord, Admiral of the Fleet Sir Dudley Pound, ordered 'On no account will heavy ships be brought south where they would be exposed to enemy air attack, torpedo-boat attack, and risk being damaged by our own and enemy minefields'. Instead, he sent submarines to form an 'iron ring' around the Brest approaches, had thousands of mines laid in the Channel, and positioned motor torpedo boats at Dover and Ramsgate.

Following the sinking of *Repulse* and *Prince of Wales* by aircraft, the RAF confidently expected the *coup de grâce* to be delivered by its heavy bomber force. It did not seem to appreciate that Japanese naval pilots had been intensively trained for low-level ship destruction, while Bomber Command specialized in high-altitude area-bombing.

Hitler Plans the Channel Dash Personally

Heavy British air raids threatened to damage the ships beyond repair, leading the Germans to review the three escape options with increased urgency. Grand Admiral Raeder wanted to resume commerce raiding in the Atlantic, but Hitler – who had been disillusioned by the loss of *Graf Spee* and *Bismark* – said, 'Battleships are no good for anything. Their big guns would be more useful and less vulnerable in emplacements ashore.'

Later, the Führer said the ships should go to Scandinavia, telling Raeder, 'The issue of war will be decided in Norway. Unless the British are fools they will attack us there. . . . With our ships at Brest, enemy sea forces are tied up to no greater extent than would be the case if they were stationed in Norway.' He dismissed the lengthy Iceland Channel passage in favour of a dash through the English Channel, brushing aside *Kriegsmarine* and *Luftwaffe* fears of annihilation in the narrow waters by saying:

The ships must not leave port in daylight as we are dependent on the element of surprise; this means they will have to pass through the Dover Straits in daytime. (However) I do not believe the British capable of making and carrying out lightning decisions. . . . Picture what would happen if the situation were reversed – if a surprise report came in that British battleships . . . were heading for the

Straits of Dover. In my opinion, even we would hardly be able to bring up (our own) forces swiftly and methodically.

Code-named *Unternehmen Cerebus*, the operation was meticulously planned and executed in complete secrecy. U-boats were diverted to make meteorological observations. Lanes were covertly swept through German and British minefields. British radar covering the Dover Straits was jammed for gradually-increasing periods each day – in such a manner as to simulate atmospheric interference.

Six escort destroyers were stealthily moved to Brest, while torpedo boat flotillas assembled at Le Havre, Flushing and Dunkirk, two E-boat flotillas were scheduled to join the escort after Cherbourg, and two more before the narrows at Cap Gris Nez. For once, inter-service cooperation was impeccable. Gunners and artillery from the *Wehrmacht* (the army) were brought onboard the big ships to supplement their own anti-aircraft armament; and *Luftwaffe* officers were assigned to each of them to control 250 fighter aircraft and thirty night fighters, scheduled to provide around-the-clock air cover.

British Countermeasures

Early in February 1942, British Intelligence accurately forecast a probable breakout on or after the tenth of the month. But they reversed Hitler's ideas, believing the ships would leave Brest in daylight, in order to pass the Straits of Dover in darkness. Detailed counter-plans were drawn up for this scenario. Code-named 'Fuller', they were classified 'Most Secret', and restricted to senior officers with a 'need to know'. As a result, most of the assigned forces had no idea why they were being redeployed.

To give early warning of any attempt to move through the Channel, the Royal Air Force arranged for Coastal Command to mount overnight radar patrols over Brest and along the western part of the English Channel, and for Fighter Command to organize daylight sweeps over the Eastern part. There was no liaison between them, and neither knew of the other. The RAF also promised the Navy that 300 of its heavy bombers would be kept on standby ready for the German ships' breakout.

Britain's most effective anti-ship weapon should have been the Beaufort torpedo bombers of RAF Coastal Command but, not being under naval command, many of their pilots had never dropped a torpedo, even in practice. One squadron, based at St Eval in Cornwall, was positioned to attack a break-out into the Atlantic. A second, stationed at Thorney Island near Portsmouth, covered the Dover Strait. A third, at Leuchars in Scotland, was poised to counter a sortie by the German battleship *Tirpitz* from Norway. It was ordered to move south to

Coltishall near Norwich, within flying distance of the Strait.

Orders were also sent to move a naval squadron of Swordfish torpedo-bombers to Manston in Kent. Unlike the Beauforts, these obsolescent aircraft were too slow and vulnerable for daytime attack. However, they would be invaluable if, as expected, the Germans tried to run the Strait in darkness. Swordfish had already proved their worth by destroying three Italian battleships in a night raid on Taranto, and by crippling *Bismark,* making her a sitting target for the guns and torpedoes of the surface fleet.

Seven modern British submarines patrolling the Brest approaches had recently been withdrawn, some to replace heavy submarine losses in the Mediterranean, others to go to the new war against Japan. One older and smaller boat was on station, patrolling the Atlantic escape route, and a newer one was sent to watch the Channel route. The Navy also placed a flotilla of six elderly destroyers at Harwich on high alert.

Execution of Hitler's Plan

The Führer's belief that the British would be 'unable to bring up forces swiftly and methodically' proved accurate. The rapid and complex sequence of events will best be illustrated by reporting them in 'real time' as they unfolded.

11 February

1930 hours (7:30 p.m.): Just as the German vessels are about to cast off, an air-raid warning sounds and the harbour is quickly shrouded with a protective shield of artificial fog. None of the ships is hit but, because photographs taken by the Wellington bombers show parts of them through gaps in the fog, the British make their first blunder by assuming the Germans are safely tied up in the harbour.

2000 hours (8:00 p.m.): Given a reduced level of alert, the nearest screening British submarine moves some fifty kilometres (thirty miles) away in order to recharge batteries. As this is only a temporary move, no replacement is sent.

2125 hours (9:25 p.m.): Almost two hours behind schedule, tugs begin pulling the ships out. *Scharnhorst*, wearing Vice Admiral Otto Ciliax's flag, leads, closely followed by *Gneisenau* and *Prinz Eugen*. They quickly work up to thirty knots (34.5 mph; 55.6 km/h) while destroyers take station on both sides and ahead.

A Coastal Command Hudson is over Brest when they leave, but its radar fails and it returns to base. Another Hudson is ordered to take over the patrol, but its engines refuse to start due to damp plugs. By the time a third aircraft is prepared and sent off, the German fleet has long gone.

12 February

0400 hours (4:00 a.m.): The fleet is crossing the Gulf of St Malo. Another Hudson should be patrolling there, but its radar has also just broken down and the pilot has been ordered to return to base. Incredibly, no replacement has been dispatched, so yet another opportunity to spot the Germans has been missed. A third Hudson, patrolling near Boulogne, is recalled when fog begins to gather over its home base. Had it remained on station, it too would have been in position when they passed.

0720 hours (7:20 a.m.): When dawn breaks, the ships go to battle stations and *Luftwaffe* nightfighters hand over to the day shift. At the same time, RAF patrols take off, with one Spitfire patrolling eastward from Cap Gris Nez as far as Le Havre, and another westward as far as Flushing. Coastal Command aircrews are briefed to report a breakout with the code word 'Fuller', but Fighter Command instructs its pilots to maintain radio silence and report verbally on return to base.

0824 hours (8:24 a.m.): British radar plotters notice air activity over the Channel near Le Havre. RAF 11 Group interprets this to be either some kind of air-sea rescue operation or air cover for a coastal convoy. However, Squadron Leader William Igoe, Controller at Biggin Hill fighter airfield, notices that the circling aircraft are steadily moving eastward at twenty-five knots. Since this is too fast for a merchant convoy, he realizes they must be escorting warships and calls 11 Group, saying 'I think it must be Fuller'. Nobody at the other end seems to be familiar with the code word. So, shortly after 1000 hours (10:00 a.m.), entirely on his own initiative, he sends a pair of Spitfires to investigate.

0900 hours (9:00 a.m.): Controllers at Kenley fighter airfield decide it is too cloudy and misty to risk sending inexperienced pilots on dawn patrols, but about an hour later, a couple of high-ranking officers, needing to log airtime, decide to fly a sweep themselves.

At the same time, fourteen Beaufort torpedo-bombers take off from Leuchars in Scotland. Four days earlier they had been ordered to Coltishall in East Anglia, but had been delayed by heavy snowstorms and administrative inefficiencies.

1016 hours (10:16 a.m.): Another RAF radar station plots three large ships near Boulogne and tentatively identifies them as German battle-cruisers. Flight Lieutenant Gerald Kidd tries to telephone a warning to naval headquarters in Dover Castle, but finds the lines out of service.

1030 hours (10:30 a.m.): The senior officers from Kenley spot the ships. Group Captain Beamish, who is in the loop, need only transmit the single code word 'Fuller' but, mindful of standing orders, decides to maintain radio silence.

By coincidence, the Spitfires from Biggin Hill arrive at the same time and, unlike his superior, Squadron Leader Robert Oxspring decides this is the time for initiative. He doesn't know the code word, but radios in plain language 'Three large German ships, probably battle-cruisers, escorted by twenty-plus other craft, sailing off Le Touquet, heading towards Dover.'

1040 hours (10:40 a.m.): Flight Lieutenant Kidd finally manages to contact naval HQ by routing the call to Dover Castle via Portsmouth.

1110 hours (11:10 a.m.): Beamish returns to base and immediately tries to report the sighting to Air Vice Marshal Leigh-Mallory. Officious staff officers say he is too busy to be interrupted for a mere Group Captain.

1135 hours (11:35 a.m.): The naval plan – which assumes any attempt to pass the Narrows will be made in darkness – visualizes a couple of pathfinder Swordfish dropping flares to illuminate the targets, followed by a simultaneous torpedo attack by ten more Swordfish and thirty-two motor torpedo boats (MTBs).

Now the daylight passage throws everything out of gear. Only five MTBs are ready to move out, and only six Swordfish have arrived at Manston. Admiral Ramsey is hesitant to send the Swordfish to almost certain death in daylight, but is overruled by Admiral of the Fleet Sir Dudley Pound who says 'The Navy will attack the enemy whenever and wherever he is to be found.'

1139 hours (11:39 a.m.): Leigh-Mallory finally becomes aware of the breakout, when Wing Commander Constable-Roberts, RAF liaison officer on Admiral Ramsey's staff, officially requests fighter cover for the Swordfish. It is agreed that two Spitfire squadrons from Hornchurch will provide close support against shipborne anti-aircraft gunfire, while three squadrons from Biggin Hill fly combat air patrol against German fighters.

As the fifty Spitfires assemble, it is discovered that the Intelligence Officer has locked the Battle Plan for Operation Fuller in his safe and gone away on leave without turning over the key. Pilots are simply ordered to rendezvous with the six Swordfish over Manston and follow them across the Channel. None of them is told what the naval airmen are hunting, or what they themselves might have to face.

1145 hours (11:45 a.m.): The Beauforts from Scotland land at Coltishall. There, thanks again to the RAF obsession with security, they are simply told to find and attack a German convoy. But two have developed engine trouble and three are unarmed. Unaware of the urgency of their mission, they decide to hold back the eight serviceable aircraft until the other five are ready.

Being a fighter base, Coltishall has no torpedoes for the unarmed Beauforts, so a message is sent to a Mobile Torpedo Servicing Unit near Grimsby about 240 kilometres (150 miles) away. Again, no immediacy is specified. The missiles and compressed air could be rush-delivered within three hours, but the Unit takes its time on slippery roads, stops for a leisurely tea, and does not arrive until the Germans are nearing home waters.

1155 hours (11:55 a.m.): An RAF staff officer orders fighters to escort seven Coastal Command Beaufort torpedo-bombers from Thorney Island. They are supposed to catch up with the slower Swordfish and make a coordinated attack. But two of the aircraft are armed with bombs which have to be unloaded and replaced by torpedoes, while a third develops a technical fault. Once again, urgency is not specified, so the four serviceable aircraft are held back until the others are ready. No-one thinks to tell Fighter Command they will be late at the rendezvous.

1158 hours (11:58 a.m.): The six old destroyers from Harwich are having a target shoot in the North Sea when a signal comes in reading 'Enemy cruisers passing Boulogne. Speed about twenty knots. Proceed in execution of previous orders.' Ordering his anti-aircraft shield of 25-knot Hunt Class destroyers to return to Harwich, Captain Mark Pizey sets off to intercept at full speed of thirty-plus knots.

1200 hours (12 noon): Guarding the narrows between Dover and Cap Gris Nez are two modern 14-inch naval guns in fixed emplacements, and four railway-mounted 13.5-inch guns of First World War vintage. Both batteries require five minutes to reload, meaning they can only get off a single shot before fast ships move out of range.

Potentially more dangerous to the Germans is a battery of four 9.2-inch guns on the South Foreland, which can fire one round every minute. Newly installed, they have not yet completed firing and ranging practice. All these batteries are directed from the Army Plotting Room which is five minutes walk from the Naval Operations room, with no direct communication between them.

South Foreland Battery is alerted at 1203 hours (12:03 p.m.). Visibility is so bad that fire control will have to be by radar, a technique which is still experimental and never before used in action. Six 9.2-inch ranging shots are fired, but the radar cannot accurately record fall of shot, so range and bearing corrections have to be estimated.

1215 hours (12:15 p.m.): Exactly on schedule, the German armada reaches the narrows. By this time the three big ships are accompanied by ten destroyers, three torpedo-boat flotillas of five ships each, and three E-boat flotillas. So far they have been unopposed, but will now have to face heavy guns, surface ships and aircraft.

1228 hours (12:28 p.m.): The Swordfish are circling over Manston, but only Squadron Leader Brian Kingscombe has arrived, and he is leading a mere ten Spitfires instead of the promised fifty. Due to jumbled orders, two fighter squadrons have flown straight to Calais, where they find neither ships nor aircraft. The other two are merely behind schedule. However, with a top speed of about ninety knots when carrying torpedoes, the Swordfish will have to hustle to catch up with their targets. Lieutenant Commander Eugene Esmonde decides to go ahead, without waiting for more fighter cover.

1229 hours (12:29 p.m.): South Foreland Battery opens up and fires a total of thirty-three rounds before the radar blips move out of range. Three or four are near-misses, causing the German ships to make violent changes of course, but no damage is done.

1233 hours (12:33 p.m.): Lieutenant Commander Nigel Pumphrey, commanding the MTB flotilla transmits the sighting code followed by the plain language message '3 battleships bearing 130 degrees, 5 nautical miles distance, course 70 degrees'. This is the first positive confirmation of the breakout, a full fifteen hours after it began.

The German fleet is making thirty knots, and the E-boats escorting it can make thirty-five, whereas the British MTBs are flat out at twenty-seven knots. They try desperately to close up to firing distance, constantly harassed by E-boats, strafed by *Luftwaffe* fighters, and only just being missed by friendly 9.2-inch shells from the South Foreland battery. The seas are too rough for accurate aiming, and they have to fire too long a range, so none of their torpedoes does any damage.

1243 hours (12:43 p.m.): Esmonde's six Swordfish begin skimming the waves for their torpedo run. Their ten-Spitfire escort is too small to hold off all the German fighters, let alone engage shipborne gunners as well, so the slow antiquated biplanes are sitting targets. All are shot down without scoring a single hit.[29] [30] Only five of the eighteen crewmen, three of them badly wounded, survive to be picked up by the retreating MTBs.

1258 hours (12:58 p.m.): The last two of the five Spitfire squadrons, having missed Esmonde at Manston, fly across the Channel and engage German fighters. They are just fifteen minutes too late to save the naval aviators.

1300 hours (1:00 p.m.): Pizey is told the twenty-knot estimate he was given an hour ago is ten knots below the Germans' true speed. On his present course he will miss them, so he takes a chance, slows down to twenty-eight knots, and diverts through one of the British minefields, hoping to intercept off the Hook of Holland. Destroyer *Walpole* falls out due to an overheated bearing, but Pizey's *Campbell* carries on, followed by *Vivacious*, *Worcester*, *Mackay* and *Whitshed*.

1325 hours (1:25 p.m.): Someone makes the belated decision to send off the four serviceable Beauforts from Thorney Island. Five minutes later their escorts arrive at the rendezvous and circle for a while before asking what happened to their charges. As the Beauforts have only just taken off, it is hastily decided that Manston Control will send the fighters across the Channel, and re-route the bombers to meet them over the target. However, no-one tells Manston that Coastal Command has switched to radio telephone and no longer uses Morse code. As a result the controllers are unable to make contact when the Beauforts arrive and start circling, waiting for their escorts.

1337 hours (1:37 p.m.): Pilot Officer Carson takes the initiative and leaves the circling aircraft in search of the 'convoy'. Another Beaufort follows him. Not knowing what he is looking for, or how fast it is going, he searches fruitlessly fifty miles behind the Germans. The other two obey orders and circle until shortage of fuel forces a return to base.

1411 hours (2:11 p.m.): Twelve destroyers leave the Thames Estuary to support Pizey. A few minutes later, another eleven destroyers are sent to patrol off Harwich, awaiting further orders.

1415 hours (2:15 p.m.): After waiting at Coltishall for the Torpedo Unit to arrive, the nine armed Beauforts are ordered to take off. They are to rendezvous with eleven Spitfires, and then follow eleven Hudson bombers for a coordinated strike on the target. All arrive on schedule and the Beauforts line up behind the Hudsons as ordered. Then they keep circling around and around, waiting for orders which, once again, fighter control tries to send by Morse code to aircraft which can only communicate by radio telephony.

1420 hours (2:20 p.m.): The first of three waves of heavy bombers takes off. The RAF has secretly reneged on its pledge to keep 300 on standby for this operation, and has assigned most of the promised reserve to strategic operations.

Only seventy-three are immediately available, but Bomber Command eventually manages to scrape up another 169 – from crews supposed to be resting after spending the previous night flying over Germany. The tired airmen, trained for high-altitude area-bombing of static targets, have virtually no success against fast-moving ships taking evasive action in bad visibility.[31]

1430 hours (2:30 p.m.): Twelve Beauforts from St Eval finally arrive at Thorney Island and are sent on to Coltishall for arming. The Mobile Unit has still not arrived, and they are ordered back to Thorney Island.

1432 hours (2:32 p.m.): Just as Pizey's flotilla exits the minefield some twenty-eight miles north-west of the Germans, *Scharnhorst* hits a mine off the Scheldt Estuary. Damage is not severe, and she is underway within thirty minutes. At about the same time, Pizey's five destroyers are misidentified and bombed by an RAF Hampden.

1500 hours (3:00 p.m.): Still circling behind the Hudson bombers,

Squadron Leader Cliff decides to break orders and takes his nine torpedo-carrying Beauforts toward the last reported position of the 'convoy'. Six of the bombers decide to follow, while the other five continue circling. The two groups lose contact in heavy overcast and, shortly afterward, the Hudsons detect ships on radar. Diving below the clouds, they bomb German E-boats and destroyers, losing two aircraft in the attack.

1543 hours (3:43 p.m.): Captain Pizey's destroyers open fire on *Gneisenau*, whose lookouts are so preoccupied with the bombers and fighters wheeling overhead that shells bursting nearby are their first warning. Soon, *Prinz Eugen* also comes under British fire. The smaller vessel opens up with her 8-inch main armament, while the battle-cruiser fires 11-inch and 5.9-inch salvoes. Pizey's flotilla is hidden by a smokescreen, laid by German destroyers, so none is hit.

1545 hours (3:45 p.m.): *Mackay* and *Whitshed* launch torpedoes at *Prinz Eugen* from 4,000 yards. The heavy cruiser, which has misidentified them as part of its escort, takes no precautions. At the last minute, purely by chance, she makes an emergency turn to dodge a British bomber and the torpedoes pass harmlessly by.

1546 hours (3:46 p.m.): The remaining five Thorney Island Beauforts fly through a major dogfight between RAF and *Luftwaffe* fighters and drop their torpedoes, all of which miss. Below the dogfight, there is an equally confused surface mêlée. Visibility is too poor for either side to see the other clearly but, from the air, some of the British destroyers are so close to the Germans they seem to be part of the escort.

1547 hours (3:47 p.m.): Barrelling in at 30 knots, under fire from every German gun which can be brought to bear, *Campbell* and *Vivacious* fire nine torpedoes at *Gneisenau* from 3,500 yards. *Kapitän* Brinkmann immediately turns to starboard to comb (run between) the tracks.

1550 hours (3:50 p.m.): Pizey's fifth destroyer, *Worcester*, holds her fire, closing the range to about 2,200 yards. Then, seconds before launching, she is struck by three heavy shells, causing mortal damage. Unable to hear firing orders from the bridge, torpedo-gunner Wellman uses his own initiative to send off three torpedoes, which miss narrowly, close astern of *Gneisenau* and close ahead of *Prinz Eugen*. Moments later four more shells strike, and it seems *Worcester* will have to be abandoned.

1556 hours (3:56 p.m.): Squadron Leader Cliff's nine Beauforts from Coltishall positively identify the German capital ships, noting that one of them (it must have been *Scharnhorst*) is 'listing badly, with smoke pouring from her bows'. Taking serious damage, they barrel in to drop their torpedoes but, once again, they all miss.

In the confusion, one of the Beauforts aims at Pizey's destroyer. It is a straight shot and *Campbell* only escapes by applying emergency full-astern. At about the same time, German destroyer *Hermann Schoemann* is bombed by a *Luftwaffe* Dornier 217. Other ships and aircraft undoubtedly come under 'friendly fire' in the mêlée.

1700 hours (5:00 p.m.): The St Eval Beauforts, armed at last, arrive over Manston only to find no fighter escort waiting for them. After circling for a few minutes, they set off by themselves.

1718 hours (5:18 p.m.): *Worcester* gets underway again, using sea water to raise steam. Slowly she limps her way home, waterlogged and rolling badly, with a huge rent in her starboard side.

1741 hours (5:41 p.m.): The St Eval Beauforts arrive at their target coordinates. Since these had been given to them hours before and never adjusted, the German fleet is eighty kilometres (fifty miles) away. All they see are a few German minesweepers which fire at them. Base orders them to fly back with their unfired torpedoes, but they never arrive. They are believed to have hit the waves while flying too low in the growing darkness.

1816 hours (6:16 p.m.): The German crews thankfully watch the last British aircraft fly off into the night. A few minutes later, their *Luftwaffe* escorts also leave. The ships have successfully run the gauntlet of everything the enemy could throw against them and, although a total of 694 British aircraft have been deployed – 398 Fighter Command, 242 Bomber Command, forty-eight Coastal Command and six Naval – they have inflicted only minor damage.

1930 hours (7:30 p.m.): The German fleet stands down from battle stations and resumes normal cruising routine.

1955 hours (7:55 p.m.): *Gneisenau* explodes a previously air-dropped British magnetic mine which is too far away from her hull to do any serious damage. A collision mat is dragged over the hole and she gets under way again.

2135 Hours (9:35 p.m.): *Scharnhorst* hits a second mine, which stops her engines and leaves her drifting towards Terschelling Shoals. Thirty-five minutes later, rudder and engine damage have been repaired enough for her to start moving slowly under reduced power.

13 February

0100 hours (1:00 a.m.): Admiral Pound telephones Prime Minister Churchill: 'I am afraid, sir, I must report that the enemy battle cruisers should by now have reached the safety of their home waters.' He is right, but *Kriegsmarine*'s impeccable planning has finally gone awry. No-one has thought to lay on pilot boats or tugs to assist the crippled warships enter harbour. Not until mid-morning are they brought in to tie up alongside.

Aftermath

Referring to the Dutch raid of 1667, the London *Times* newspaper sums up the melange of tardiness, inefficiency, equipment failure, jumbled orders, lack of inter-service cooperation and plain bad luck, by saying: 'Nothing more mortifying to the pride of British seapower has happened in home waters since the seventeenth century.' Later, attempting to rationalize a failure of monumental proportions, Winston Churchill wrote:

> The news astonished the British public, who could not understand what appeared to them, not unnaturally, to be proof of the German mastery of the English Channel. . . . (However) viewed in the after-light and in its larger aspects the episode was highly advantageous to us.

Germany's stunning tactical victory had, in fact, been a strategic error. The Allies had no intention of attacking Norway, while removal of the threat to Atlantic shipping was a great relief for them.

JUNE 1942 –
THE WRONG MUNITIONS AT MIDWAY

Having failed to destroy the United States' aircraft carriers along with the rest of the Pacific Fleet at Pearl Harbor, Admiral Isoroku Yamamoto planned to complete the task by luring them into an ambush. While a diversionary force lured the carriers north by attacking the Aleutian Islands, the island of Midway would be invaded. He knew the Americans would have to react against a Japanese presence so near to Hawaii and would rush south again, straight into the jaws of his trap.

Unknown to Yamamoto, the Japanese naval code had been broken, so the Americans knew that Midway was the main target. Ignoring the diversion, they decided to commit virtually all their remaining assets and, by 1 June 1942, had two task forces totalling three carriers, eight cruisers and fifteen destroyers deployed north-east of the island.

These were greatly outnumbered by the enemy who had fielded one light and four large carriers, eleven battleships and some 200 other vessels. Moreover, Japanese naval aircraft were superior in performance as well as numbers, and were flown by more-experienced pilots.

Vice Admiral Chuichi Nagumo's carrier task force was north-west of Midway; the invasion force of troop transports was approaching from the west, and Yamamoto's battleship support force was between them and to their rear. Both sides had screening forces of submarines.

The Midway Bombardment

At dawn on 4 June, Nagumo began 'softening up' the island with an air raid of seventy-two bombers escorted by thirty-six fighters. Then, while his cruisers catapulted-off reconnaissance aircraft to search for the enemy carriers, he armed another ninety-three bombers with torpedoes and armour-piercing bombs ready to attack as soon as they were sighted.

At 7:15 a.m., the commander of the Midway strike radioed, recommending a follow-up raid. No carrier sighting had been reported, so – losing sight of his main objective – Nagumo ordered the standby aircraft to be struck below and re-armed with high-explosive bombs for use against ground targets. While this was going on, one of the scouts reported an enemy formation of ten ships about 500 kilometres (310 miles) away. Since no carrier was said to be present, Nagumo allowed re-arming to continue.

At 8:20 a.m., the scout reported there was a carrier in the group after all. Nagumo reversed his plans and ordered the reserve aircraft re-armed for anti-ship operations. However, before they could be brought up and flown off, the Midway force returned and had to be landed-on, refuelled and re-armed. This took about an hour, during which the flight decks were criss-crossed with fuel hoses, while piles of bombs, torpedoes and machine-gun ammunition were everywhere.

The Naval Air Battle

In the midst of all this orderly confusion, the Americans struck. Three squadrons of torpedo bombers – one each from *Enterprise, Hornet* and *Yorktown* – came in at low level, only to fall victim to alert anti-aircraft gunners and the Japanese combat air patrol. Only six of forty-one aircraft survived, while not a single torpedo struck home. However, they had diverted the attention of gunners and fighter pilots, allowing fifty-four dive bombers from *Yorktown* and *Enterprise* to swoop in on three of the four carriers.

Four 1,000-pound bombs struck *Kaga*, rupturing fuel lines and setting off secondary explosions in the aircraft park. Engulfed in flames, she was abandoned before sinking. It took three bombs to finish off *Soryu*, but two were enough to deal with *Akagi*, whose flight deck was ripped open and covered with blazing aircraft. She too was abandoned and sunk by escorting destroyers.

Thanks to bad visibility, the fourth Japanese carrier, *Hiryu*, had not been attacked. From her, Rear Admiral Tamon Yamaguchi launched two strikes about an hour apart. The first, consisting of eighteen dive bombers, scored three hits on *Yorktown*. Then just as the damaged carrier got underway again, the second force of ten torpedo bombers swept in to score two more hits.

Aftermath

Yorktown was abandoned, but refused to sink. Taken in tow, she was later sunk by Japanese submarine *I-168*. Meanwhile, dive-bombers from *Enterprise* found *Hiryu,* which was defenceless with all her fighters engaged on the *Yorktown* strike. Their four hits damaged her so badly that she had to be scuttled.

In the space of a few hours, Japan had lost four fleet carriers and a heavy cruiser, along with 234 aircraft, and some 2,500 men, including a cripplingly high proportion of its front-line naval aviators. Yamamoto retreated, knowing Japan had lost its commanding naval supremacy in the Pacific, surrendering the strategic initiative to America.

JULY 1942 – CENTRALIZED INTERFERENCE WITH AN ARCTIC CONVOY

Of all the supply routes in the Second World War, by far the most hazardous was the Murmansk Run. Forced by pack ice to sail close to the coastline of Nazi-occupied Norway, convoys were within easy range of German submarines, aircraft and surface warships.

In summer they were exposed by twenty-four hours of daylight, in winter they faced fierce storms and brutal cold. Winter was preferred though, because foul weather and long nights provided better cover for the slow-moving merchantmen. The matériel they delivered was essential to the faltering Soviet war effort, as expressed by Premier Stalin in a telegram to Prime Minister Churchill on 7 May:

> I have a request of you . . . steamers loaded with various important war materials for the U.S.S.R. are bottled up at present in Iceland or in the approaches from America to Iceland. I understand there is a danger that the sailing of these ships may be delayed . . . because of the difficulty to organize convoy, escorted by the British naval forces. I am fully aware of the difficulties involved and of the sacrifices made by Great Britain in this matter. I feel [it] however incumbent upon me to approach you with the request to take all possible measures to ensure the arrival of all the above-mentioned materials . . . this is extremely important for our front.

The Allies had sensibly planned to suspend Arctic convoys until autumn, but this precaution was overruled by the political need for Washington and London to demonstrate ongoing support to the hard-pressed Russians, who were reeling before the brutal German invasion.

The Ill-fated Convoy Departs

On 27 June, Convoy PQ17 left Reykjavik, Iceland with thirty-five merchant ships, escorted by six destroyers, four corvettes, two anti-aircraft ships, three minesweepers and four armed trawlers. In close support was British Rear Admiral Hamilton with four heavy cruisers – British *London* and *Norfolk;* American *Tuscaloosa* and *Wichita* – and another three destroyers.

Not directly concerned with convoy protection, but standing-off ready to pounce if the heavy ships of Germany's powerful Norwegian battle-group sortied, was British Admiral Tovey, with battleships HMS *Duke of York* and USS *Washington*, aircraft carrier HMS *Victorious,* two cruisers and eight destroyers. Both sides were acutely aware of the stakes; destroying any of the heavy German ships, but especially super-battleship *Tirpitz*[32], would be a major strategic and propaganda victory for the Allies, while decimating the convoy would seriously impact the Russian war effort.

On 3 July, British aerial reconnaissance reported *Tirpitz*, accompanied by pocket-battleships *Lützow* (formerly *Deutschland*) and *Admiral Scheer,* heavy cruiser *Admiral Hipper* and a dozen heavy destroyers, steaming northward towards North Cape. At this stage it was unclear whether they planned to wreak havoc on PQ17, or to try to break out into the Atlantic. The Admiralty believed the former and calculated they would reach the convoy by late on the 4th or early on the 5th. Tovey's force was placed on high alert, ready to respond to either threat.

Pound's Controversial Order

Long experience had shown that ships were best protected in convoy, where escorts could keep submarines submerged and at a distance, while the combined firepower of escorts and merchantmen deterred aerial attack. Hence, British Convoy Instructions required the order to scatter be issued only as a last resort, by agreement between escort commander and convoy commodore, when about to be overwhelmed by superior surface forces.

In spite of this, Admiral of the Fleet Sir Dudley Pound, professional head of the Royal Navy, made a decision which should clearly have been left to commanders on the spot. From London, he ordered the convoy to disperse and individual ships to make their own way to Archangel or Murmansk.[33] At the same time he ordered the close support group to withdraw westward and join Tovey for the expected battle. Admiral Hamilton took not only his own three destroyers, but the six destroyers of the close escort as well.

In fact, Pound's reaction was premature. Unknown to Allied naval intelligence, *Lützow* had run aground off Narvik, after which the other heavy warships had stopped at the naval anchorage in Altenfjord to await further orders. Not until noon on the 5th, a full day after the order to scatter, were they dispatched. However, before the convoy dispersed, a U-boat had sighted its only air cover – a lone catapult-launched Hurricane fighter – and mistakenly reported the convoy was escorted by an aircraft carrier. The battlegroup was only a few hours out when this news reached Hitler and, unwilling to put his prestigious ships in harm's way, he intervened and ordered them back to Altenfjord.

Disastrous Consequences

Meanwhile, the convoy had broken up, not as individual ships, but into several small clusters around the remaining corvettes, armed trawlers, anti-aircraft ships and rescue vessels. Most headed north-eastward, seeking the protection of bleak islands and pack ice. This did not help them much. With the withdrawal of depth-charging anti-submarine escorts, shadowing U-boats were able to move in and radio homing signals to other submarines and aircraft which converged on each of the clusters. An American merchant seaman writes in *Attack on an Arctic Convoy 1942*:

> They came early, the Heinkels, the Messerschmitts, the Stukas, the Junkers. . . . They used everything: 1,100-pounders, 550's, 250's, aerial torpedoes, mines, their cannons, and their machine guns; while outside, always trying to get in . . . (were) their submarines. . . . It was Hell. There was no other word for it. Everywhere you looked aloft you saw them, crossing and recrossing us . . . bombs . . . screaming to burst furiously white in the sea. All around us, as so slowly we kept on going, the pure blue of the sea was mottled blackish with the greasy patches of their bomb discharges. [Copyright © Ibis Communications 2001]

Their attacks were lethal, destroying a rescue ship and twenty-four merchantmen.[34] With them went 210 aircraft, 430 tanks, 3,350 other vehicles, and 99,316 tons of war matériel. Eleven freighters and the remaining small escorts finally staggered into Russian ports, with varying degrees of battle damage. German losses totalled five aircraft.

OCTOBER 1942 – PREOCCUPATION IN MID-ATLANTIC

The world's largest ship, Cunard liner RMS *Queen Mary*, had been converted to a troop transport and was crossing the North Atlantic carrying 15,000 American troops, or seven times her peacetime passenger load. She was too fast to travel in convoy and, relying on speed for protection, was steaming unescorted at 28.6 knots (53 km/h; 33 mph) following a random zigzag course.

On 2 October, thirty-two kilometres (twenty miles) off the southern coast of Ireland, on a day of brilliant sunshine and perfect visibility, she rendezvoused with Royal Navy cruiser *Curacoa*, who was to escort her to the port of Glasgow in Scotland. For some unexplained reason, the two ships did not establish voice communication.

Because *Curacoa* was slower than *Queen Mary*, Captain John Boutwell tried to keep on station by steering a straight course while the big liner continued to zigzag. However, he gradually lost ground and *Queen Mary* came progressively closer. As they converged, Boutwell assumed it was the liner's responsibility, as overtaking ship, to stay clear of his cruiser. This would be the normal rule of the sea, but Captain Gordon Illingworth assumed that, because he was zigzagging and *Curacoa* was not, it was the escort's duty to stay clear.

Eventually one of *Queen Mary*'s turns brought her head-on to the cruiser, but the bridge watches and lookouts on both ships were so busy scanning the horizon for U-boats that neither of them noticed they were on a collision course. At precisely 2:12 p.m., *Queen Mary* struck the cruiser at an acute angle, riding over and cutting her in two. By the time the liner's entire 311 metres (1,020 feet) had passed through, her bow wave had pushed the two halves apart by about 100 metres (328 feet).

Aftermath

Not daring to put the lives of so many passengers at risk, Captain Illingworth maintained full speed and headed for port with a hole the size of a large mansion in *Queen Mary's* bow. Although this was undoubtedly the right decision, it doomed many of *Curacoa*'s crew, since the nearest rescue craft – destroyers *Cowdray* and *Bramham* – were two hours' fast-steaming away. They rescued Captain Boutwell and 100 of his crew, but 338 had died before they arrived.

Under wartime secrecy, the collision was not made public until January 1947, when the Admiralty laid charges against Cunard. However, the Court blamed *Curacoa*, agreeing with Captain Illingworth that a convoy in wartime was a special case in which the general rule for overtaking ships did not apply.

NOVEMBER 1942 – CRITICAL DELAY AT TASSAFARONGA

After destroying the American battle fleet at Pearl Harbor and sinking *Prince of Wales* and *Repulse* in the Gulf of Siam, Japanese amphibious forces fanned out in all directions virtually unopposed. Their northward thrust towards the Aleutian Islands was only a sideshow, while the naval Battle of Midway in May 1942 stopped their eastward advance. But their westward offensive through the Dutch East Indies (now Indonesia) and Malaya into Burma (Myanmar) still seemed invincible; and so did a southward attack through the Philippines and New Guinea to the Solomon Islands. The latter threatened strategically-important Australia, leading the United States to mount its first counter-offensive.

The Solomon Islands Campaign

The American landing on Guadalcanal, on 7 August 1942, was a disorganized shambles but, fortunately for the United States Marines, the enemy had been taken by surprise and they faced no immediate opposition. Next day, in a battle off Savo Island, a Japanese cruiser squadron shattered Australian Rear Admiral Sir Victor Crutchley's screening force, forcing the invasion fleet to withdraw before landing the rest of its troops.

Those marines who were already ashore had to face ferocious counter-attacks for two weeks. Then American combat aircraft landed on hastily-constructed Henderson Field and regained control of the strait between Guadalcanal and Florida Island. America then poured in reinforcements at the eastern end of the island, while Japan landed troops on its western tip. For three months ground fighting was bloody, but inconclusive.

Late in October, a premature report led the Imperial Navy to believe Henderson Field had been taken by Japanese ground forces. A large fleet promptly moved towards eastern Guadalcanal, but was intercepted off the Santa Cruz Islands by numerically inferior American carrier task groups. The two-day battle was more-or-less a tactical draw.

Sixteen days later, an even larger Japanese force approached western Guadalcanal. It was detected by the Americans and the three-day Battle of Guadalcanal began. When it ended, so many ships had been sunk in the Florida Strait that it was nicknamed 'Ironbottom Sound'; that said, the United States Navy had acquired effective control of the waters around the island, forcing the Japanese onto the defensive.

Japanese Destroyer Convoys

No longer able to mount troop or supply convoys in daylight, Rear Admiral Raizo Tanaka initiated overnight round-trips from Bougainville, using Destroyer Division Two as high-speed transports. Because their timing was as regular and punctual as a railway timetable, the Americans called them 'The Tokyo Express'. Tanaka's Chief of Staff, Commander Yusami Toyama, was less than enthusiastic about the new arrangement, as he confided to his friend Tameichi Hara, captain of destroyer *Amatsukaze:*

> We are more a freighter convoy than a fighting squadron these days. . . . We transport cargo to the cursed island, and our orders are to flee rather than fight. What a stupid thing! It is doubtful if we could fight anyway. Our decks are stacked so high with supplies that our ammunition supply must be cut in half. . . . It is a strenuous and unsatisfying routine.

On 27 November, Tanaka started another run, passing down New Georgia Strait – a narrow 450-km (280-mile) passage between two roughly parallel island chains – which Americans called 'The Slot'. Destroyer *Takanami* scouted about 3,000 metres ahead of the main body, which was led by Tanaka in his flagship *Naganami*. In line astern of him were *Makinami, Oyashino, Kuroshio, Kagero, Kawakaze* and *Suzukaze.*

The Americans Mount an Ambush

Effective signals-intelligence alerted American Rear Admiral Carleton Wright, who set out intending to 'Cross-their-Tee' with overwhelming force. His extended line-ahead was led by destroyers *Fletcher, Perkins, Maury* and *Drayton,* followed by heavy cruisers *Minneapolis (*flag*), New Orleans, Pensacola, Honolulu* and *Northampton,* each armed with nine 8-inch guns (or 'rifles'). Holding the rear were destroyers *Lamson* and *Lardner.*

At 2316 (11:16 p.m.) *Fletcher*'s radar sighted the Japanese convoy, just slowing down as it neared its cargo drop-off point. Commander Cole immediately contacted the flagship by TBS,[35] requesting permission to launch a torpedo attack from 7,000 yards (6,400 metres). Admiral Wright, a 'desk warrior' with little combat experience, doubted a launch could be successful at that distance, but agreed after discussing the matter for four critical minutes.

During the delay, both columns steamed ahead and, by the time *Fletcher* launched her torpedoes, the angle-of-attack had changed from full-abeam of the convoy to a difficult shot on its starboard quarter.

Perkins and *Drayton* fired from similarly unfavourable angles. All twenty missiles missed their targets, but alerted the unsuspecting Japanese.

The Japanese React Rapidly

Without waiting for Tanaka's orders, *Takanami* took the initiative, raced out of the scout position, launched all eight torpedoes, and opened fire with her pathetic little 5-inch guns. She was immediately pounded by heavy 8-inch counter-fire from all five American cruisers and turned into a blazing hulk, but she still had a vital role to play. Lying between the opposing columns, her bulk masked the American radar, allowing Tanaka to go to battle speed, make a sweeping turn, place his column on a parallel course, and take the offensive.

Illuminating *Minneapolis* with searchlights, *Naganami* launched a spread of eight torpedoes, one of which destroyed the 10,000-ton cruiser's bow, while another hit her No.2 boiler room. Still defiant, *Minneapolis*' forward turret fired three more salvoes before her shattered bow scooped up enough seawater to short-circuit its power supply. The cruiser slewed to a halt with a starboard list.

Coming up fast from astern, *New Orleans* barely avoided collision with the flagship and, while taking evasive action, was struck by one of *Makinami*'s topedoes. This ignited both forward magazines, blowing off thirty-six metres (120 feet) of her bow, as far as No.2 turret. As the broken section slid along her hull, it gouged huge holes in the big cruiser's side, further disabling her.

Closing rapidly on the two stationary cruisers, *Pensacola* made an emergency turn to port, while *Honolulu* turned sharply to starboard. The former's change of course took her straight into the path of one of *Kawakaze*'s torpedoes, which turned her midships fuel tanks into an inferno. The latter, having turned out of harm's way without any battle damage, sighted two more destroyers and opened fire. Fortunately her aim was off, because they were her own rearguard *Lardner* and *Lamson*.

The last cruiser in line, *Northampton*, also undamaged, was about to follow *Honolulu* when she sighted two Japanese destroyers heading westward and gave chase, firing as she went. *Kagero* and *Oyashino* responded by launching eight torpedoes, two of which struck home, crippling the fourth heavy cruiser.

Aftermath

Away from the combat zone, Tanaka paused to assess battle-worthiness. None of his seven remaining destroyers had sustained more than minor damage, but four had expended all their torpedoes, and a fifth had launched half of its supply. Two had not achieved favourable firing angles and still had their full complement.

Not realizing the extent to which he had harmed the Americans, he decided not to risk returning for a second round. Had he taken that chance, he might had destroyed the crippled cruisers, or forced them to be scuttled. In the event, *Northampton* had to be abandoned, but heroic damage control saved the other three for repairs, which took almost a year to complete.

The Battle off Tassafaronga ranks as one of the United States Navy's most humiliating engagements. With advance knowledge of enemy intentions, its carefully-planned ambush achieved complete surprise but – thanks to four minutes of indecision, followed by unwise concentration of fire on a single opponent – an audacious and quick-thinking enemy turned the tables and inflicted disproportionate damage on the vastly superior American force.

PART SEVEN

The Second World War
War
– The Allies Strike
Back

APRIL 1944 –
SURFACE INFILTRATION OFF THE DEVON COAST

Slapton is a pleasant little village on a slope rising from Start Bay on the Devonshire coast of England. Below it, an unspoiled beach of coarse gravel faces a long freshwater lake. During the Second World War, it suddenly assumed special importance when planners of the invasion of Nazi-occupied Europe realized its bluffs and beaches closely resembled those of Utah Beach in Normandy where Americans were scheduled to land.

All civilians were moved inland, leaving Start Bay and nearby Torbay free for US Army live-ammunition training exercises, the culmination of which were to be full-scale rehearsals during April and May of 1944. The final practice for forces scheduled to land on Utah Beach started on 22 April, when troops and equipment began boarding the actual ships, and at the actual ports they would use for the real thing.[36]

Because German high-speed torpedo and gun boats (E-boats) frequently hunted the Channel by night, the British Royal Navy maintained a regular motor torpedo boat (MTB) patrol off Cherbourg where most E-boats were based. While the practice exercise was on, it planned to throw an additional protective screen of three MTBs, three motor gun boats (MGBs), and Canadian destroyers *Athabaskan* and *Haida*, across the mouth of Lyme Bay.

The Practice Convoys Set Out

Marshalling and embarkation were completed by late on the 26th, and the main force set out into Lyme Bay, led by minesweepers, as if actually crossing the Channel. Following a live ammunition naval bombardment of the beach, the lightly-armed infantry assault wave landed successfully on the morning of 27 April.

Meanwhile, a follow-up convoy (code-named T-4) was on its way, carrying engineer and quartermaster troops, trucks, tanks, artillery and heavy engineering equipment. This convoy departed from two different ports. Leaving Plymouth were five Tank Landing Ships, one of which was towing two pontoon causeways while, coming from Brixham there were three more LSTs.

These large-capacity flat-bottomed ships were crammed with troops, vehicles and equipment. After merging, they were to be escorted by British destroyer *Scimitar* and corvette *Azalea,* but an American vessel collided with the destroyer, which docked for repairs. No replacement was available.

Shortly before midnight the Canadian screening destroyers were withdrawn for other duties and, about forty minutes later, *Azalea* heard that a flotilla of nine E-boats had somehow evaded the remaining patrols. Since the LSTs should have picked up the same message, she did not pass it on. However, due to a clerical error, the British and Americans were on different radio frequencies, so they had not received it.

The Battle off Slapton Sands

The convoy's first indication of trouble came without advance warning at 2:04 a.m., when a huge explosion was heard. Most soldiers and seamen thought this was just another live ammunition exercise, at least until *LST-507* burst into flames. Angelo Crapanzano from Cliffside Park NJ was at the engine room controls when she was hit. Later he reported:

> There was this terrific roar, and I got this sensation of flying up, back, and when I came down I must have bumped my head and must have been out for a few seconds. When I came to . . . it was pitch black. I knew the engine room like the palm of my hand. . . . I ran to the ladder and I went up. When I got topside I couldn't believe what I saw. The ship was split in half and burning, fire went from the bow all the way back to the wheelhouse . . . the water all around the ship was burning . . . it was like an inferno. And the soldiers were panicking. You couldn't blame them because they're not trained for disasters at sea. They're trained for land.
>
> Now we've got to go into the water, because it's getting worse. . . . It got so hot on deck that their shoes start smoking. . . . All right so you've got to jump. . . . In the engine room I knew the reading on the salt water coming in was 43 degrees. What I didn't know was what 43 degrees felt like. So when I hit the water, it took my breath away, that's how cold it was. It was frigid. It was unbelievable, un-believable cold. [*Slapton Village Community Website*]

In fact, many of the deaths on this frightful night were from hypothermia. Many more were because the soldiers had not been told how to use their life belts. Those who tied them around their waists found themselves tipped forward, with heads under water, drowned by their own safety device. One of those who wore his properly, tied under the armpits, was Patsy Giacchi, from Hackensack NJ, private in a quartermaster railhead company. He said:

> Then we got a direct hit, BOM! . . . I flew up ten, fifteen feet. . . . Bradshaw landed on the side of me. I hit . . . a piece of sharp square metal . . . and I started to bleed. . . . We turn and look and we could see the ship, the 507, was in half. So it was going down. He said

'Pat, we got to get out of here' . . . It seemed to be about forty feet, Oh my God! So we had to go. We inflated our life jackets, held hands, we hit the water. Boom! You go down, salt water, about 40 degrees. Oh! Cold! . . . We started to drift away . . . we held hands. . . . I'll never forget the water was on fire, there was a gasoline smell, but the worst thing was the death cry of the sailors and the soldiers, 'Hellp! Hellp! Hellp!' And there's nobody to help. [*Slapton Village Community Website*]

Minutes later, *LST-531* was torpedoed and sank in six minutes. *LST-289* opened fire on the E-boats, but was herself torpedoed, although she did not sink. Amazingly, *Azalea* stayed out of the fight. For some inexplicable reason, US Rear Admiral D.P. Moon had ordered her not to engage if attacked. However, the remaining LSTs opened fire on the E-boats. They were soon joined by two British destroyers, which had rushed to the scene.

Their arrival caused *Korvettenkapitän* Günther Rabe to throw down a smoke screen and retreat at 37 knots (69 km/h; 43 mph). His E-boats had had no casualties, but the US Army had suffered 551 deaths and the Navy 198 more than three times as many deaths as the total of killed, missing and wounded at the real Utah Beach on D-Day.

September 1944 – POW Nightmare off Sumatra

Although his radar and high-power periscope were both out of service, Lieutenant Commander S.L.C. Maydon, of British submarine *Tradewind,* decided to spend one more day off the west coast of Sumatra before aborting his offensive patrol. At 1516 (3:16 p.m.) on 18 September, somewhere between Benkulen and Padang, the officer of the watch, Lieutenant P.C. Daley, sighted a plume of smoke through the low-power periscope.

Thirty minutes later the vessel was close enough to be identified as an old-fashioned three-island merchantman of 4,000- to 5,000 tons, escorted by a corvette and a motor gunboat. Maydon was manoeuvring into attack position when the ship obligingly changed course to present a perfect shot. A spread of four torpedoes was fired, and two struck the target – now known to be Japanese steamship *Junyo Maru* sailing from Java to Sumatra.

Tradewind reloaded her torpedo tubes and set off for home. Maydon, who was congratulating himself on a 'clean kill', would have been horrified if he knew the sunken vessel had been carrying 4,200 Javanese slave labourers and 2,300 American, Australian, British and Dutch prisoners of war – all destined to work on the Sumatran railway line.[37]

Junyo was so full that there had only been space for 100 of these prisoners to lie down. Some of the others had managed to squat, but most had had to stand erect since setting out two days earlier. Nineteen-year-old Dutch POW Willem Wanrooy reports that they:

> Suffered from the blazing sun during the day and bone-chilling rains at night. It was horrid below deck. Without enough drinking water, food or medicine, many broken-down prisoners gradually lost the will to live. A third of them suffered from malaria or dysentery. Many went mad, and some ranted deliriously in the stifling, fetid hold that smelled of urine, excrement and putrefying flesh. As men died, the living stood on the dead . . . more than two thousand souls, melting in their own sweat and body wastes, gasping for every breath. . . . A sudden jolt shook the ship. As I looked up, I saw human bodies, wood pieces, metal and other debris blown high in the sky. [Copyright © *Veterans Outlook* 1988]

While the few surviving slaves and prisoners spent an horrific night clinging to whatever floated, escorts picked up the Japanese crew and guards and ferried them to Padang, some six hours away. Finally, one of the gunboats reappeared out of the morning mist to pick up those who still had enough strength to grab ropes trailing over the side. After being hauled in, those who were too exhausted to stand were thrown back overboard.

Aftermath
Of 6,500 passengers, only 680 POWs and 200 Javanese were rescued. They were then sent as slaves on the Pakan Baru to Muaro railway until the war ended, almost a year later. Conditions were so terrible that many wished they had gone down with the ship. None of the Javanese, and only ninety-six of the POWs survived, bringing the final death toll to 6,404.

DECEMBER 1944 –
INACCURATE METEOROLOGY IN THE PACIFIC

By the autumn of 1944, the American advance across the Central Pacific had been so rapid there had been no time to establish meteorological (aerological in US Navy parlance) stations on captured enemy territory. Pacific Fleet Weather Central at Pearl Harbor issued forecasts twice daily, while weather reports were broadcast four times a day from Kwajalein and Manus, but these stations were too distant to accurately cover local conditions at the spearhead of the naval thrust.

On 11 December 1944, Admiral William ('Bull') Halsey's United States Third Fleet steamed out to strike Japanese airfields on Luzon in support of amphibious landings on the Island of Mindanao. The fleet's principal fighting unit was Vice Admiral John McCain's fast carrier group, designated Task Force 38. It was huge, containing seven fleet carriers, six light carriers, eight battleships, fifteen cruisers and fifty destroyers. The bunkers of many of these combatant vessels were dangerously low following three days of intensive action.

Refuelling the Fleet

Early on Sunday 17 December, they rendezvoused with a support group which included twelve fleet oilers and five escort carriers carrying replacement aircraft. Bunkering started immediately, despite a 20–30 knot wind which made the operation risky and difficult. By noon, the wind had increased to 40 knots (force 8) and the combination of wind and waves led Halsey to order the ships to belay fuelling. Later, Chief Warrant Officer Steven Yorden of USS *Dewey* (DD-349) told interviewers from the Washington Naval Historical Foundation:

> Captain Calhoun . . . had a heck of a job to keep station so that the hoses don't part. . . . They were parting so many fuel hoses that they were down to one last section. . . . That's when they decided to call it off. They were going to move to another location and commence fuelling in the morning again.

About mid-afternoon, on the advice of his weatherman, Halsey designated a third refuelling point. An hour later he heard that a scouting seaplane from Ulithi had sighted a storm centre about 300 kilometres (190 miles) from his present position. Angrily asking why the report had taken some twelve hours to reach him, he was told the pilot had returned to base before reporting, after which the message had been encrypted using the slow laborious cipher used for low priority communications, rather than the high speed coding machines used for operational orders.

At this stage there was no indication that the weather was anything more than a nuisance. Despite the Ulithi report, Fleet Aerologist Commander Kosco estimated the cyclonic disturbance to be 750 kilometres (450 miles) distant, and on a course which would miss the fleet. In fact, it was only 200 kilometres (120 miles) away and heading towards it.

Realizing the ships could not possibly reach the third fuelling rendezvous in daylight, Halsey cancelled it. Later, he ordered the carriers and escorts to change course in the hope of finding calmer water, and designated a fourth meeting point for Monday morning. Sunset on Sunday evening left a sinister afterglow which worried experienced seamen. Indeed, during the small hours, the weather did deteriorate, but the barometer held steady.

The wind had not changed direction, and had dropped to about force 7, creating the impression that nothing exceptional should be expected. Halsey studied Kosco's weather maps, but made no decision on what should be done until 0500 hours on Monday morning. Then he cancelled the fourth rendezvous and told his ships to refuel on their own initiative whenever they found it practicable. By 0830, bunkering had proved impossible due to high seas and continuous driving rain, so he cancelled the operation and ordered the fleet to resume course.

The Typhoon Strikes

There was no sign of serious weather until 1000 hours when the barometer took a nose-dive and the wind was observed to be backing anti-clockwise – both typical warnings of an approaching tropical cyclone. By this time, the Third Fleet was spread out over about 6,500 square kilometres (2,500 square miles). Each ship was experiencing different weather conditions, and some were too close to the storm to escape.

At 1345, Kosco issued a typhoon warning. This was the first official message to reach Fleet Weather Central. By this time the storm had reached its peak, with winds of over 97 knots (180 km/hr; 110 mph) and gusts estimated at 160 knots (295 km/hr; 185 mph). Chief Warrant Officer Yorden continues:

> I'm talking about waves that were fifty and sixty feet high. Sometimes you'd see a destroyer. He'd be sitting on top of a wave and the next time he'd be down so low that you couldn't even see the mast. That's how deep the troughs were.

Samuel Morison's official *History of US Naval Operations* describes the same scene from a broader aspect:

> All semblance of formation was lost. Every ship was labouring heavily; hardly any two were in visual contact. . . . The weather was so thick and dirty that sea and sky seemed fused in one aqueous element. At times the rain was so heavy that visibility was limited to three feet, and the wind so powerful that to venture out . . . a sailor had to wriggle on his belly. . . . *Hancock*'s flight deck, 57 feet above her waterline, scooped up green water. . . . Planes went adrift, collided and burst into flames.

Fletcher-class destroyer USS *Spence* (DD-512) was top-heavy from lack of fuel in her bunkers. Suddenly, mountainous waves and a gust of wind blew her over at a 72-degree angle (the greatest measured that day). Water poured in and shorted her electrical system. Then the rudder jammed, she completed her roll, and foundered. Twenty-four men survived, nine of them badly-injured, but 317 went down with the ship. Yorden's USS *Dewey* was luckier:

> We finally made the big roll. We went over and the helmsman, the water was up to his arms. That's how deep the water was over the ship . . . it took the stack off. That's what really saved us . . . and a wave just happened to hit us right. It started to right us . . . and when she came up she went back again but didn't go quite as far because now the stack was off you know and we got less wind laying us over.

Two other destroyers – USS *Hull* (DD-350) and USS *Monaghan* (DD-354) – also riding light with almost-empty bunkers, capsized and sank with virtually all hands, while a cruiser, five aircraft carriers and three more destroyers were seriously damaged. Numerous other vessels were hurt and 146 aircraft were destroyed.

In mid-afternoon, the wind began to moderate and the sky brightened slightly. By nightfall it was down to 60 knots and it was clear that the eye of the storm had passed. The heavy armoured battleships had ridden out the storm safely, although Admiral Halsey, who was in *New Jersey* writes in his autobiography:

> No one who has not been through such a typhoon could conceive its fury. The seas smash you from all sides. The rain and scud are blinding; they drive you flat-out until you can't tell the ocean from the air. At broad noon I couldn't see the bow of my ship, 350 feet from the bridge. . . . This typhoon tossed our enormous ship as if she were a canoe . . . we could not hear our own voices above the uproar.

Altogether, 788 officers and men had been killed or swept overboard, and eighty more had been seriously injured.

Aftermath

Pacific Fleet Hedquarters established new weather stations in the Caroline Islands and later, as they were captured, at Manila, Iwo Jima and Leyte. Offices for coordinating weather data were also set up on Guam and Leyte. A Court of Inquiry advised 'Weather ships should be stationed in the area and at least two planes daily be assigned as weather reconnaissance.' However, as we shall see, these recommendations were not implemented in time for the next typhoon, seven months later.

JANUARY 1945 –
ACTS OF WAR OR RUSSIAN WAR CRIMES?

During the 1930s German liner *Wilhelm Gustloff* had been the flagship of Hitler's 'Strength Through Joy' worker's recreational programme. Then, when the Second World War began, she became a stationary base for training U-boat crews. In 1945 she was recommissioned to take part in the largest organized maritime movement of all time – the evacuation of some 2 million civilians and large numbers of wounded or frost-bitten troops, ahead of the advancing Red Army. All available passenger ships, freighters, ferries, naval auxiliaries and even some combatant warships, were pressed into this service.

Towards the end of January, some 65,000 military and civilian refugees were gathered in the Polish port of Gotenhafen (Gdynia) hoping for transportation home. It was snowing, the temperature was fourteen degrees below zero and, in the midst of military collapse, the loading of *Gustloff* was chaotic.

A proper count was not taken, but post-war research by Heinz Schon[38] estimates that 8,956 women, children and elderly people had scrambled on board, along with 162 badly-wounded soldiers, 918 U-boat officers and men, and 173 female naval auxiliaries. At the last minute, Captain Friedrich Petersen found room for another 373 female auxiliaries by packing them into the empty swimming pool.

At 12:30 p.m. on 30 January, four tugboats pulled *Gustloff* out of her berth and into the harbour mouth, from where she proceeded under her own power. A small minesweeper led the way. The Baltic Sea was blustery, with occasional ice floes and, as night fell, it grew even colder, and ice began to form on her decks and superstructure. At approximately 9:00 p.m. the liner was off the coast of Pomerania, near Stolpmunde, when she was sighted by Russian submarine *S-13*.

Orlogskapitajn (Commander) Alexandre Marinesko fired a spread of four torpedoes, one of which missed. The second struck *Gustloff* deep below the waterline near the bow, the third hit the engine room amidships, and the last exploded further aft, just below the swimming pool where the naval auxiliaries were quartered. In a letter held by the World War II Preservation Society, *Oberbootsmannsmaat* (Boatswain Petty Officer) Karl Hoffmann reported:

> The desperate crowd of thousands had only one thought: to reach the upper decks, away from the massive flood of water. They clawed their way upward, pushing and shoving mercilessly. Those who fell were lost. Children that slipped from their mothers arms were trampled to death. . . . Many of the ice-covered lifeboats

could not be lowered . . . I saw boats full of people snag and hang by the bowline, spilling screaming people into the waves. . . . I saw families shoot themselves rather than suffer slow and terrifying death.

At almost exactly 10:00 p.m., *Wilhelm Gustloff* sank beneath the icy waves. Hoffman jumped overboard into bone-chilling water and:

What I saw then was terrible. Children hung in lifejackets, their stiff legs sticking straight up. Elderly people bobbed dead in the water. Death screams and cries for help filled the air. . . . For about twenty minutes, the most dreadful moments of my life, I swam through the water. Time and again I was covered by sheets of ice. Occasional cries for help became fewer and fewer. What happened then bordered on the miraculous. I saw a dark shadow coming directly towards me and recognized the outlines of a ship. I screamed with the last of my strength. I was noticed and pulled into . . . German torpedo boat *T-36*.

Hoffman was one of 1,239 snatched from the frigid water by mine-sweepers and torpedo boats, while an estimated 9,343 had frozen to death or drowned.

Aftermath
Eleven days later, just after midnight on 10–11 February, at almost exactly the same place, Commander Marinesko's *S-13* hit *General von Steuben* with two torpedoes. The liner sank in seven minutes, killing some 3,500 civilians and wounded servicemen.

Two months after that, freighter *Goya* left Hela near Danzig (Gdansk) with over 7,000 refugees crammed into her cargo holds. Just before midnight on 16 April, two torpedoes from Russian submarine L-3 struck *Goya*, which sank in less than four minutes, long before her deep holds could be evacuated. Only 183 were rescued.

These three submarine sinkings, in the closing days of the war in Europe, took between 16,000 and 20,000 non-combatant lives. Some sources claim the Russians knew they were attacking civilian evacuation ships, but deliberately sunk them in revenge for Nazi atrocities.

APRIL 1945 –
BREACH OF TRUST OR AMERICAN WAR CRIME?

Every spring, the area around Washington DC's tidal basin bursts into a riot of colour, attracting visitors from near and far. The National Cherry

Blossom Festival dates from 1912, when freighter *Awa Maru* delivered 3,020 cherry trees as a gift of friendship from the Japanese government.

Three decades later, during the Second World War, the United States gave a Guarantee of Safe Passage to another *Awa Maru*, this one being a hospital ship authorized to carry wounded Japanese soldiers, and also to deliver food and medicines to Allied POWs and interned civilians.

Early in March of 1945, the second *Awa* picked up 2,000 tons of Red Cross parcels from a stockpile at the Russian port of Nakhoda on the Sea of Japan and dropped them off at various ports, ending at Singapore, where Captain Hamada Matsutaro took aboard some wounded soldiers, and about 2,000 Japanese diplomats, technicians and other civilians. So far, everything was in accord with Japan's agreement with the United States.

However, by this stage of the war, American submarines had achieved in the Pacific what Hitler's U-boats had marginally failed to accomplish in the Atlantic: they had virtually destroyed the enemy's fighting capacity by interdicting trade routes. Since only ships with safe passage could expect to reach the home islands, the Japanese began to break the rules.

While at Singapore, and later during a stop at Jakarta, *Awa Maru* secretly loaded an illegal cargo of tin, tungsten, rubber, drilling machinery, aircraft parts, ammunition, crude oil and other war matériel. She was also rumoured to have picked up a fortune in gold and diamonds, but this has never been confirmed.

The Americans knew Japanese mercy ships were carrying contraband, but ignored the breach in order to ensure desperately-needed humanitarian relief continued to reach the prison camps. Advised of her prearranged course, Admiral Lockwood instructed submarines patrolling the Taiwan Strait:

> Let pass safely the *Awa Maru* carrying prisoner of war supplies. She will be passing through your areas between March 30 and April 4. She is lighted at night and plastered with white crosses.

One of these boats was USS *Queenfish* whose skipper, Lieutenant Commander Charles Loughlin, was upset that he had made no kills on this patrol. Shortly before 1000 hours on 1 April, *Queenfish* made radar contact with a vessel which seemed to be in a hurry, steaming a straight course without zigzagging. Loughlin reported being unable to take a visual periscope sighting because of fog (US naval weather records indicate a clear night, but local surface mist is a possibility).

The contact was, of course, *Awa Maru*, but she was eighteen kilometres (eleven miles) off the prearranged course and, thanks to her heavy cargo and many passengers, was so low in the water that her radar profile looked more like a destroyer than a merchantman. Satisfied he had a legitimate target, Loughlin fired a spread of four torpedoes from his stern tubes. All struck, and *Awa Maru* went down with 2,003 passengers and crew. A lone survivor, First Class Steward Shimoda Kantaro, was rescued by *Queenfish*.

Aftermath

Tokyo furiously denounced the incident, calling it 'A most outrageous act of treachery, unparalleled in the world history of the war'. Afraid of jeopardizing the distribution of aid to POWs, Washington issued an unprecedented apology to its wartime foe, offered to replace the lost ship, relieved Loughlin of command, and tried him by court martial.

The Court accepted his attorneys' defence of 'lack of criminal intent', substantiated by his rescue of the lone survivor who denied any atrocity. Its verdict acquitted him of 'culpable inefficiency in the performance of duty' and 'disobedience to the lawful orders of superior officers', but convicted him of the lesser offence of 'negligence in obeying orders'.

He received a letter of admonition from the Secretary of the Navy, but his career was far from over. He worked out the war as Operations Officer for the Atlantic Submarine Fleet. Then he commanded a submarine division, became an instructor at Annapolis, captained the cruiser USS *Toledo*, and finally raised his flag as Rear Admiral before retirement.

MAY 1945 –
TRAGIC ERROR OR BRITISH WAR CRIME?

Russian submarines were not the only ones to destroy German merchant ships evacuating non-combatants ahead of the advancing Red Army. During the last days of April 1945, former passenger liner *Cap Arcona* lay at Neustadt Bay near Lübeck loading some 5,000 prisoners and 400 SS guards from Neuengamme Concentration Camp. She carried a crew of seventy-six and a naval gunnery detail of about 500.

A much smaller vessel, *Thielbek*, crammed in another 2,800 camp inmates and their guards. Most of the overcrowded prisoners were sick and malnourished, but there was little food or water for them. There seemed no point because, under secret orders issued by SS chief Heinrich Himmler, both ships were to be taken out to sea and scuttled, with the prisoners battened below to drown.

On the afternoon of 3 May, several waves of British Typhoon fighter-bombers swept in with bombs and rockets. *Thielbek* sunk in about fifteen minutes. Then the Typhoons machine-gunned swimmers, killing most of the ship's crew, the prisoners and their SS guards. Next, *Cap Arcona* was set afire, burning many of her passengers to death. Eventually she sank in shallows with her upperworks visible. Only about 500 from the two ships survived. Five days later, Germany surrendered and the European phase of the Second World War was over.

Aftermath

German revisionist sources say both ships were flying large white flags, making the attacks violations of international law and war crimes. The British claim no such flags were visible and hence they had every reason to suppose the ships were conveying combat troops to defend the German heartland. In fact, the argument seems irrelevant in view of Himmler's murderous intent.

June 1945 – Aerological Lessons Unlearned

Six months after Halsey's typhoon, few of the recommendations for improved warning systems had been implemented. With the American net closing ever closer on Japan, the Third Fleet's striking component, Task Force 38, was operating in three sections known as Task Groups (TG's).

Admiral Halsey in USS *Missouri* and Vice Admiral McCain in USS *Shangri-la* were off Okinawa, accompanied by Rear Admiral Clark's TG38.1. Rear Admiral Radford's TG38.4 was about 225 kms (140 miles) south-east, at a fuelling rendezvous with the oilers of Rear Admiral Beary's TG30.8. Rear Admiral Sherman's TG38.3 was resting at Leyte.

On 3 June 1945, ships and aircraft began reporting a tropical storm to the south. Halsey ordered command ship USS *Ancon* to head for the disturbance and advise weather conditions. Pending her report, the Third Fleet aerologist recommended staying where they were because he believed the typhoon would miss Okinawa. However, Halsey decided to avoid the risk of being forced into shallow waters by moving away, and the aerologist recommended a south-easterly course to miss the storm.

On the evening of 4 June, Halsey, McCain and Clark were joined by Radford's group and Beary's oilers. Next morning Halsey received a signal from *Ancon* confirming there was indeed a typhoon, closer than originally reported. Once again, the signal had been sent in the cumbersome, low-priority weather code and had waited about eight hours before being decoded. The storm seemed to be on a collision course with the Third Fleet, but the delayed warning left little time to avoid it.

The Admiral ordered a complete reversal of course from south-east to north-west, hoping to cross in front of the storm and into its safer western semicircle. Then he transferred tactical command to McCain. The three task groups were strung out over fifty-five kilometres (thirty-four miles), with the flagships and TG38.4 in the van, TG38.1 at the centre and TG30.8 to the rear.

After a while Beary signalled, 'Believe this course is running us back into the storm.' McCain authorized a change of direction, but the ships rode so heavily he reverted to the original bearing. At 0420, Clark signalled that he had the typhoon on radar, adding, 'I could get clear of the center . . . by steering 120 degrees.' McCain replied, 'Nothing on our scope to indicate storm center', and Clark answered, 'Well, we definitely have.'

McCain then consulted Halsey, who told him not to scatter the fleet if he could avoid it. These discussions took time, and it was twenty minutes before McCain gave Clark local discretion, saying, 'Intend holding present course, use your own judgement.' It was too late. While McCain, Halsey and Radford were steaming across seas so calm that Halsey said, 'It's possibly not a typhoon after all', Clark and Beary found themselves in the grip of a small and tight, but fierce storm.

Sustained hurricane-force winds, with gusts up to 127 knots (235 km/hr; 146 mph) hit Beary's fuelling group first. Most of his forty-eight ships came through with superficial injuries, but two escort carriers lost part of their flight decks, while a tanker and a destroyer suffered severe superstructure damage.

Clark's group entered the storm about ninety minutes later. This time, the destroyers had full bunkers and came through rather well, but heavy cruiser *Pittsburgh* lost thirty-two metres (104 feet) of her bow.[39] Two other cruisers received serious hull damage, and the flight decks of all four fleet carriers were buckled or otherwise injured.

In total, the two task groups suffered damage to thirty-three ships and lost seventy-six aircraft. Fortunately, only a single officer and five men had been killed or swept overboard. On 14 July 1945, Halsey expressed his frustration in an official report:

Commander THIRD Fleet has made strong representations in the past, including recommendation in his top secret serial 0085 of 26 January 1945, for the establishment of aircraft weather reconnaissance squadrons composed of long range aircraft. He again emphasizes the absolute necessity of improved typhoon warning communications. . . . These recommendations are repeated here and Commander THIRD Fleet will continue to repeat them until a satisfactory typhoon warning service is established; and until then the Fleet will be in constant jeopardy from these vicious and unpredictable storms.

JULY 1945 –
OVERLOOKED AND FORGOTTEN IN MID-PACIFIC

'You are relieved, Mr Twible.' Newly commissioned and still un-accustomed to the boredom of a night watch, Ensign Harlan Twible greeted his replacement, climbed out of the after crow's nest and started down to the main deck of USS *Indianapolis (CA35)*. Later he recalled:

> I heard the explosion and felt the tear in my side, then another explosion. . . . I reached down to my side and felt wetness. . . . There was no time to think about my problem. . . . When you blow a ship to smithereens . . . virtually everyone is wounded or injured. . . . When I arrived amidships our starboard side was about one foot above the water and sinking fast. I yelled 'over the side'. No one moved. . . . Then I yelled 'follow me' and jumped into the water. The crew followed. [Copyright © *New American* 2001]

Some four months earlier, while Twible was still a Midshipman at the United States Naval Academy, a Japanese suicide bomber had plunged into the heavy cruiser's port side. Despite holes in her bottom, ruptured fuel tanks and damaged propeller shafts, she managed to limp across the Pacific to Mare Island Navy Yard in California. As soon as extensive repairs had been completed, *Indianapolis* was ordered to forego the normal shakedown cruise and pick up a special high-priority cargo for delivery to the United States Strategic Air Forces on Tinian Island.

An Unusual Assignment
At San Francisco, two trucks came alongside. One carried a huge crate which was winched off and stored in the port hangar. Then two army officers (who looked and talked like civilians) carried a mysterious canister from the second truck and clamped it to ring-bolts welded to the deck of the vacant admiral's cabin. Captain Charles McVay told his senior officers he had no idea what this strange cargo was, adding, 'But I have been told that every day we take off this trip will be a day off the war.'

He then did his best to shorten the conflict, setting a record by covering the 8500 kilometres (5300 miles) to Tinian in ten days, at an average speed of 29 knots (54 km/h; 33mph). Once the cargo (consisting of uranium and components for the world's first operational atomic bomb) was off-loaded, *Indianapolis* reported to Pacific Fleet Headquarters on Guam and received orders to proceed to Leyte Gulf for gunnery practice with battleship *Idaho*, preparatory to rejoining the fleet for the invasion of Japan.

Naval Intelligence had intercepted Japanese signals indicating that two of its few surviving submarines were operating along *Indianapolis'* route. However, being anxious to keep its code-breaking capability top-secret, it had not passed this information down the chain of command. As a result, Captain McVay's request for the usual destroyer escort was denied because, he was told, the Japanese submarine force had been virtually destroyed. For the same reason, zigzagging was to be discretionary.

Indianapolis Torpedoed

At 2305 hours (11:05 p.m.) on 29 July, Japanese submarine *I-58* picked up an echo on her passive sonar. Commander Mochitsura Hashimoto later reported, 'We waited until it got close enough to see what it was. When we saw what a big ship it was, I aimed my torpedoes and fired.' By this time it was just after midnight and, at 0014 (12:14 a.m.), two of Hashimoto's six-torpedo spread struck the big cruiser.

The first blew off a 12-metre (40-foot) section of her bow and wounded Ensign Twible. Still barrelling ahead at 17 knots (31.5 km/h; 19.5 mph) the open bow scooped up water, the pressure from which collapsed forward bulkheads. The second hit an engine space amidships, igniting a fuel bunker, exploding an ammunition magazine, and knocking out electric power throughout the ship. More water cascaded through this gaping hole. Captain McVay gave his recollection of the event in a recording made on 27 September 1945:

On Saturday night, the 29th of July, we had been zig-zagging until dark. We did not zig-zag thereafter. . . . After midnight, I was thrown from my emergency cabin bunk by a very violent explosion, followed shortly thereafter by another. . . . I got out onto the bridge. I asked the Officer of the Deck if he had any reports. He said 'No Sir, I have lost all communication.' . . . I ran into the damage control officer . . . (who) told me that we were going down rapidly by the head, and wanted to know if I desired to pass the word to abandon ship. I told him 'No.' . . . we had been through a hit before and were able to control it. . . . Within another two or three minutes the executive officer, Commander Flynn, came up and said, 'We are definitely going down and I suggest that we abandon ship.' . . . Having utter regard for his ability, I then said 'Pass the word to abandon ship.'

Between 200 and 300 of 1,199 seamen and marines on board had been killed by the explosions, or trapped in rapidly-flooding enclosed decks. But the watch had just changed, so half the crew was at cruising stations and the rest were still out and about. As a result, perhaps as many as 1,000 were able to jump overboard, or simply walk off the side. Many were badly burned or severely injured. Some had kapok life jackets, although quite a few had none. A few life rafts floated free, but most went down with the ship.

Survivors Forsaken

Before the cruiser sank, radio operators managed to send distress signals. They were not received by the Navy, but an army signalman claimed to have monitored the calls and reported them to a naval contact. This was denied by the Navy, and was just one of many controversial factors contributing to failure to recognize the plight of *Indianapolis*. These included:

- Naval intelligence intercepted Commander Hashimoto's report that he had sunk a battleship of the Idaho class. However, since no battleship was missing, the report was assumed to be a false claim. No one noticed that the coordinates of the sinking were exactly where *Indianapolis* ought to have been.

- Regulations required the delayed arrival of non-combatant vessels to be reported. However, fighting ships (which might have been diverted for secret operations) were excluded. Hence, although alerted to expect the cruiser, Leyte made no report when she did not arrive as scheduled.

- Battleship *Idaho* had been advised of *Indianapolis'* orders to join her, but the coded message was garbled by decoders, who did not ask for a repeat transmission of the low-priority non-operational signal. In consequence her arrival was not anticipated.

With no-one looking for them, the survivors endured four-and-a-half days of horror and terror, during which they drifted 160 kilometres (100 miles), and spread out along a line some thirty kilometres (eighteen miles) long. Panic, shock, pain, hunger, thirst, burning daytime heat and chilling night-time cold debilitated and exhausted them.

Then came the sharks. At first they only ate floating corpses, but later they closed in for a feeding frenzy on the living. Some survivors became delirious, others committed suicide by taking off their life jackets and sliding under water. In an interview, Seaman First-Class Ed Brown remembered:

The thirst and dehydration was terrible and many men went mad from drinking the sea water. And the sharks, of course. But even worse than the terror of the sharks was the anguish of feeling utterly deserted and alone out there in this huge expanse of sea. It seemed at times so hopeless, that help would never come.

It almost didn't. Huge B-29 Superfortresses flew overhead on their way to bomb Japan. On the return trip to Tinian they were briefed to scan the surface for downed aircrews, but the survivors were too far south-west of their course to be seen. Finally, on 2 August, Navy Lieutenant Chuck Gwinn, piloting a PV-1 Ventura on anti-submarine patrol, leant out to fix a recalcitrant radio antenna and, purely by chance, spotted a large oil slick.

Last-Minute Rescue

Thinking the oil must have come from an enemy submarine, he descended for a depth-charge run, sighted the swimmers, and radioed base, giving his position and saying, 'Many men in water'. At first they refused to believe him, thinking he was playing a joke but, after about three hours a Catalina PBY flying boat was dispatched. Arriving at the scene, Navy Lieutenant Adrian Marks dropped to thirty metres (100 feet) and his crew began tossing out life rafts and supplies. Then they were horrified to see sharks circling the swimmers and eating them alive.

Ignoring standing orders, which prohibited landing in the open sea where damage could be extensive, Marks bravely made a power-on stall between wave crests.[40] Taxiing his seriously-injured aircraft to the nearest group, he filled the fuselage and crammed the wings with fifty-six survivors, who were transferred to surface vessels which began arriving shortly after midnight.

The first to arrive, Destroyer Escort *Cecil Doyle (DE-368)*, stripped Marks' unserviceable aircraft of instruments and secret gear before sinking her by gunfire. Only 316 were plucked from the sea alive. The death toll was 883, and decomposing cadavers and body parts were still being picked up six days later.

AUGUST 1945 – JAPANESE WAR CRIME

Terrified screams broke out as water gushed into sealed compartments, but the cries soon diminished, stifled by compressed air forcing its way into lungs struggling to expel it. Oblivion was mercifully swift, as 10,000 tons of steel sank gently to the ocean floor.

A week earlier, 5,000 Koreans, who had been working as conscripted slave labourers in Aomori Prefecture, at the extreme north of Japan, happily clambered aboard freighter *Ukishima Maru*. They had been told they were being repatriated because their work was done, and the war was almost over.

After boarding, they steamed southward along the west coast of Honshu Island to Maisuru Naval Base at Kyoto. There, explosive charges were placed inside the hull and hatches were battened down. Then *Ukishima Maru* went into the Sea of Japan, where she was scuttled, murdering 4,920 of the Koreans.[41]

PART EIGHT

The Current Period

DECEMBER 1948 –
LURKING LEFTOVER IN THE WANGPOO RIVER

When Japan opened the Second World War by mounting its full-scale invasion of China, the civil war between the Kuomintang National Government and the Chinese Communist Party turned into reluctant cooperation. Then, after the Japanese surrender, the Soviets armed the Communists with captured Japanese weaponry, and even fiercer civil conflict erupted.

By 1948, the rebels were in the ascendant and soundly defeated Nationalist ground forces in the Battle of Hwai Hai River. Communist armies were then expected to close in on Shanghai, which became a city of panic and terror. Tens of thousands of frightened citizens headed for the harbour, pushing and shoving to find a means of escape. Rickety piers collapsed under their weight, dumping screaming crowds into the murky waters.

One of the ships targeted by this chaos was *Kiangya*, a rusty old coastal steamer which had just arrived. Licensed to carry 1,186 passengers, she was already overloaded with 2,250 paying customers from Nanking. Dozens of them threw previously-purchased tickets to friends sighted on the shore. Some tickets fell into the water and desperate escapees dived into the scummy filth to recover them. Others landed on the wharf creating mad scrambles of mayhem and even murder.

Hundreds of refugees scrambled up *Kiangya*'s rusty sides from sampans and junks which pulled alongside. Despite the efforts of officers and crew to fend them off, an estimated 1,200 additional people crammed themselves on board. At 6:30 p.m., the grossly overloaded vessel cast off and steamed into the Wangpoo (Huangpu) River.

Explosion

While the crushed passengers were settling down for the long journey ahead, the ship suddenly shuddered; there was a blinding flash of light, plates buckled, and bulkheads shattered. Water flooded in and many of those below were instantly drowned, although several hundred managed to shove and pummel their way to the open decks.

After its initial inrush, the river water bubbled upward slowly, and it took *Kiangya* three hours to settle, but the radio shack had been destroyed so no SOS was possible. As deck after deck was swamped, dozens of the weaker refugees were pushed over the side, while mothers were seen throwing infants into the water hoping they would somehow survive.

Finally, the remaining passengers all congregated on the top deck, standing in waist-deep water and screaming for help. It seemed so helpless that one of the ship's officers told several elderly women to 'be of good cheer' and shot them in the head before killing himself.

The tiny vessel *Hwafoo* was the first to sight the wreck and her SOS summoned the bigger steamship *Mouli*. Her captain tried to bring her alongside the now almost totally submerged *Kiangya* but sheered off, afraid the seething mob would leap across and capsize his own ship.

In the end, a resourceful *Kiangya* officer quietened them down, and some 700 were taken off the rapidly sinking vessel by twos and threes. Later, about 1,000 bodies were plucked from the brackish Wangpoo waters, while another 1,750 or so were thought to have gone down with the ship.

Aftermath

At the time, *Kiangya* was believed to have been hit by an artillery shell fired by Communist forces, but she was later determined to have struck a submerged Japanese mine left over from the Second World War. Ironically, much of the panic which had overloaded her in the first place was unnecessary, because the Communists did not occupy Shanghai until the following May.

SEPTEMBER 1949 –
'WRONGFUL DEFAULT' AT TORONTO

From the late nineteenth century until the Second World War, the ultimate dream vacation for much of middle-income America was a cruise on the Great Lakes or St Lawrence-Saguenay River system. After being dormant during the war, this holiday pastime enjoyed a brief but vigorous revival which extended throughout the 1950s.

From the start, Great Lakes cruise ship *Noronic* was regarded as lucky. By chance, she delayed her maiden voyage and so escaped the 'Great Storm' of 1913 (a once-in-centuries event which stranded twenty vessels on reefs and islands, and sank nineteen more, eleven of them with all hands). Since then she had made more than 1,000 voyages and was considered the safest, finest and largest passenger vessel plying the inland waters, rivalling the luxury and sophistication of great ocean liners.

On 14 September 1949, she left her berth at Detroit, crossed Lake Erie to pick up more passengers at Cleveland, and passed through the Welland Canal into Lake Ontario. At 6:00 p.m. on the 16th, she moored at Pier 9 in Toronto, starboard side to the dock. Many passengers, officers and crew members went ashore to visit the city, which was enjoying a post-war boom. When Captain William Taylor returned at 2:00 a.m., only sixteen of 171 crew were on duty, but most of the 624 American passengers had reboarded, along with a substantial number of Canadian guests.

Inferno

Shortly before 2:30 a.m., a passenger named Church noticed smoke coming from a small room on C Deck, and heard 'a rustle and crackling' from within. When he tried to open the door he found it locked. Running down the alleyway, he met bellboy O'Neill who fetched the key and a fire extinguisher. However, when flames began to spill into the corridor, they realized the futility of their efforts. Joined by passenger Gibson, they moved aft to pull a hose from the fire station, but when they opened the valve nothing happened. By this time the blaze was spreading down the corridor in both directions.

Church climbed to D Deck, woke his family, and took them ashore, while O'Neill went forward to break the glass on the fire alarm and provide the crew with its first indication of trouble. First Officer Wood realized the fire was serious and ran to the wheelhouse to sound the klaxon. However, instead of the five-blast fire warning – one long, three short, one long – the whistle seized and produced a continuous strident shriek.

On the dock, night watchman Harper promptly telephoned the Toronto Fire Department (TFD), which dispatched a supervisor with pumper, hose wagon, aerial ladders, high-pressure unit and rescue squad. Barrelling down Yonge Street at 2:38 a.m. with his siren wailing, District Fire Chief Jim Stevens could see flames billowing from the three upper decks. Before even reaching the dock he called in a second alarm, soon followed by a third, plus a call for the TFD fireboat.[42]

Aerial Ladder Five arrived near *Noronic*'s bow, but had barely extended to B Deck when a woman jumped on, closely followed by six or seven men. With a horrible crunch, the overloaded ladder snapped, throwing its load of escapees into the water. Aerial Ladder One had been held up by parked cars, but finally arrived and, learning from Five's collapse, braced its 100 foot (thirty-three metre) length with hand ladders. This allowed a number of individuals to escape. Many more were trapped in their staterooms behind flaming corridors. Those who did manage to reach the open deck had to face cremation or jump – risking broken bones on the dock to starboard, or drowning in the harbour to port.

Between 3:00 and 4:00 a.m., the volume of water pumped into the ship by thirty-seven fire hoses caused a list, which forced fireboat and shore-based units to withdraw for their own safety. After a short while, *Noronic* righted herself and sank to the bottom, allowing hoses and fireboat to return and pour water into the still-blazing superstructure. By 5:00 a.m., the fire was under control, but *Noronic*'s metal parts were still unbearably hot and it was almost noon before she could be boarded.

Aftermath

Locating and identifying the dead in any disaster is difficult and unpleasant, but in this case it was uncertain how many guests were aboard, while many corpses had been completely incinerated, and most of the others were charred beyond recognition. Finally, the body count was determined to be 114, with another fourteen missing. They were all passengers; the entire crew had managed to escape.

A Court of Inquiry failed to identify the exact cause of the blaze, but castigated the crew as 'disorganized and ineffectual', adding 'complete complacency had descended upon both the ship's officers and management. . . . The loss of life was caused by wrongful default of the owners and master.' Captain Taylor's certificate was suspended for a year, but he never returned to the lakes, working as a hotel night clerk until his death in 1965.

JANUARY 1950 – 'AVOIDANCE OF RESPONSIBILITY' AT NORFOLK

Captain William Brown was elated. His appointment to USS *Missouri (BB63)* – which would be his first seagoing assignment for almost six years, and first ever capital-ship command – almost guaranteed promotion to flag rank. However, once on board, he seemed to discourage intimacies. During sea trials in December 1949, he responded to suggestions from Commander Peckham by saying. 'George . . . let's have it understood that I am the skipper and you are the executive officer'. Word soon got around that the former destroyer captain did not welcome unsolicited advice.

On 17 January, the huge battleship left Norfolk Navy Base to make a run through the Fort Munroe acoustic test range. Her navigational aids were at less than peak efficiency – fathometer incorrectly adjusted, magnetic compass not compensated, and search radar overdue for calibration. Captain Brown was piloting the ship from the open bridge. Commander Peckham was four levels below in 'secondary conn', ready to take over if required.

Missouri had been provided with several charts of Hampton Roads, but they were incompatible, showing different numbers and markings of buoys. Moreover, the flag was missing from one of the more important ones. As *Missouri* headed for the range, developments came rapidly, one on top of another, and were recorded in the ship's message logs:

➤ Brown: 'Does anyone know if those spar buoys and this other buoy are part of the range?'

➤ No-one answers him.

➤ Brown, who has mistaken a line of spar buoys for range markers, orders the helm to come left.

➤ Commander Peckham sees the ship swinging to port but, probably remembering his earlier reprimand, only tentatively suggests keeping to the right. There is no response from the bridge.

➤ Minutes later he becomes more positive, saying, 'The executive officer recommends we come right immediately – the ship is standing into shoal water.'

➤ A soft-spoken telephone talker relays this message to the captain on the windswept open bridge.

➤ He does not acknowledge, but the talker does not repeat it, although he should have.

➤ Moments later the navigator, Lieutenant Commander Frank Morris, speaks up for the first time, telling Brown, 'The bearing is getting high, we should come right now.'

➤ Brown replies, 'We can't come right now, or we'll spoil the run.'

➤ Morris steels himself and shouts, urgently, 'We must come right, sir, we must come right immediately.'

➤ Brown then orders 10-degrees right rudder, but says to Commander John Millett, 'The navigator doesn't know where he is; go find out.'

➤ Peckham then issues his third warning: 'The executive officer recommends full back, or twist to the right' (engines full astern, or an emergency turn to starboard).

➤ Almost simultaneously the helmsman reports the rudder is sluggish, while stern lookouts report 'the propellers are kicking up mud'.

➤ Captain Brown orders 'Full right rudder. Engines full astern', but it is too late.

➤ The engine room reports all engines must be shut down, due to mud clogging water intakes, plus the danger of stripping propeller gears.

For ninety seconds *Missouri* ploughed ahead; the momentum of 57,000 deadweight tons travelling at 12.5 knots (23 km/h; 14 mph) driving her some 2,500 feet (760 metres) onto the mudbank, and lifting her more than six feet (almost two metres) into the air. She had grounded at the worst possible time – at the peak of an unusually high tide. Salvage efforts began at once.[43]

Aftermath

A Court of Inquiry determined there had been 'no teamwork' between officers and men, a majority of whom had shown 'An intangible and elusive . . . avoidance of responsibility, and a belief that someone else was taking care of the task at hand.' It recommended individual Courts Martial for three senior officers.

Navigator Morris was convicted of 'culpable inefficiency', Captain Brown and Operations Officer Millett of 'negligence in suffering a vessel of the Navy to be hazarded . . . and stranded.' In addition, all three were found guilty of 'neglect of duty'. Each court recommended clemency, and all three were sentenced to be reduced on their respective promotion lists. Brown never held another seagoing command, and only pinned stars on his uniform under the US Navy's 'tombstone' programme of promoting senior captains to flag rank after their retirement.

Some years later, Rear Admiral Harold Smith summed up what he believed to be the true reason for the incident, saying:

> The navigator didn't have the courage to contradict the operations officer and the captain, and forcibly point out to them that the ship was standing into danger. All he did was call out the ship's position, course and speed. Until too late he left it to the captain to discover that the course put them out of position for a safe transit.

JULY 1956 –
RELIANCE ON TECHNOLOGY OFF NEW YORK

Immediately after the Second World War, when mass air travel was still a thing of the future, the maritime nations started a race to recapture the former glory of their trans-Atlantic steamship lines. Italy's bid began with the launch of *Andrea Doria* in 1951. Named after a famous sixteenth-century Genoese statesman and admiral, this sleek vessel and her sister ship *Cristoforo Colombo* were designed for luxury rather than speed, and intended to take advantage of the sunnier southern route.

In addition to being a floating art gallery, *Doria* was one of the safest vessels in service. She was equipped with two sets of radar to guard against collision or other hazards and, even if both sets failed, she was – like *Titanic* and *Empress of Ireland* before her – claimed to be 'unsinkable'. She had a double-hull and eleven watertight compartments, with bulkheads reaching as high as 'A' Deck, designed to keep her afloat if any two were breached. Under these conditions, her architects said she would never heel more than 15 degrees. Her lifeboats were given a safety-margin, designed to be launchable at up to 20 degrees of list, and their capacity exceeded *Doria*'s complement of passengers and crew.

The Swedish entry in the trans-Atlantic race was far more modest. Built in 1946 and remodelled in 1952, *Stockholm* was one of the smallest postwar liners. At just under 13,000 tons, she was almost exactly one-third the size of *Doria*. Although far less luxurious than the Italian vessel, her yacht-like profile was equally beautiful and modern-looking. She too was radar-equipped, and had a reinforced bow for breaking ice in her home waters.

Inward and Outward-Bound

On 25 July 1956, *Stockholm* was outward-bound, heading for Nantucket Lightship, which guards the crowded lanes leading to New York Harbor. The night was cloudless, the moon was bright, and the radar screen was clear. Captain Gunnar Nordenson followed common fine-weather practice, saving time and distance by veering slightly north of the recommended outbound sea-lane, and steaming at close to full speed. At 8:30 p.m., Third Officer Johan-Ernst Carstens-Johannsen took over the watch, and Nordenson retired to his cabin.

After a mostly sunny crossing, inward-bound *Doria* had been steaming in patchy fog since mid-afternoon. It became thicker as she approached Nantucket Lightship, so Captain Piero Calamai posted extra lookouts and ordered watertight doors closed. These were standard precautions but, confident his twin modern radars would give ample warning of any approaching traffic, he maintained fast cruising speed to keep on schedule. At 10:20 p.m., he altered course for Ambrose Lightship which marks the harbour mouth. The two ships were now on parallel courses but invisible to one another.

About twenty-five minutes later, *Stockholm* came up on *Doria*'s radar, about four degrees off the starboard bow, some seventeen sea miles (31.5 km; 19.5 miles) distant and, according to the radar image, veering slightly to the right. They were converging at a combined speed of some 40 knots (74 km/hr; 46 mph), but *Doria* judged they would pass safely starboard-to-starboard by holding their present courses.

When they were twelve sea miles (twenty-two km; fourteen miles) apart, *Stockholm*'s shorter-range radar picked up *Doria*'s blip, slightly to port. Unlike the Italian practice of 'eyeballing' an oncoming ship's course on the radar screen, Swedish procedure was to plot the course by taking two radar fixes. By the time this was completed, the distance was down to six nautical miles, so they would meet in about nine minutes. To *Stockholm* it seemed they would pass port-to-port, clearing each other by about a mile. The two navigating officers had come to opposite conclusions. Either one of them had misread the radar, or one of the sets was out of adjustment.

Shortly after 11:00 p.m., when separation was less than four sea miles, Captain Calamai ordered a small turn to port, intending to open up the passing distance. Then *Doria* came out of the fogbank, and the two ships – which had previously seen each other only as radar images – came into visual contact. They were barely three minutes apart. Because of Calamai's turn, they were converging at an angle which, at the moment of sighting, showed the Swede's lights to starboard of *Doria*, and the Italian's lights to port of *Stockholm*. Thus each saw the other exactly where expected.

However, in order to give the oncoming ship a wider berth, Carstens ordered a sharp turn to starboard. He was about to signal with the conventional blasts of *Stockholm*'s whistle, when the bridge telephone rang. He turned away to answer it, losing sight of the Italian at a critical moment. Aboard *Doria*, Third Officer Eugenio Giannini screamed, 'She's turning! She's turning! She's coming towards us!'

Captain Calamai responded instantly, ordering '*Tutto sinistra*' (hard left). With faith in *Doria*'s speed and manoeuvrability he expected to move left faster than the other ship was moving right. Almost simultaneously, Carstens hung up the telephone and looked ahead. He, too, reacted quickly: 'Hard a'starboard, full speed astern!', but *Stockholm* was moving too quickly for either of their orders to be effective.

Collision

At almost full speed, her ice-breaking bow plunged deep into *Doria*'s hull like a can-opener, breaking through seven full decks from the keel up. Sparks flew and metal screamed horribly. For a brief moment she remained impaled, but *Doria* was also close to full speed and she was torn away, leaving a gaping hole for water to rush into. She bumped down *Doria*'s side, creating more holes.

In the First-Class salon, the band was thrown off the podium and crashed onto dancers on the floor. In Tourist-Class, there was momentary panic when the cinema was plunged into darkness in the middle of a film. But most of *Doria*'s 1,134 passengers had turned in early, anticipating an early morning arrival. Many of those on the port side were jolted awake when thrown out of bed onto the floor, but to starboard the impact was far greater.

Passenger Peterson actually saw *Stockholm*'s bow crashing into cabin 56 before being knocked out by it. When he regained consciousness, it had retreated and his wife Martha lay dying under the wreckage. Next door, in cabin 54, Jane Cianfarra was trapped but alive. Next again, in number 52, one of her daughters had been killed, but the other, Linda Morgan, woke up to find herself unhurt but perched on *Stockholm*'s retreating bow.

That bow had done immense damage: at least three watertight compartments had been compromised and *Doria* was doomed. Realizing this, Captain Calamai organized evacuation by lifeboat but, probably to avoid panic, did not actually signal 'Abandon Ship!' However, before boats on the port side could be launched, the ship had heeled five degrees beyond the 20 degree limit and they were wedged against the side. Suddenly the surplus of lifeboat space had become a deficit – the starboard boats could only accommodate 1,044 of the 1,660 people still alive.

Aftermath

An urgent SOS was transmitted, and soon nearby freighters and Coastguard cutters joined *Stockholm*'s rescue effort. Between them they picked up over 900 survivors, but many were left floating. Two hours fast steaming away, still blanketed by fog, Baron de Beaudean, captain of French liner *Ile de France,* thought he was too far away to help.

However, the messages became more and more frantic, so he took the risk of running to the scene at full speed through the fog. He arrived in time to rescue 735 swimmers. Amazingly, apart from fifty-one who had died in the collision or gone down with the ship, all passengers and crew were safe. Five of *Stockholm*'s crew had also been killed, and her bow was badly crumpled, but her bulkheads held and she slowly limped back to New York.[44]

MAY 1967 – EXCESSIVE SECRECY OFF THE SINAI

By 1967, Israelis had been living in constant peril for eighteen years. Guerrilla raids, terrorist action and bombardment by Syrian artillery, had encouraged the development of a siege psychology. Not one of Israel's neighbours had negotiated a peace settlement, or even recognized its right to exist, while no part of the tiny country was beyond the range of their firepower.

Countdown to War

On 16 May, Egypt mobilized its armed forces, and demanded withdrawal of United Nations peacekeeping patrols. Procrastination might have allowed time for saner counsel, but Secretary-General U Thant complied immediately. Within days, Egyptian armour was rolling up to the frontier, and the Navy had sealed the Strait of Tiran, Israel's only outlet to the Indian Ocean. Other Arab nations rushed to Egypt's support. Israel had previously and publicly announced that it would consider a renewed State of War existed under any one of the following:

- Closing the Strait of Tiran
- Withdrawal of United Nations Forces
- Alliance of Egypt and Jordan
- Iraqi forces entering Jordan

Amazingly, although all four preconditions had been met, neither Egypt nor its allies seems to have considered the possibility of Israeli pre-emptive action. Early on 5 June, while Arab commanders were still discussing strategy, the entire air branch of the Israeli Defence Forces flew westward, at wave-top height above the Mediterranean. After outflanking early warning systems, the aircraft turned south, to strike from an unexpected direction at all nineteen Egyptian military airfields. Fierce ground combat and naval engagements followed.

Unidentified Intruder
Three days later at 0600 hours, a mysterious merchantman, cruising twenty-six kilometres (sixteen miles) offshore, was spotted by aerial reconnaissance and marked 'unknown' on the plotting table at *Heyl Yam* (the maritime branch of Israeli Defence Forces). A second sighting at 1000 determined it was an American vessel, and the marker was changed to 'neutral' but with the original sighting time. By 1100, the vessel had steamed off the plot, and the incoming shift removed the marker. However, at 1130, the ship reversed course back into the combat zone. It was re-entered on the plot, again identified as 'unknown'.

At 1145, the retreating Egyptian army blew up an ammunition dump near el Arish. The advancing Israeli ground force interpreted the explosion and billowing smoke to be bombardment from the unidentified ship which, by then, was cruising offshore. At their request, another air patrol investigated the vessel and tentatively identified it as Egyptian freighter *El Quesir*. To avoid an international incident, foreign Embassies were asked if they had any ships in the area. All replied negatively, so Defence Force Headquarters authorized its destruction.

Air and Surface Attacks
A pair of Mirage fighter-bombers opened the attack with rockets, machine-guns and cannon. After raking the target's gun-mounts to

eliminate counter-fire, they destroyed her antennae to cut off external communication, and then turned against the command centre on the bridge. At some time during their six punishing runs, the ensign was blown off the vessel's masthead. As soon as they flew away, a Super Mystere moved in to drop napalm on foredeck and bridge.

Next, three MTBs attacked with guns firing, and launched torpedoes. Four missed, but the fifth struck amidships just below the waterline. While the boats were turning to make a second run, the target's crew raised a new ensign on a jury-rigged temporary mast. Seeing the Stars and Stripes, the horrified Israelis realized they had mistakenly been attacking their strongest ally. Their target was the world's most advanced electronic surveillance vessel USS *Liberty*, but the American Embassy in Tel Aviv had denied her presence because the mission was classified 'Top Secret'.[45]

Aftermath

US Rear Admiral Geis, commanding the Sixth Fleet carrier force, responded to the target's distress call by launching fighter aircraft, but Washington ordered them recalled, saying the attack was considered accidental and President Lyndon Johnson did not want to embarrass his allies.

Thirty-four American officers and men had been killed, with 172 wounded (totalling 70 per cent of her complement of 294), while damage to the ship was extensive. *Liberty*, however, refused Israeli assistance; shored-up the torpedoed compartment, plugged over 800 shell and bullet holes, doused fires forward and amidships, and steamed away, listing heavily (30 degrees) to starboard. She was soon joined by the cruiser *Little Rock* which escorted her to Malta for repairs. Israel offered, and the United States accepted, a full diplomatic apology.

JANUARY 1968 –
EMBARRASSMENT OFF NORTH KOREA

In contrast to the *Liberty* affair, a 'secret' mission has seldom been conducted so openly as that of *Pueblo*. While she was still docked at Saigon, and before the crew had been briefed on their mission, bar girls told them where they were going. At the same time, Hanoi Radio blew their cover by denouncing the 'Imperial Aggressor' for planning the 'provocative acts' of sending disguised 'spy ships' into North Korea's territorial waters.

The little ship was unsound; a US Navy pre-departure inspection had uncovered an amazing 462 defects in electronic surveillance ship USS *Pueblo*, but only seventy-seven were remedied before she sailed. She was underpowered, with only two small six-cylinder engines. And she was effectively unarmed, because her two 50-calibre machine guns could not be fired for fear of damaging the sensitive listening devices she was crammed with. She was also unsuitable, eighty-three seamen and electronic technicians having been squeezed into quarters and toilet facilities designed for thirty.

Almost half the crew and most of the technicians had never been to sea and suffered from seasickness. Her captain, Commander Bucher, in his first seagoing command, had no authority over the electronics officer, Lieutenant Harris, who reported directly to the National Security Agency.

Onerous Alternatives

On 22 January, *Pueblo* took station in International Waters off Wonsan, and soon found herself accompanied by North Korean 'fishing boats', which had no nets but were loaded with antennae. Shortly afterward, two MiG-21 fighter jets started circling overhead, while a submarine-chaser and four torpedo boats closed in with crews at battle stations. Bucher ordered the Union Flag to be hoisted, whereupon the leading torpedo boat signalled 'heave to' and sent off an armed boarding party.

Fight was impossible, so Bucher had to decide between flight and surrender. Choosing the former, he began to move. The Koreans immediately opened fire. Suffering from an agonizing bullet wound in the rectum, and another on the ankle, Bucher managed to gasp out 'flank speed', but it was hopeless. *Pueblo* raced off at her maximum 12.5 knots, with no chance of outdistancing 50-knot torpedo boats.

Capture was certain, so Bucher and Harris ordered their respective secret documents destroyed; but the water was too shallow to jettison them, and there were far too many to shred or burn. When the Koreans gave *Pueblo* another burst of machine-gun fire, Bucher had no option but compliance with their order to follow them into Wonsan.

Aftermath

In North Korean hands, the commander was subjected to physical and mental torture until he gave way and confessed that *Pueblo* was not on oceanographic survey, as claimed, but spying for the CIA. He and his crew were held in captivity for eleven months. Then a complicated and cynical diplomatic compromise was reached. The prisoners were released in return for a signed American admission of espionage, which was immediately repudiated, by prior agreement with North Korea.

AUGUST 1971 – EMBARRASSMENT AT ATHENS

Suddenly, and without warning, supercarrier USS *Saratoga (CV60)*[46] settled gently towards the bottom of Piraeus harbour. As she went down, the Aviation Department sprung into action and catapulted fifty-three aircraft in quick succession. Their screaming jets created panic among inhabitants of Athens, who feared the Third World War had started.

The weather was calm, and the ship's engineers were unable to find any reason for the disaster which had flooded two machinery spaces. She was pumped out and refloated, only to flood and founder once again. Then it was discovered that the mighty warship had suffered a mishap which could have affected any simple household appliance, let alone one of the world's most high-tech vessels. After fifteen years in service, a rubber gasket – deep down on her underwater hull – had deteriorated and was leaking. At a stateside navy base, the event would have been an indignity. When 'showing the flag' in a foreign port it was an humiliation.[47]

MAY 1982 –
SELF-DEFENCE OR ANOTHER WAR CRIME?

The Falklands, also known as the Malvinas, is an archipelago of two main islands and about 100 islets, lying some 480 kilometres (300 miles) east of the Straits of Magellan. Their ownership has long been a subject of controversy.

They fell on the Spanish side of the Papal Line of Demarcation promulgated in 1493, but remained unknown to Europeans until sighted by English navigator John Davis in 1592. Following his report, they were visited by Dutch navigator Sebald van Weert in 1600, and English sea captain John Strong in 1690. Strong named the sound between the main islands after Viscount Falkland.

In the mid-1760s, British settlers landed on West Island, naming it after the sound. At about the same time, French settlers from Saint-Malô arrived on East Island, giving rise to the alternate name of Malvinas. In 1770, Spain bought out the French and, four years later, the British left of their own accord.

In 1820, after throwing off Spanish rule, Argentina declared ownership and established a whaling colony on the islands but, in 1831, following a dispute over whaling rights, American warship USS *Lexington* expelled the small settlement. Two years later, Britain took control of the unoccupied territory, but Argentina refused to relinquish its claim to sovereignty.

Invasion and Counter-attack

Long-lasting attempts to settle the dispute through United Nations mediation seemed to be getting nowhere, and in 1982 – with the 150th anniversary of British occupation looming – the Argentines lost patience. On 2 April, they launched a surprise attack which overwhelmed the small Royal Marines garrison. The UN Security Council condemned this unilateral action, but Argentina ignored its demand to withdraw. Britain then assembled a forty-five-ship counter-invasion fleet which set out on the 12,500 kilometre (7,800 mile) journey to the Falklands.

On 12 April, Britain declared a 320-kilometre (200-mile) maritime exclusion zone around the islands, warning it would be patrolled by nuclear-powered submarines with orders to destroy any Argentine ship which entered. Two weeks later, heavy cruiser *General Belgrano*[48] sortied from Ushuaia Naval Base and headed towards the islands.

Torpedo Incident

British intelligence incorrectly believed *Belgrano* had been retro-fitted with Exocet guided missiles. She had not, but accompanying destroyers, *Hipolito Bouchard* and *Piedra Bueno,* were armed with these deadly anti-ship weapons. On 2 May, they were patrolling the Burdwood Bank, just outside the exclusion zone, but close enough to the British task force for Exocets to threaten its vital aircraft carriers.

Prime Minister Margaret Thatcher authorized the cruiser's destruction and, at 4:00 p.m., nuclear submarine HMS *Conqueror* sank her with two wire-controlled torpedoes, killing many seamen and forcing others to take to the sea on rafts.[49]

In an exemplary rescue operation, under appalling weather conditions with high storm-driven waves, 770 survivors were saved by the *Armada Argentina* (Argentine Navy). Some died later of hypothermia or wounds, bringing the total death toll to 323.

March 1987 –
'The Disease of Sloppiness' off Zeebrugge

As the giant ferry gathered speed, some passengers sat down to dinner, while others stood quietly watching the lights of Belgium fading behind. Suddenly, without even a hint of warning, the deck tilted sharply, and they had to grab hold of furniture or slide across the deck. They were still gasping and wondering what had happened, when a second lurch threw the ship onto her beam ends and the lights went out.

Startled light-watchers on the open decks were tossed overboard. They were the lucky ones. Those below suddenly found themselves hurled against port-side bulkheads and drenched as water flooded into the passenger decks. Some clawed their way upright and escaped, but many drowned while panicking, disorientated and screaming for loved ones.

The Ro-Ro Ferries

During the Second World War, a new class of vessel, the Landing Ship had been designed with loading doors in the bow and a stem-to-stern through deck, from which tanks and trucks could drive straight onto land during invasions. An inherent flaw in this design was its lack of bulkheads and watertight compartments. If the doors leaked, water immediately flooded the entire vehicle deck. This risk was acceptable in wartime but, after the conflict, the design was adapted to civilian ferry boats, many being provided with doors at both ends to create 'Ro-Ro' (roll-on, roll-off) capability for rapid loading and unloading of vehicles.

The record-size *Herald of Free Enterprise* was built in 1980 with a new pattern of horizontal clamshell doors which, unlike conventional doors, could not be seen from the bridge for visual check on their opening and closing. She had two main vehicle decks which could be loaded simultaneously via double ramps at her normal ports of Dover and Calais. She was certificated to carry 1,400 passengers and a crew of eighty.

On 6 March 1987, *Herald* was in the port of Zeebrugge, where she loaded eighty-one cars, three buses and forty-seven trucks, and took aboard 459 passengers bound for Dover in England. Driving on was slower than usual, because the Belgian port had only one access ramp. After the lower vehicle deck had been loaded, bow tanks were filled with water ballast to lower the upper deck into line with the ramp. By 6:40 p.m., loading was complete and *Herald* slowly backed out stern first, and then turned to go ahead. The wind was light, the sea was calm, the sky was clear, and Captain Lewry anticipated an uneventful routine crossing.

Carelessness Brings Catastrophe

Mr Stanley, the assistant Bo'sun, who was responsible for closing the bow doors, was sleeping in his cabin and did not hear the call to 'harbour stations' on the public address system. His boss Mr Ayling, the Bo'sun, later told a court of inquiry, 'It has never been part of my duties to close the doors or to make sure anyone is there to close the doors.' In consequence, they were still wide open.

By 7:05 p.m. the ship had speeded up to fifteen knots (28 km/h; 13 mph) and built up a bow wave. The ballast tanks were still being pumped out, and she was down by about a metre (three feet) in front. The lower vehicle deck began to ship water at about 200 tons per minute. Almost immediately, *Herald* developed a thirty-degree list to port and, within ninety seconds capsized onto that side. Thanks to a last moment change of course, she landed in shallow water with the starboard half of her hull exposed.

Aftermath

Since she was still close inshore, rescue boats were on the scene in moments, and were soon joined by naval and fishing craft. They rescued 351 people, but 150 passengers and thirty-eight crew had perished, some while trapped inside the capsized vessel, others due to hypothermia in the frigid water alongside. The findings of a Court of Formal Investigation, held under the Merchant Shipping Act, were devastatingly critical, saying:

> A full investigation into the circumstances of the disaster leads inexorably to the conclusion that the underlying or cardinal faults lay higher up in the Company. The Board of Directors did not appreciate their responsibility for the safe management of their ships . . . did not have any proper comprehension of what their duties were. . . . All concerned in management . . . were guilty of fault . . . From top to bottom the body corporate was infected with the disease of sloppiness . . .
>
> (A year before the accident) there was a meeting of senior Masters with management, at which Mr Devlin (a Director and Chief Superintendent) was in the chair . . . Mr Devlin said that, although he was still considering writing (job descriptions) . . . he felt it was more preferable not to define the roles but to allow them to evolve. This attitude was . . . an abject abdication of responsibility . . . (demonstrating) an inability or unwillingness to give clear orders.

As this investigation progressed it became clear that shore management took very little notice of what they were told by their Masters . . . did not listen to complaints, or suggestions or wishes . . . the voice of the Masters fell on deaf ears ashore.

DECEMBER 1987 –
UNCERTIFICATED OFFICERS OFF MINDORO

Ferries are the principal form of transport between the 7,000 Philippine islands, and the only method most Filipinos can afford. What is thought to be the worst ever peacetime maritime catastrophe occurred on 21 December 1987, when trans-island ferry *Doña Paz* was struck by oil tanker *Vector* in the Strait between Mindoro and Tabias Islands.

The ferry was dangerously overcrowded, with many of the people who had bribed, pushed or fought to get on board being migrant workers going home to spend Christmas with their families. The collision threw oil from the ruptured tanker over both vessels and on the adjacent water. In an interview published in *The Times* newspaper on 22 December, passenger Paquito Osbel described the result:

> I was sleeping when I heard an explosion. I looked out and saw another ship was on fire. In just two seconds there was a big fire on our ship and I heard everybody screaming and wailing. The fire spread rapidly and engulfed our ship. There were flames everywhere. People were screaming and jumping. The smoke was terrible. We couldn't see each other and it was dark. I could see flames in the water below, but I jumped anyway.

Osbel clung to a plank for over an hour before he and a few other survivors were rescued. They were lucky because uncounted thousands died in the burning shark-infested waters. Few details are available. Estimates of the death-toll vary widely, from a minimum of 2,903 to a maximum of 4,341. No one seems to have determined exactly how the collision occurred, or why so many passengers and crew were on board at the time.

Aftermath

During a series of lawsuits between 1987 and 1999, the Philippines Supreme Court determined that the Master of the tanker had no certificate to command or navigate; its Mate was licensed only for bays and rivers; there was no Third Mate or Radio Operator as required by law; its engines were defective, and the Chief Engineer was not qualified to operate them. The Justices concluded: 'MT *Vector* was improperly manned, ill-equipped, unseaworthy, and a hazard to safe navigation; as a result it rammed MV *Doña Paz* in the open sea setting MT *Vector*'s highly flammable cargo ablaze.'

DECEMBER 1991 – OVERCONFIDENCE ON THE RED SEA

While cars and trucks trundled up the ramps, streams of pilgrims, still dressed in their best robes after the *Hajj* to Mecca, clambered aboard Egyptian Ro-Ro ferry *Salem Express* at the Saudi Arabian port of Jeddah. Her master, Hadsan Moro, a former instructor at the Egyptian Naval Academy, was generally regarded as one of the most experienced and knowledgeable of Red Sea navigators.

He prided himself on cutting the 835 kilometre (518 mile) journey from Jeddah to Safaga by two or more hours, thanks to steaming inside the treacherous Hyndman Reefs. This was a route no other captain cared to risk, preferring the deeper water further offshore. On 16 December, a westerly gale blew up soon after *Salem Express* left Jeddah, so Moro considerately hugged the Egyptian shore even closer than usual. Many of the pilgrims could only afford deck space, and the land would give them maximum protection from wind and rain.

Around midnight, the ferry was approaching Hyndman Reefs. The offshore wind had blown her slightly to the east of the clear passage, but at night, with the sea roiled by gusts, it was impossible to distinguish water from reef. Entering the passage, *Salem Express* touched the southernmost ridge. It was just a glancing blow, which only created a small hole forward. But it also jarred the visor, knocking it upward.

Just as the open door on *Herald of Free Enterprise* instantly flooded the vehicle deck, so did the damaged visor on *Salem Express*. An immediate list to starboard was increased by the gale-force wind pressing on the port side. In moments she went down with no time at all to launch a single life boat or raft. Officially, she was carrying 578 passengers and seventy-two crew, of which 180 were rescued by ships anchored nearby to ride out the storm. It is probable, however, that many more had squeezed or bribed their way on board, bringing the death toll closer to 1,000.

SEPTEMBER 1994 – DESIGNED FOR DISASTER

Twenty-four-year-old Silver Linde, the duty able-seaman, stumbled from side to side, bumping into bulkheads, grabbing hold of stanchions, trying to make his way forward on a routine hourly safety inspection. As he approached the automobile loading ramp, an exceptionally heavy wave hit the bow. He almost fell over and, simultaneously, heard 'a noise like two heavy metal objects clashing with great force'. He notified the Second Officer on the bridge by radio-telephone, and was told to try and identify the source of the unusual sound. He made a thorough check and found nothing out of the ordinary.

He was aboard Estonian-flagged Ro-Ro passenger ferry *Estonia*, en route from Tallinn, capital of Estonia, to Stockholm, capital of Sweden, with a crew of 186 and 803 passengers. Over 300 cars and some fifty trucks were aboard. Her former Chief Mate, Sakari Kleimala, described *Estonia* as 'Not really suitable for sea traffic. She had not been designed like a ship, rather more like a trunk, and travelling in her especially in side winds was not that comfortable.'

Indeed, her hull was simply a square container, except at the bow where the front of her forward ramp was screened by a 'visor' shaped like a normal prow. This fifty-six ton steel structure was pivoted to swing upward around hinges mounted on an extension of the collision bulkhead at the upper deck level. It was well sealed and secured in its down position by both hydraulically-operated and manually-controlled locking devices.

She had been underway for about six hours, and was in Finnish waters, almost at the halfway point. The moderate weather had gradually worsened and, after passing Osmussar Lighthouse, she lost her land shelter and wave heights reached three to four metres (ten to thirteen feet). By 12:50 a.m., when Silver Linde heard the strange clang, the billows had risen to between four and six metres (thirteen to twenty feet), with intermittent crests of twice that height.

The extreme flare of the bow visor made it vulnerable to heavy wave impact, but this normally produced more of a boom than a clang. Because the sound was annoying to passengers, *Estonia* usually slowed down or changed course in heavy weather. On this occasion, her normal 19-knot cruising speed was reduced to 14 knots, and stabilizers were extended to counter increased rolling. Shortly after one o'clock a number of passengers and off-duty crew members reported hearing strange noises from forward and, about fifteen minutes later, Linde was sent back to the car deck to re-investigate.

Catastrophic Failure

Before he reached that level, the visor separated from the bow and tilted over the stem, pulling the ramp fully open and allowing water to flood the car deck rapidly. The ship developed a heavy list to starboard, slewed to port, and slowed down.

Minutes later, the passenger public address system came to life, and a female voice called out in Estonian '*Häire! Häire! Laeval häire!*' (Alert! Alert! On-board alert!). This was followed by an internal warning for the crew and, seconds later, by the general lifeboat alarm. By this time all four main engines had stopped, and the ship was drifting broadside-on to the waves.

The main generators cut out, but emergency equipment started automatically, providing full power to essential equipment and limited lighting in public areas and on deck. Twenty-nine-year-old Kent Härstgedt, who was in the bar, reports that ' . . . the cosy atmosphere . . . with people singing, laughing, having a good time . . . in just a few seconds changed to total chaos . . . people fell onto the wall breaking arms and legs.'

Passengers began to rush up staircases toward the boat deck, some calmly, but most pushing and shoving in panic. Many more were in bed, trapped in their cabins. They had little chance of getting out before the list increased and water began to flood the accommodation decks. Lifejackets were distributed to those who reached the boat deck and they jumped, or were washed into the sea. A few life-rafts were released, but the heavy list and high seas prevented any lifeboats from being launched.

Aftermath

By 1:30 a.m., the Maritime Rescue Coordination Centre in Turku, Finland, had responded to *Estonia*'s distress signals and dispatched four other passenger ferries and several air-sea-rescue helicopters to the scene. *Estonia* was lying on her beam ends, with her starboard side fully submerged. From there she subsided quickly, stern first, and by 1:50 a.m. had disappeared from the rescue ships' radar screens. During the night, they picked up forty-three crew and ninety-four passengers, one of whom died in hospital. They also collected ninety-five bodies, but 757 had gone down with the stricken ship.

A nine-member International Joint Accident Investigation Committee was set up with nine Commissioners, three from each of Estonia, Finland and Sweden. It determined that the vessel was seaworthy, well maintained, and properly manned by qualified personnel; cargo was properly stowed; and the visor was fully closed and secured.

However, *Estonia* was originally Finnish, and the Committee noted that Finnish (and Swedish) Maritime Administrations frequently approved passenger ferries with forward-mounted bow ramps extending from the upper collision bulkhead, even though this was contrary to regulations of the SOLAS (Safety of Life at Sea) Convention.

The Committee attributed the accident to engineering design error. The visor had been given enough strength to withstand 'normal' wave action, but not extreme conditions, which its architects should have foreseen. Under the continual working of unusually heavy waves, its hinges and locking devices had failed, allowing it to work its way forward, pulling the ramp open as it went.[50]

AUGUST 2000 –
PIPE FRACTURE UNDER THE BARENTS SEA

'The time when Russia could be kept out of the world's oceans has gone forever. . . . We shall sail all the world's seas – no force on earth can prevent us!' So spoke Marshal Zakharov, Soviet Chief of Staff, in 1968, initiating a policy of naval growth which Russia had not seen since Peter the Great. Led by Fleet Admiral Sergei Gorshkov, the Soviet Navy embarked on the largest peacetime expansion in history, soon outnumbering the US Navy in almost every category except aviation and long-range fleet support.

A Magnificent Force Declines

On 26 December 1991, the Soviet Union collapsed. Its successor, the Russian Federation, was bankrupt and, in consequence, naval budgets dropped precipitously; ships were left to rust at anchor; maintenance was skimped; machinery sank into perilous disrepair; weapons and equipment became obsolescent; and crews were unable to accumulate sea time and their meagre pay became irregular. Needless to say, morale reached low levels despite residual pride in the service.

Even with this overall decline, it became a matter of national prestige to keep a select few vessels at (supposedly) peak efficiency. One of these was enormous, state-of-the-art, nuclear-powered submarine *Kursk* (NATO code name Oscar II). In August 2000 she prepared for fleet manoeuvres. The vessel was equipped with some two dozen weapon systems, of which the most significant were her SSN-19 cruise missiles, and two types of torpedo – standard 533-mm (21-inch) weapons, and huge 650-mm (25.6-inch) high-speed, long-range, Type 65 HTP missiles.[51]

While loading one of the larger torpedoes at Vidiayevo, part of the tackle snapped, dropping one end onto the deck. It was not inspected for damage, and loading continued. On 8 August, *Kursk* left, to participate in Northern Fleet exercises. Under the command of Captain (1st-rank) Gennadiy Liachin of the Volgograd Naval Regiment were five officers, two naval architects and 111 crewmen.

Catastrophic Explosions

At 8:51 a.m. (Moscow time) on the morning of 12 August, *Kursk* radioed for permission to launch exercise torpedoes, and received '*dobro*' (okay) in reply. At 11:29 a.m., the Norwegian seismic service recorded an explosion measuring 1.5 on the Richter scale. Two minutes later a second explosion of magnitude 3.5 occurred. Similar recordings were made by seismic stations in Alaska and Canada, and by surface ships and submarines nearby. All pinpointed *Kursk*'s last position in the Barents Sea. Worried by these reports, Northern Fleet Headquarters signalled the submarine: 'Report coordinates and operations'. When no reply was received, a Fleet Emergency Alarm was declared, but *Kursk* had vanished without a trace.

Although the Russian Navy's deep-sea rescue and recovery facilities were obsolete, under-funded and inadequate, national pride led to the initial rejection of offers to help, which poured in from the United States, Canada, Israel, and five European and two Scandinavian countries. The subsequent failure to search for and rescue possible survivors drew massive criticism at home as well as abroad, especially when it was determined that twenty-three crewmen had survived in the stern of the vessel for about eight hours before dying from carbon monoxide poisoning.

Cause of the Disaster

At least fifteen 'explanations' of the accident were advanced, ranging from the probable (result of an internal fire), via feasible (striking a left-over Second World War mine), to absurd (intervention by a UFO). For almost two years, Russia insisted that *Kursk* must have been sunk by collision with a NATO submersible, or some unknown surface ship. Western sources, however, tended to blame the premature explosion of an ASW rocket[52] during launching.

On 31 October 2000, another possible explanation was put forward by Captain Sergey Oveharenko of the cruiser *Petr Vilikiy*, who told the newspaper *Zhizn* he had launched a Vodopad ASW missile with a live warhead in violation of exercise rules. He and his officers thought they saw unusually large explosions on impact and believed they might have struck an American observer submersible, only later learning *Kursk* had been sunk at about that location.

In October 2001, *Kursk* was raised by Dutch salvage companies Mammoet Worldwide and Smit-Tak International and was towed to the Russian naval shipyard at Murmansk.[53] Over the next eight months she was closely examined in dry dock by naval architects and technical investigators from the State Prosecutor's Office, allowing the real cause of the explosion to be determined.

On 26 July 2002, General Prosecutor Vladimir Ustinov reported the findings to President Vladimir Putin, who ordered him to inform the Russian public and media. Ustinov said:

> The disaster occurred at 11:28 and 26.5 seconds Moscow time because of the explosion of a practice torpedo inside the fourth torpedo tube, which in turn triggered explosions in torpedo charge chambers in the submarine's bow section. . . . No one was to blame for the disaster and no criminal charges will be laid. . . . Russia has already pulled from service all torpedoes of the type that malfunctioned, which use highly volatile hydrogen peroxide as propellant.

Experts theorize that the fall onto the dock at Vidiayevo had cracked one of the propellant supply lines, allowing hydrogen peroxide to drip onto kerosene and metal, causing the initial explosion and starting a fire. Warheads in the compartment would then have overheated and spontaneously exploded, creating an unextinguishable conflagration, whose fumes killed the surviving crew.

SEPTEMBER 2002 – OVERLOAD OFF SENEGAL

A motley crowd pushed and shoved its way onto ferryboat *Joola* at the Senegalese port of Zinguinchor. There were traders taking dried fish, mangoes and palm oil to markets in the capital, Dakar, students returning to school or university after their holidays, visitors from neighbouring Guinea-Bissau, and about thirty Europeans from Belgium, France, Holland and Spain.

The coastal ferry route is especially important to Senegal because the country is almost bisected by the Republic of The Gambia, which hugs the banks of its eponymous river. Never more than forty-eight kilometres (thirty miles) wide, it penetrates 475 kilometres (295 miles) inland, separating the agrarian south from the more urbanized north.

Asian and African ferry boats are often ancient and unseaworthy, with low safety standards, and renowned for their frequency of disastrous accidents. In contrast to these floating coffins, *Joola* had been built in 1990 and recently overhauled. However, like the others she was plagued by corrupt administration, inadequate maintenance, and frequent overloading.

Operated by the Senegalese Army, she was designed to carry forty-six crew and 536 passengers, but almost that number had crowded onto the open upper deck alone, while at least as many more scrambled into the interior. Tickets had been officially issued to 1,064 passengers, but children under five were not counted, and ferry officials were known to take kickbacks to allow unticketed travellers on board.

Fatal Voyage
Flat-bottomed *Joola* was originally intended for lake service, but had been licensed to travel up to thirty-seven kilometres (twenty-three miles) offshore. Shortly after 2:00 a.m. on 26 September, she was about that distance off the Gambian coast when a local storm came up. Strong offshore winds blew torrential rain onto the deck passengers, and they all rushed for shelter on the port side. Their weight would normally have been counter-balanced by up to forty cars in the hold but, on this occasion, there were only one or two. The ship listed heavily, and the wind pushed her onto her side. Minutes later she turned turtle, trapping hundreds of helpless passengers below decks.

Those lucky enough to have been on the open deck clung to the keel and one of them, Moussa Ndong, said, 'It was horrible, because we could hear people screaming from underneath'. Another, Ben Bechir Badji, a student returning to university, reported they were 'Thrown about by the wind and huge waves until about four in the morning'.

Sixty-four survivors were lifted off by fishermen who risked their lives in dangerous seas to affect the rescue, but an estimated 1,863 had died in Africa's worst maritime disaster. France, the former colonial power provided aircraft, helicopters and boats for the recovery of bodies.

Aftermath

The Senegalese public was outraged by the disaster, and President Abdoulaye Wade rushed into political damage control, by accepting resignations from the Ministers of Transport and Armed Forces, and firing Colonel Ousseynou Kombo, the officer responsible for ferries. This did not satisfy the relatives of victims, some 300 of whom decided to sue the government for manslaughter and negligence.[54] President Wade then dismissed Prime Minister Madior Boye and her entire government.

December 2002 –
Four Times Looks Like Carelessness[55]

The English Channel is like a very wide river, thirty-five kilometres (21.7 miles) across at its narrowest point. Between 400 and 500 ocean-going ships travel along the waterway every day, numerous ferries cross from shore to shore, and private yachts and fishing boats scurry in between. Powerful tides change direction every six hours or so. These factors combine to make it a very dangerous passage, as outlined by the British Maritime and Coastguard Agency:

> The Dover Strait and its approaches are among the busiest shipping lanes in the world and pose serious problems for the safety of navigation. The traffic separation scheme, its associated inshore traffic zones, the Channel Navigation Information Service . . . and the mandatory reporting system . . . have been designed to assist seafarers to navigate these waters in safety. There is therefore a need for careful navigation in this area in accordance with International Regulations for Preventing Collisions at Sea. . . . The risk of collision is ever present and heightened if vessels do not comply with the requirements of the scheme.

Early on Saturday 14 December 2002, two large ships on almost parallel courses were ploughing through heavy fog some forty-nine kilometres (thirty miles) off the English port of Ramsgate. They were heading for the most-complex and least-effective point of the separation scheme, where French-controlled north/east and British-controlled south/west lanes cross one another.

Bahamas-registered *Kariba*, a 21,000-ton container ship, was heading from Antwerp in Belgium, to Le Havre in France, while Norwegian-flagged *Tricolor*, a thirteen-deck, 50,000-ton Ro-Ro vehicle transporter, had left Zeebrugge in Belgium, en route for the United States via Southampton in England. Her cargo of 2,862 luxury cars and seventy-seven containers was valued at US$49 million.

The Initial Collision

At about 1:20 a.m., *Tricolor* shuddered abruptly and tipped sideways. Instead of passing astern as required by the Rule of the Road, *Kariba* had run directly into the bigger ship's port side. Andrew Linington, a spokesman for the maritime union NUMAST, told the UK Press Association:

> About ninety percent of accidents like this are the result of the human factor. People are the key to shipping safety . . . (but) there is a constant drive to reduce crewing levels and people can be working 80 to 90 hours a week on busy waterways like these.

Later, Diosdada Remollo, *Tricolor*'s duty engineer, recounted his frightening ordeal as the transport abruptly heeled over:

> I got the phone to contact the Chief Engineer, but nobody answered . . . I grabbed the railings, then heard a lot of alarms as well as the general alarm. I saw water going inside the engine room from . . . car deck No.9. I proceeded to the starboard side of the control room, but unfortunately – together with the computer, printer and chairs – I tumbled again to the portside corner. This hurt my body. . . . I grabbed the shelves to give access for me to open the door exit going to the workshop. When I was inside the workshop I proceeded to the . . . stairway, but the door was blocked . . .
>
> I opened the emergency exit hatch located at the ceiling of the elevator. I climbed up the ladder, and at the top tried to open (the manhole). I went down and tried to open the door of the level deck . . . then there was a blackout. The emergency light and emergency generator were activated. I climbed up again and punched with all the force I could give. It took me approximately four minutes to open the manhole . . . I proceeded to the starboard life raft . . . we floated on the water for twenty minutes until a tugboat rescued us. [Copyright © Barber *Ship Management*]

Belgian warship *Wandelaar* escorted *Kariba* back to Antwerp for inspection and repair, but *Tricolor* rapidly heeled over and sank. The water was so shallow that her starboard side was exposed at low tide creating a serious hazard to navigation. Along with Engineer Remollo, *Tricolor*'s Norwegian master, her Swedish mate, and twenty-two Filipino officers and seamen took to the lifeboats. They were soon picked up, and the French Maritime Service reported: 'All the lives have been saved and our action now will involve providing nautical safety around the wreck.'

The Second Collision

In spite of the French Maritime Service's efforts, at about 2:00 a.m. on Sunday morning, *Nicola*, a 3,000-ton German ship registered in the Dutch Antilles, travelling from La Coruna in Spain to Rotterdam in Holland, drove herself on top of *Tricolor* and was stuck there until Monday, when the tide rose enough for two tugboats to pull her off. She had suffered no serious damage. Paul Gunton, Managing Editor of *Fairplay Shipping Weekly,* speculated in the London *Times*:

> How has this latest collision happened? One has to wonder if anyone was on watch, as ships do use autopilots. This area is very busy and I expect many ships would have pre-programmed routes that take them over this spot. Could this ship have forgotten to amend its route to avoid the wreck?

Nicola's owner, Intersee, claimed there were no visible markers and that the wreck coordinates provided by the French authorities were five kilometres (three miles) too far east. The French Maritime Prefecture denied this, saying that, not only was their location correct, but a warning buoy had been anchored near the wreck, and French frigate *Geranium* was patrolling the area to alert vessels to the hazard.

Third Collision Averted

By nightfall on Sunday, four more warning buoys had been strategically placed, all of them fluorescent, and one specially designed to throw a bright warning symbol on ships' radar screens. Written warnings were being handed to all vessels leaving Belgian ports. Coastguards broadcast warnings every half-hour from both Dover and Cap Gris Nez, and additional radio warnings were made on the maritime distress frequency which all ships were supposed to monitor. French Police vessel *Glaive* and British HMS *Anglesey* took station nearby, soon to be joined by French frigate *Flamand*. All in all it seemed inconceivable that any mariner could be unaware of the wreck and its location.

Nevertheless, on Monday, Cyprus-based NDS *Provider* was spotted heading directly for the wreck, and was only about 100 metres (330 feet) from hitting it when a British Coastguard aircraft flew over, waggling its wings in warning. *Provider* sheered off just in time, but the mystery of its collision course deepened when Jim Nelson, a director of the owners, said, 'Our understanding is that the vessel was aware the wreck was there'.

The Third Collision Occurs

All was quiet until Wednesday, when Turkish-registered *Vicky*, a 43,000-ton tanker bound for New York with nine million litres (two million gallons) of kerosene, diesel fuel and heavy oil ignored all warnings and slammed into the wreck at about 7:00 p.m. The ship's master, Bulent Yamac, initially told Britain's *Times* newspaper:

> I had no idea it was there. I saw some light buoys but I didn't under-stand what it meant or why they were there . . . I tried to change course and turn to starboard. Visibility was normal and I could see waves breaking, then I knew it must be a wreck because there were no shallows in the area.

This testimony was contradicted by Michel Botlla-Gambetta, of the Cherbourg Maritime Prefecture, who said, 'The duty officer on the *Vicky* received clear instructions but did not make the right manoeuvre', while Antoine Goulley, another spokesperson for the Prefecture, told BBC News:

> The markers should have been understood by a trained sailor. In this case, *Vicky* should have known the position of the shipwreck. The ship had got in contact with the (French) navy patrol ship *Flamand* just before the collision and it is not known why the tanker continued on its route towards the shipwreck.

Later, according to French newspaper *Le Soir,* Captain Yamac changed his story and told Belgian authorities that *Flamand* had directed him onto the wreck instead of away from it. *Vicky* remained on top of *Tricolor* until the tide rose enough to float her off. Despite her double-hull, she lost some oil and developed a list. The big tanker drew too much water to enter any nearby port, so she anchored in Belgian waters off Ostend. An approaching storm with 100 km/h (60 mph) winds made it impossible to examine *Vicky*'s hull or pump out cargo.

A spokeswoman for the Belgian Transport Ministry said French maritime authorities were improving the way they alerted ships to avoid future collisions, but Lars Walder, of Dutch salvage company Smit Tak[56], said he did not believe the French could do more than they already had. Peter Legg, watch officer of Dover coastguard concurred, telling the

BBC, 'There is a possibility this could happen again, but at the present moment we have done all we can to make this wreck obvious to the mariner.'

The Fourth Collision
On Wednesday 22 January, with strong winds and a high swell, a wave picked up one of the tugboats sent by Smit Tak to check for leaks and slammed it onto *Tricolor*'s hull – in the worst possible place, directly above a fuel oil tank. The crack was quickly patched, but not before a thin film of bunker fuel had spread for about eight kilometres. A spill response vessel was sent to the scene to mop it up but, sadly, animal protection activists reported about 5,000 oil-soaked seabirds being found on Belgian beaches. 2,200 were dead, but the rest had been rescued and taken to cleaning centres.[57]

Epilogue

In these pages we have seen tragedies resulting from gale, fog, ice and other natural causes, or just plain bad luck. All too often, however, catastrophe has been due to human factors such as navigational error, faulty design, timidity, complacency, inflexibility, bad timing, misinterpretation of orders, procrastination, incompetence, and many other stupidities.

From every such event, lessons can be drawn and new precautions introduced. That said, blunders will doubtless continue to occur partly, in the words of Andrew Bonar Law, 'due to want of human wisdom', and partly because technological marvels, such as radar and global positioning systems, are subject to software bugs and errors of human interpretation. Moreover, Nature still has, and probably always will have, power beyond human control and technology.

Appendices

APPENDIX A:
THE RECOVERY OF MARY ROSE

After several early salvage attempts had failed, the location of the wreck of the *Mary Rose* was forgotten until rediscovered in 1971. Eight years later, the *Mary Rose* Trust was formed 'to find, record, excavate, raise, bring ashore, preserve, report on, and display for all time . . . the *Mary Rose*'.

A team of 500 divers made over 28,000 descents, uncovering and examining the silted-in vessel. By 1982, they had gathered enough information, and the Trust had raised enough money, to go ahead. On 11 October, watched by 60 million viewers of the world's first underwater television broadcast, the wreck was gently lifted onto a purpose-built cradle.

For twelve years, the hull was protected by constant spraying with chilled water. Then in 1994, final conservation began, using water-soluble wax-polyethylene-glycol. It will take ten years for this to penetrate and replace the water in the ship's timbers. Then the wreck will be slowly air-dried. When this twenty-two-year treatment is finished, it is expected to have prevented wood decay and eliminated microbiological contamination.

Over 19,000 artefacts were recovered. In addition to quantities of weapons and ammunition, there are everyday items such as a pepper mill, a manicure set, pewter plates and flagons, and a complete set of barber-surgeon's instruments. These and the ship itself are on display in the *Mary Rose* Museum at Portsmouth, which includes air-conditioned viewing galleries to shield visitors from the chemicals used in conservation.

APPENDIX B:
THE SPANISH ARMADA AND ITS ENGLISH OPPONENTS

The Armada was essentially a large escorted convoy; a hodgepodge of combat vessels, cargo ships, and troop transports, divided into eight squadrons, drawn from different parts of the Spanish Empire, each with its own admiral and vice admiral. Little ships called *zebras* and *patches* served as messengers and scouts. Out of a total of 130 vessels, only about half were fighting ships.

The English Fleet was divided into three parts – the Main Fleet of thirty-four 'Queenes Shippes' was commanded by Howard himself, while Vice Admiral Drake led thirty-four privateers; they were both based at Plymouth. The Narrow Seas Squadron, with Lord Henry Seymour in command, consisted of a couple of galleons and twenty-three armed volunteer vessels (mostly small pirates or privateers). It was positioned to guard the straits where Parma was expected to launch his invasion. The third Squadron, stationed at London, also under Seymour's command, included armed merchantmen coasters. The Fleet totalled 197 vessels, but the number of purpose-built warships was numerically equal to the Spanish.

Ships: The Armada's fighting component consisted of relatively large troop-carrying sailing galleons, rowing galleys and galiots, and hybrid oared-and-sailed galleasses. Except for seven huge Spanish vessels, the English combat ships were of about the same size, but longer, narrower, and more manoeuvrable. They were direct descendants of *Mary Rose*, but without the cumbersome castles.

Tactics: Spanish doctrine was still based on the age-old manoeuvre of grappling and boarding, so they regarded their ships as floating fortresses, to be garrisoned by land soldiers. In contrast, English tacticians had grasped the potential of artillery for distance fighting. Their ships seldom carried soldiers, but seamen and gunners were trained to leave their posts and arm themselves from stacks of pikes and cutlasses when required to board or repel boarders.

Guns: The Spaniards carried hundreds of anti-personnel weapons, plus a few short-range cannon firing twenty-three kilogram (50-pound) ship-crushing balls. The English were equipped with long culverins, firing broadsides of eight-kilogram (17-pound) round shot over greater distances, but they were only accurate to about 500 metres (550 yards).

Crews: Most Spanish sailors were recently-impressed landsmen, and many of their officers owed their commissions to social status. Those who were experienced mariners were accustomed to convoying treasure fleets. The English, by and large, were old sea dogs with combat experience gained while raiding the Spanish Main.

Pilotage: In the entire Armada there were only forty qualified pilots. They knew the Channel, but had little understanding of the northern waters around the British Isles. The English were in home waters, knowing every rock and tide.

APPENDIX C:
BLOK'S EXPLORATIONS

The Dutchman was the first European to dare the perilous whirlpools of the East River Passage, which he named *Hellegat* (now Hell's Gate). Sailing eastward on Long Island Sound, Blok discovered the Housatonic and Connecticut Rivers (which he named the Redhills and Freshwater Rivers respectively). Pushing further east, he named *Roode Eiland* (Red Island) after the colour of its clay, and *Blok Eiland* after himself. These are now, of course, Rhode Island and Block Island. He explored Narragansett Bay and, by circumnavigating Long Island, proved it was in fact separated from the mainland.

APPENDIX D:
RAISING *VASA*

In 1956, after years of searching, shipwreck explorer Anders Franzén located the remains of *Vasa*. She was thirty metres down, but in 1959 the Swedish Royal Navy undertook her recovery. Divers used specially designed nozzles to flush six tunnels through the mud under the fragile timbers. Steel cables threaded through these tunnels hoisted the hull and moved it to shallow water in sixteen gentle stages, spread out over five years.

After being submerged for 332 years and 8 months, the Swedish royal flagship surfaced at 9:03 a.m. on 24 April 1961. Using the same technique as was later applied to *Mary Rose*, marine archaeologists preserved the ancient woodwork and skilled craftspeople reconstructed lost elements. The virtually complete seventeenth century warship now stands proudly in the *Wasavarvet* (*Vasa* Museum) in Stockholm.

APPENDIX E:
EIGHTEENTH CENTURY NAVIGATION

Latitude refers to a ship's position on one of the north-south Meridians which divide the earth into theoretical wedges (like the segments of an orange). It could be accurately calculated from celestial observations, but these were only possible when skies were clear without overcast.

In contrast, the determination of **Longitude** – a ship's position east or west of the standard meridian at Greenwich in England – was one of the greatest scientific challenges of the period. Its calculation depended on knowing the exact time at the ship's location, relative to the exact time at Greenwich, and that in turn demanded an astronomical observation, or a timekeeper infinitely more accurate that anything available in the early 1700s.

In its absence, longitude was estimated by **Dead Reckoning**. This involved recording every change of course, the length of time heading in each direction, and the speed of the ship. With variable currents and fickle winds, this was a very unreliable technique.

Speed was measured with a log-chip or log-ship. This was a thin wooden quadrant with a weighted circumference to keep it upright and retard its passage through the sea. Attached to its 'sharp end' was a thin line wound around a reel. This line had knots tied at regular intervals. One man held the reel over his head, while the officer threw the log-ship overboard to windward and clear of the ship. When the first knot passed his hand he shouted 'turn' and an assistant upended a twenty-eight-second sandglass. When it ran out the assistant shouted 'stop' and the log-line was nipped. Then the number of knots and fractions which had run out equalled the speed of the vessel in nautical miles per hour – known for obvious reasons as knots.

APPENDIX F:
THE RACE TO CALCULATE LONGITUDE

A decade after the disaster at the Scillies, the English Parliament posted a reward of £20,000 (equal to several million dollars today) for a practical solution to the longitude riddle. The criterion was accuracy to within half a degree (about fifty-six kilometres or thirty miles at the equator) after a voyage from England to the West Indies. This translates to a time-keeping error of less than two minutes.

The immensity of the prize attracted many crackpots, including the only woman to enter the competition, Jane Squires, who proposed dividing the sky into more than a million segments relative to the meridian of the manger at Bethlehem. Navigators would have to memorize these astral 'cloves' (as she called them) in order to determine their position.

Another hare-brained proposal came from a man who claimed to have invented the 'Powder of Sympathy'. If this came into contact with a knife, any thing or person previously wounded by that knife would immediately feel pain, no matter where they were. Each ship was to be provided with one or more dogs who had been hurt by a knife kept at Greenwich. Precisely at noon, this knife would be plunged into a jar of Sympathy Powder, causing all the dogs to howl.

More realistically, a race developed between astrologers (who planned to tell the time by the relative positions of sun, moon, stars and planets) and horologists (who hoped to construct a timepiece which could maintain its accuracy under all conditions likely to be encountered during a long sea voyage).

The winner was a self-taught clockmaker named John Harrison, a carpenter's son and apprentice, who had never been to sea. After fifty years of trial and error, his genius produced a chronometer which kept time in pitching-and-tossing ships, under arctic cold or tropical heat, with breathtaking accuracy, losing or gaining less than a single second in a month – three times better than required to win the prize.

APPENDIX G:
THE DEVELOPMENT OF STEAM-POWERED
IRONCLADS

Rigid naval conservatism long delayed the introduction of innovations spawned by the Industrial Revolution. As early as 1783, Marquis Claude de Jouffroy d'Abbans managed to steam-propel a small boat upstream on the River Saône, but it was not until 1802 that the first practical steamboat was built. Then, in a trial on the Forth-Clyde canal, the sternwheeler *Charlotte Dundas* towed two loaded barges against a strong wind.

This test was witnessed by Robert Fulton who, five years later, built the more famous *Clermont* which plied the Hudson River between Albany and New York. Fearing instant obsolescence of the Royal Navy's immense investment and overwhelming superiority in wind-powered ships, the British Admiralty pronounced:

> Their Lordships find it their bounden duty to discourage to the best of their ability the employment of steam vessels, as they consider the introduction of steam is calculated to strike a fatal blow at the naval supremacy of the Empire.

This was a golden opportunity for rival navies to catch up with or surpass Britain, but reactionary European admirals procrastinated – arguing that the risk of boiler explosion was unacceptable, that the burden of fuel and machinery reduced the weight of ordnance which could be carried, that range was limited by the size of a ship's bunkers, and that paddle-wheels were vulnerable to cannon fire. Consequently, steam was usually restricted to harbour tugs and messenger vessels and it was left to less-hidebound Americans to develop the concept.

During the war of 1812, Fulton designed the world's first completely unrigged warship for the defence of New York Harbour. USS *Fulton*, was a thirty-eight-ton catamaran, whose steam-driven paddle wheel was mounted centrally, protected from cannon-fire by her twin hulls. Then, during the 1830s, the underwater propeller was invented by American John Ericsson and others. Once again, the Admiralty tried to stifle a development calculated to reduce Britain's advantage in sail. In 1837, Sir William Symonds, Surveyor of the Navy, said:

> Even if the propeller had the power of propelling a vessel it would be found altogether useless in practice, because of the power being applied to the stern it would be absolutely impossible to make the vessel steer.

Two years later, the Ericsson-designed frigate USS *Princeton* not only proved him wrong, but had boilers and machinery below the waterline, where they were protected and their weight stabilized the ship. Six years after that, the British Admiralty organized a tug-of-war between steam sloops of comparable deadweight and shaft horsepower. On a calm day with no wind-effect, propeller-driven HMS *Rattler* towed paddle-wheeled HMS *Alecto* backward at nearly three knots (5.6 km/h; 4.5 mph).

Experimental cladding of wooden warships with thick metal plates produced vessels too heavy to manoeuvre properly under sail, so that technology was also rejected – often with the comment 'wood floats, iron sinks'. Even when a more-mobile all-iron frigate was built by private enterprise in 1842, the British Admiralty refused to consider such a radical departure from oaken hulls. Its developers sold it to the Mexican Navy instead.

Because of this stubborn professional resistance, most of the Anglo-French fleet which bombarded Sebastopol in 1854 would have been familiar to veterans of the Napoleonic Wars (which many of its senior officers were). A few frigates had auxiliary steam propulsion, and one or two French floating siege batteries had armoured decks. Otherwise, it consisted of square-rigged, wooden-hulled vessels, firing broadsides of solid shot from smoothbore cannon through side-ports.

Appendix H:
One Survivor's Story

The collision with *Geiser* occurred off Sable Island, and *Thingvalla* limped into Halifax, Nova Scotia, where survivors were landed. The *Halifax Morning Herald* of 20 August 1888 gave a number of their stories. One of them (much abbreviated) tells in the flowery hyperbole of the era:

Only one cabin passenger of the *Geiser* was saved. She is Mrs Hilda Lind . . . a pretty, fair-haired woman of twenty-eight, but looks at least ten years older now, and is half-crazed with grief . . . 'I was asleep when the collision came' said Mrs Lind to our reporter . . . 'An old woman took my baby from me and said she would take care of him. Poor little dear, I hated to let him go out of my arms, but the old lady was so good and kind . . . I never saw his face again'.

Here the little woman buried her face in her hands and her frame shook . . . it was some minutes before she was able to speak . . . then she said, 'I hugged my little girl to my breast and went on as fast as I could . . . I forgot all about being sick and was standing in the doorway . . . when something struck me an awful blow. My little girl was knocked out of my arms and all I can remember was that there was water all around and it rushed with a roar. I found myself going down, and I thought I shall never stop . . . next thing I remember I struck . . . it was a big wide board, with some other pieces nailed to it that must have been torn off something on the steamer'.

'My poor babies! My darling little ones!' sobbed the unhappy woman, and it seemed as though she would go into hysterics . . . big, stalwart First Mate Petersen came along and spoke to her in her native tongue . . . the poor woman moaned 'Oh, my home! My home! How can I go there!' . . . she muttered something in Swedish and then started up affrighted. The recital of her story has affected the woman so deeply that brave muscular Mate Petersen had almost to carry her . . . and it is feared her mind may be affected by the terrible experience . . .

She was sent home in a cab by the steamship company . . . clad in a dress lent by a passenger. Her ring was answered by her little five-year-old niece. . . . Next moment the husband ran out and the woman fell into his arms crying: 'You have no children, Oscar! They are all drowned!' The husband could not speak, and Mrs Lind lost consciousness. Little by little the frightful tale was revealed . . . and the husband began to realize the awful truth. Mrs Lind is completely prostrated, and it is feared she may not recover.

APPENDIX I:
A DARING CUTTING-OUT OPERATION

When Commodore Preble learned the Corsairs had refloated *Philadelphia*, he realized he would have to do something before she was seaworthy, giving the Corsairs a vessel to match anything in his fleet. He gave the task to twenty-five-year-old Lieutenant Stephen Decatur, who recruited the help of Salvadore Catalano, an Arabic-speaking Sicilian.

On the moonlit night of 16 February 1804, sailing a captured Corsair raider re-named USS *Intrepid*, they entered the harbour and headed for *Philadelphia*, whose brightly-lit open gunports were easily identifiable. When they came near, Decatur ordered most of his seventy-four carefully chosen officers and men below decks, while he and a few others wearing Arab dress stayed topside.

The prize crew was alert, but recognized *Intrepid*'s familiar profile and lateen rig. So, when Catalano answered their challenge in fluent Arabic, saying his ship had lost its anchor and would like to tie up alongside, they agreed. The Americans swarmed aboard through the open gunports, quickly subdued the small harbour-watch, set the ship afire, and withdrew before the Corsairs could react.

As they sailed away from the blazing vessel, 141 coastal guns opened up on them, but the greatest danger came from *Philadelphia* herself, whose double-shotted cannon fired spontaneously as the flames reached them, spraying the Americans with 'friendly fire'. No less a personage than Horatio Nelson applauded Decatur's feat, calling it ' . . . the most bold and daring act of our age'.

APPENDIX J:
THEORIES ABOUT THE *MAINE* EXPLOSION

Modern research makes it almost certain the explosion which sank *Maine* was caused when fire in a coal bunker spread to an adjacent powder magazine. What is unclear and a source of much controversy is what set fire to the coal, and especially whether it was internal or external.

Admiral Hyman Rickover's 1975 suggestion of spontaneous combustion seems unlikely, because a bunker fire would had been noticed long before reaching the magazine, and anyway the coal had passed its critical hydration time.

The author subscribes to the theory that it was a mine which ignited the coal, but does not believe it was set by the Spanish, since they were on the verge of crushing the rebellion and had nothing to gain from American intervention. Probably Cuban revolutionaries planted it for the same reason they had been burning American sugar plantations: to involve the United States in their struggle.

APPENDIX K:
NAVIGATION LIGHTS, RULES OF THE ROAD AND FOG SIGNALS

Navigation Lights on a steamship underway are designed to show precisely in which direction she is travelling. On each side of the bridge is a light – red on the left or port side, green on the right or starboard. Each is screened so as to be visible only from dead ahead to slightly (two points) abaft the beam. When dead ahead to another vessel, both lights are visible, but even a slight change of course will leave only one showing. Neither is visible from astern.

Range Lights are mounted on the mastheads, the forward one lower than the aft. When in line above one another, they confirm the evidence of the red and green lights that the ships are head on. If separated, the distance between them tells an experienced observer the other ship's angle of approach.

The Rule of the Road allows ships on parallel courses to steam ahead, passing in accordance with the old adage 'green-to-green or red-to-red, perfect safety go ahead'. When two ships are head-on to each other, the simple rule is for each to move to starboard, so that they pass 'red-to-red', while if they are on converging courses it is the duty of the ship seeing the other's port light to steer clear.

In fog, ships are normally expected to avoid any changes of course when they have been in sight of one another while visibility was still good. They confirm this to one another, or warn ships which are not previously visible, with long, single blasts of horn or whistle. If any changes are made while in fog, three short blasts mean 'going astern on engines' – normally to slow down the ship, rather than actually move it backward. Then, two long blasts in succession mean the ship no longer has way on (i.e. it is motionless).

APPENDIX L:
QUESTIONS ABOUT THE *LUSITANIA*

The sinking raised a number of uncertainties, some of which have been answered by recent underwater examination of the wreckage:

What caused the second explosion? At the time, it was thought a second torpedo had been fired, but *U-20*'s log disproves that theory. German counter-propaganda claimed *Lusitania* carried ammunition, making her a legitimate target, but underwater exploration confirms that the magazine was intact, while the hole was adjacent to her bunkers. This makes it virtually certain that the secondary explosion was caused by coal-dust being ignited by sparks from the torpedo strike.

With her rugged construction, why did *Lusitania* sink so quickly? The structural damage was all in the vicinity of engine and boiler rooms, which were directly below her huge dining room and first class lounge. These were all large open spaces with few watertight bulkheads, allowing rapid inflow of seawater.

Was there a conspiracy to place the ship in harm's way? Several authors have suggested that First Lord of the Admiralty, Winston Churchill, deliberately put *Lusitania* in danger in the hope of creating an incident which would draw America into the war on the Allied side. The Admiralty ordered Rear Admiral Sir Charles Coke, commanding nearby Queenstown naval base, to protect the liner as best he could, which they would hardly have done had Churchill wanted her attacked. On the other hand, Queenstown squadron had no destroyers, while Coke's flagship HMS *Juno* was an elderly cruiser and far too slow to keep up with *Lusitania*.

What did the British know, and what did they do about it? Before *Lusitania* sailed, naval intelligence had intercepted and decoded Bauer's deployment order, and subsequently monitored radio transmissions from *U-20* and *U-30*. Admiral Coke was warned that three submarines were en route to his area, but does not seem to have passed on this information to Captain Turner of *Lusitania*.

Why was *Lusitania* not zigzagging? In the absence of any direct information on U-boat activity across his path, Captain Turner may have decided to proceed at full speed without the delay of zigzagging. However, he had seen the German Embassy's warning, and would have been prudent to take that precaution.

Why had no escorts been provided? Destroyers could have been sent from the flotilla at Milford Haven – but the U-boat campaign was in its infancy and, more than likely, no-one really believed a non-combatant liner would be attacked without first allowing passengers and crew to abandon ship, in accordance with naval practice and international law.

APPENDIX M:
SECOND WORLD WAR INCIDENTS INVOLVING OVER 1,000 DEATHS

During 1940
8 June: While evacuating British troops from the failed Anglo-French expedition to Norway, British aircraft carrier HMS *Glorious* and two escorting destroyers were sunk by German cruisers. 1,519 were killed.

During 1941
28 March: In the night battle of Cape Matapan, Italian cruisers *Fiume*, *Pola* and *Zara*, with escorting destroyers *Alfieri* and *Carducci*, were sunk by British battleships. 2,303 men from the five ships were killed.

16 April: Near the Kerkenah Islands off the Tunisian coast, a convoy of one Italian and four German merchantmen was attacked by the British 14th Destroyer Flotilla. Some 1,750 soldiers and seamen perished.

24 May: In the Denmark Strait, British battle cruiser HMS *Hood* was destroyed by German battleship *Bismark*. The death toll was 1,414 including Vice Admiral Sir Lancelot Holland. There were only three survivors.

27 May: After sinking *Hood*, *Bismark* was hunted down by British task forces and sunk with the loss of 2,097 lives, including Admiral Günther Lütjens. One hundred and fifteen survivors were rescued by British cruiser *Dorsetshire* and destroyer *Maori*.

3 December: Russian troop transport *Josif Stalin* struck several mines in the Gulf of Finland. Rescue ships picked up about 1800 survivors, but some 2300 died.

7 December: Japanese naval aircraft attacked the US Navy base at Pearl Harbor. Battleships *Oklahoma* and *Arizona* were sunk; *Tennessee* and *West Virginia* were damaged. Altogether 2,409 seamen and marines were killed.

During 1942

1 July: Unescorted Japanese liner *Montevideo Maru* was torpedoed and sunk by American submarine *Sturgeon* off the Philippines. All 133 Japanese crew and naval guards were rescued, but there were no survivors from 845 Australian army and 208 civilian prisoners of war on board.

9 August: The Battle of Savo Island was the worst defeat ever suffered by the United States Navy. In little over an hour, one Australian and three American cruisers were sent to the bottom by a superior Japanese force, taking 1,162 men with them.

12 September: German submarine *U-156* torpedoed and sank British liner *Laconia* carrying Italian prisoners of war, their Polish guards, and a few British military and civilian personnel. The three-boat German wolf pack picked up about 200 survivors, and another 1,083 were rescued by Vichy French naval craft, but 1,649 had died.

During 1943

2 to 7 March: A large Japanese convoy, carrying troops to New Guinea, was repeatedly attacked by a fleet of American and Australian aircraft in the Bismarck Sea. All eight troop transports and four of eight escorting destroyers were sunk, while some 3300 Japanese soldiers and seamen perished.

9 September: After the Italian surrender, battleship *Roma* was attacked by German aircraft hoping to prevent her joining the Allies. Struck by two radio-controlled bombs, she broke in two and sank. 1,351 were killed, including Admiral Carlo Bertgamini.

23 September: Former Italian MV *Donizetti*, commandeered as a German troop transport, was evacuating soldiers from Rodi Island when she was intercepted and sunk by two British destroyers. All 1800 on board were killed.

20 October: French troop transport *Sinfra*, also under German command, was attacked and sunk by British and American aircraft off the island of Crete. 2,098 died.

26 November: British troopship *Rohna*, part of a convoy bound for Bombay in India, was hit by a German glider bomb. 1,015 American soldiers and 102 Indian seamen were drowned.

4 December: Japanese escort carrier *Chuyo* was torpedoed and sunk by submarine USS *Sailfish*. Some 1,250 Japanese and nineteen American POWs died. A twentieth POW was rescued by destroyer *Urakaze* which, mistakenly, thought he was one of *Chuyo*'s crew.

26 December: German battleship *Scharnhorst*, attempting to intercept an Allied Arctic convoy for Murmansk, was herself intercepted by a British task force. Hit by shells from battleship *Duke of York*, cruisers *Belfast*, *Jamaica* and *Norfolk*, and torpedoes from British and Norwegian destroyers, she went down off the northernmost point of Europe, taking 1,933 men with her.

During 1944

12 February: Egyptian troop transport *Khedive Ismail*, under British charter, was sailing from Mombasa in Africa to Colombo in Ceylon when torpedoed by Japanese submarine *I-27*. One thousand two hundred and ninety-seven passengers and crew were killed, including eighty-two nurses and female members of the armed forces.

24 February: Japanese transport *Tango Maru* was en route from Surabaya in Java to the Molucca Islands, carrying some Javanese slave labourers and Allied POWs. She was accompanied by *Ryusei Maru* carrying 6600 Japanese soldiers. They were intercepted and sunk by USS *Rasher*. Virtually all the 3500 Javanese and 200 POWs drowned, accompanied by 4,998 Japanese – approximately 8700 lives in total.

26 April to 6 May: A troop convoy bringing reinforcements to Halmahera, largest of the Molucca Islands, was attacked by two US submarines. First, *Jack* sank *Yoshida Maru*, then *Gurnard* sank *Aden*

Maru, *Tenshizan Maru* and *Taijima Maru*. Over 10,000 Japanese soldiers went down with the four transports.

19 June: During the Battle of the Philippine Sea, Japanese fleet carrier *Shokaku* was torpedoed by American submarine *Cavalla*, rupturing fuel tanks and filling the vessel with fumes which blew her apart when ignited by an air-dropped bomb. 1,263 died.

In the same action, *Taiho*, the newest and largest Japanese carrier, was torpedoed by American submarine *Albacore*. She too was blown up by gasoline fumes and 1,650 were killed.

29 June: *Toyama Maru*, a transport carrying the Japanese 44th Mixed Brigade to Okinawa, was torpedoed by American submarine *Sturgeon*. The death toll was 5500.

4 August: A small Japanese convoy was sighted in the Java Sea by submarine USS *Ray* which sank *Koshu Maru*. Killed were 301 Japanese passengers and crew, plus 1,239 Javanese slave labourers.

24 August: Japanese transport *Tsushima Maru* was evacuating school children, their teachers and some parents, from Okinawa to Japan, when she was torpedoed by US submarine *Bowfin*. As in so many of these cases of attack on civilians or POWs, she carried no special markings and was indistinguishable from legitimate targets. The death toll of 1,788 included 741 children – almost 90 per cent of those aboard.

12 September: A Japanese convoy consisting of two tankers and three transports, escorted by four destroyers, was attacked in the South China Sea by American submarines *Growler*, *Pampanito* and *Sealion*. By unfortunate coincidence, the only ships sunk – *Kachidoki Maru** and *Rukuyo Maru* – were those taking Allied prisoners to internment on Formosa. American submarines rescued 173 surviving POWs, and another 797 were picked up by the destroyer escorts, which also rescued 104 Japanese crewmen and guards. However, 1,144 British and Australian POWs lost their lives. (*Kachidoki Maru was the former *President Harrison*, which had been sunk and later salvaged by the Japanese).

21 September: Japanese transport *Hofuku Maru*, ferrying POWs from Singapore to Japan, was attacked and sunk by American torpedo-carrying aircraft. 1,049 British and Dutch prisoners were drowned while battened-down in the holds.

27 September: American submarine *Flasher* sank Japanese transport *Ural Maru*. About 2,000 Japanese soldiers died.

24 October: A seventeen-ship Japanese convoy was attacked by US submarine *Shark* in the Bashi Channel of Luzon Strait. As fate would have it, the only ship sunk, *Arisan Maru,* was once again the only one carrying American POW and civilian slave-labourers. The vessel split in two, but both halves remained afloat for about two hours. Most of the Japanese crew and guards escaped by lifeboat, while those left behind were killed by the POWs. Seven Americans escaped by clinging to flotsam. Two were picked up by a Japanese destroyer, the other five floated in to land on Formosa (Taiwan). Apart from the murdered guards, the death toll was ninety-eight American civilians and 1,782 POWs.

25 October: In the night Battle of Surigao Strait, Japanese battleships *Fuso* and *Yamashiro* and destroyer *Yamagumo,* were torpedoed by American light craft. Ten survivors were picked up by USS *Claxton,* but all who swam to shore were murdered by Filipinos. More than 2900 seamen died, including Admiral Masami Ben and Vice Admiral Nishimura Shoji.

26 October: During the Sibuyan Sea phase of the Battle of Leyte Gulf, Japanese super-battleship *Musachi* received seventeen bomb- and six torpedo hits from American naval aircraft. She rolled over and sank, taking Rear Admiral Inoguichi Toshihira and 1,023 of his men with her.

12 November: German battleship *Tirpitz,* sister ship of the more famous *Bismark,* spent most of the war in Norwegian waters, where her presence tied down a large Allied fleet. Repeated attempts to destroy her by both air and sea were unsuccessful, until British Royal Air Force bombers hit her with several 12,000-pound 'blockbuster' bombs. She capsized at her berth, trapping most of the crew below deck. Welders cut escape holes, but only eighty-seven managed to get out, leaving 1,204 to suffocate inside the hull.

21 November: Japanese battleship *Kongo,* badly damaged in the Battle of Leyte Gulf, was limping home via the Formosa Strait when she was torpedoed by American submarine *Sealion,* along with escorting destroyer *Urakaze.* Other destroyer escorts picked up 237 survivors, but some 1,557 died.

27 November: Norwegian troop transport *Rigel,* under German control, was in a southbound convoy when attacked by naval aircraft from HMS *Implacable.* She was carrying military equipment, 580 German soldiers, 2,248 Russian POWs, and ten Norwegian crewmen. 2,571 of them were killed.

29 November: Seventeen hours after setting out for sea trials after being converted from super-battleship to the world's largest and most heavily armoured aircraft carrier, Japanese *Shinano* was torpedoed by American submarine *Archer Fish*. Escorting Japanese destroyers closed in to lift off her crew and civilian dockyard workers, but many panicked and leaped into the sea to drown. Losses were 1,467 naval personnel and 308 civilians.

During 1945

7 April: As American forces prepared to invade Okinawa, the Japanese planned a suicidal counter-mission. An air assault by 355 kamikaze and 340 conventional aircraft was to cripple the invasion fleet, which would be finished off by monster battleship *Yamato*, accompanied by cruiser *Yahagi* and eight destroyers. These ships were crammed with ammunition, but had only enough fuel for a one-way trip. The massive air assault only managed to sink five small American ships and damage twenty-four, while the maritime forlorn hope was met by wave after wave of American carrier aircraft. After nearly four hours of constant pummelling with bombs and torpedoes, one of *Yamato's* magazines exploded and, shortly afterward, the great vessel capsized, taking Vice Admiral Sejichi Ito and 2,488 seamen with her. *Yahagi* and five of the escorts were also sunk, bringing the total loss to 3,656 lives.

APPENDIX N:
CAPTAIN MCVAY'S TRIAL AND EXONERATION

The Navy withheld any public report on the *Indianapolis* disaster for almost two weeks, hoping the detrimental news would be overshadowed by President Truman's announcement of the Japanese surrender.

Nevertheless, it felt the need for a scapegoat to cover up the breakdown of its ship tracking and reporting system and, more importantly, the failure to warn McVay that signals intelligence knew he was steaming into harm's way. Vice Admiral Raymond Spruance and Fleet Admiral Chester Nimitz recommended against court-martialling the captain, but were overruled by Commander-in-Chief, Fleet Admiral Ernest King.

The first charge – 'Failure to issue timely orders to abandon ship' – was dismissed, because the ship sank in twelve minutes, at a time when the electrical system had been knocked out, and orders could only be passed by word of mouth.

The second – 'Hazarding his ship by failure to zigzag in a combat zone' – should have been disallowed because no Navy directive required zigzagging in low visibility at night and, even if it had, McVay's orders specifically left the matter to his discretion. However, the charge was pressed by the prosecution, in spite of mitigating evidence by two of its own witnesses.

On cross-examination, American submarine ace Captain Glynn Donaho admitted that the evasive zigzag manoeuvre ' . . . is of no value to surface ships', while Commander Hashimoto testified he could easily have sunk the cruiser even if it had been zigzagging. In an interview shortly before his death in 2000, Hashimoto said, 'I had a feeling it (the verdict) was contrived from the beginning.'

McVay was the first officer in US naval history to be court-martialled as a result of enemy action. He was sentenced to lose 100 points in both his acting rank of Captain and permanent grade of Commander. The promising career of a much decorated officer with an exemplary record had been irretrievably damaged, even though, two months later, in February 1946, the Navy granted him clemency.

He never went to sea again, and was retired in 1949 with the 'tombstone' rank of Rear Admiral. In retirement he was constantly harassed by 'hate' mail and telephone calls from friends and relatives of the victims until, in 1968, he committed suicide by shooting himself in the head.

Twenty-nine years later, an American seventh-grader named Hunter Scott decided to undertake a school project on the *Indianapolis* disaster. After his findings were aired on national television, Representative Julia Carson sponsored legislation to clear McVay's name. The bill was opposed by the Pentagon and did not pass but, two years later, Congress did approve such a resolution.

Finally, in July 2001, Navy Secretary Gordon England ordered the captain exonerated of both wrongdoing and responsibility for the loss of *Indianapolis* and members of her crew. Unfortunately, the US military has no process for reversing the findings of a court-martial, so the conviction remains on record.

APPENDIX O:
SALVAGING USS *MISSOURI*

Bunkers were pumped free of fuel. Ammunition, provisions and other movables were taken off on lighters. Pontoons designed to raise sunken submarines were towed down from Boston to provide buoyancy. Civilian dredgers were hired and together with an Army dredger they dug a channel behind and around the vessel. Then a huge network of anchors, tackles, and other gear was designed and laid out.

Fifteen days after the grounding, at another high tide, a small armada assembled to try and pull *Missouri* off her ignominious perch. The battleship herself winched in nine kedge anchors laid out around her hull. Simultaneously, six fleet salvage tugs pulled directly astern, while five hauled alongside the huge vessel, and another three swung the bow to pry her loose from the glutinous muck.

At the same time, a couple of big salvage ships reeled in tackles attached to *Missouri*'s stern, while each pulled itself backward on five anchors laid out behind it. Seven smaller tugboats scurried around, keeping the larger vessels in position. The force of these twenty-three vessels prevailed and, thanks to the soft nature of the mud, damage was limited to a few dented and ripped plates, which were repaired in less than a week.

APPENDIX P:
THE FATE OF SS *STOCKHOLM*

Three years later, after her collision with *Andrea Doria*, the Swedish liner was sold to Communist East Germany, to serve as a cruise ship for trade unionists and party members. In the late 1980s she returned to Scandinavia as a barracks ship for the Norwegian Navy and in the early 1990s was purchased by an Italian company.

When she arrived at Genoa, one of the Italian newspapers ran a banner headline, saying: *È ARRIVATA LA NAVE DELLA MORTE!* (The Ship of Death has arrived!), but her new owners undertook a major reconstruction which resulted in an almost completely new ship, named *Italia Prima*. After several seasons of cruise service, she was laid up in Havana, Cuba where she remains at the time of writing (Autumn 2003).

Appendix Q:
New Evidence Regarding the *Liberty* Incident

Some of *Liberty*'s survivors immediately challenged basic facts in the 'official' version of the incident, claiming Israel was well aware of the ship's identity and deliberately attacked her; possibly because state-of-the-art intelligence gathering equipment was threatening to uncover its tactical plans and electronic warfare secrets. The Israeli and United States governments strongly deny this assertion, declaring 'mistaken identity' to be the cause. Surviving crewmen were threatened with disciplinary action if they spoke publicly on the matter. Recently, however, two documents have raised considerable doubt:

1. On 22 October 2003, an independent committee issued the following report:

    'We the undersigned [Admiral Thomas H. Moorer (former Chairman of the US Joint Chiefs of Staff), General Raymond G. Davis (former Assistant Commandant United States Marine Corps), Rear-Admiral Merlin Staring (former USN Judge Advocate General), and Ambassador James Akins] having undertaken an independent investigation . . . hereby find the following . . .
    After eight hours of aerial surveillance, Israel launched a two-hour air and naval attack against USS *Liberty*. . . . There is compelling evidence that Israel's attack was a deliberate attempt to destroy an American ship and kill her entire crew, . . . (that) the White House deliberately covered up the facts . . . an official cover-up without precedent in American naval history . . . '

2. On 8 January 2004, in a signed affidavit, Captain Ward Boston Jr., USN (ret.) stated:

    'For more than thirty years I have remained silent . . . however recent attempts to rewrite history compel me to share the truth. In June of 1967, while serving as a Captain in the Judge Advocate General Corps, Department of the Navy, I was assigned as Senior Legal Counsel for the Navy's Court of Inquiry into the brutal attack on USS *Liberty* . . .
    The late Admiral Isaac C. Kidd, President of the Court, and I were given only one week to gather evidence . . . despite the fact that we had both estimated that a proper Court of Inquiry . . . would take at least six months . . .

Despite the short amount of time we were given . . . the evidence was clear. Both Admiral Kidd and I believed with certainty that this attack . . . was planned and deliberate, and could not possibly have been an accident. I am certain that the Israeli pilots that (*sic*) undertook the attack, as well as their superiors, who had ordered the attack, were well aware that the ship was American . . .

I know from personal conversations I had with Admiral Kidd that President Lyndon Johnson and Secretary of Defense Robert McNamara ordered him to conclude that the attack was a case of 'Mistaken Identity' despite overwhelming evidence to the contrary. Admiral Kidd told me . . . that he had been ordered . . . to rewrite portions of the Court's findings . . . we were never to speak of it and we were to caution everyone else involved that they could never speak of it again. I have no reason to doubt the accuracy of that statement as I know the Court of Inquiry transcript that has been released to the public is not the same as the one I certified and sent off to Washington . . .

APPENDIX R:
CONTROVERSY OVER THE *ESTONIA* INCIDENT

Alternative explanations of the accident have been postulated, several of them the result of extensive investigation and analysis.

1. No sooner had the Joint Accident Investigation Committee brought down its report than *Estonia*'s German shipbuilders (Meyer Werft of Papenburg) issued a vehement denial of design error, accusing the ship's technical manager (Nordström & Thulin of Stockholm) of poor maintenance, and the operations manager (Estonian Shipping of Tallinn) of slack procedures.

2. In 1999, a self-styled 'German Group of Experts' hired a team of underwater specialists to defy a ban on diving near the mass grave in order to make a detailed survey of the sunken vessel. Their findings are analysed in a comprehensive report by Lieutenant Commander B.H.L. Braidwater, a world-renowned explosives and demolition consultant, formerly Commandant of the UK Joint Services Explosive Ordnance Disposal School.

Based on the distorted nature of the hull and visible burn marks, Braidwater concluded that the starboard visor hinge had been destroyed by an explosive device. What appeared to be a similar unexploded device was found and photographed adjacent to the port hinge which, however, had fractured under excessive strain after the starboard hinge was broken.

3. A year later, another team of less highly qualified divers concluded the ship had been sunk by collision with an unspecified underwater object. They advanced little evidence to support this theory.

4. In her 2003 book *Die* Estonia: *Tragödie Eines Schiffsuntergangs*, German documentary-journalist Jutta Rabe uses official documents, eyewitness testimony and underwater video photographs to substantiate Braidwater's conclusion.

Rabe claims to have hard evidence that the Swedish government hired divers from Rockwater (a subsidiary of BRES, which is, in turn, owned by Haliburton, US Vice President Dick Cheney's former company). According to her, these divers had to sign lifetime contracts to remain silent about their search of the wreck which, she suggests, was to locate a black attaché case owned by passenger Alexandr Voronin, a major dealer in contraband Russian space and weapons technology.

She contends the sabotage had been commissioned or carried out by the 'Felix Group', a clandestine organisation of hard-line nationalists from former Soviet intelligence agencies, dedicated to preventing the clandestine transfer of technology to the west, one of whose members was Vladimir Putin (later President of the Russian Federation).

All of these theories are strongly denied by the authorities, who stick to the Joint Accident Investigation Committee's finding of 'Design Error'.

APPENDIX S:
SALVAGING *KURSK* AND *TRICOLOR*

These were two of the most difficult and technologically-advanced maritime lifting operations ever attempted. Both were entrusted to consortia led by Dutch salvage experts Smit. Unsurprisingly, the methodology was similar even though the circumstances were substantially different.

Kursk lay in fifty-nine fathoms (108 metres; 354 feet) of turbulent near freezing Baltic water, while *Tricolor* was barely submerged in the (relatively) calm and warm English Channel. *Kursk* had a displacement tonnage of 14,700, versus *Tricolor*'s 50,000 – to which must be added the weight of almost 3,000 automobiles, making it one of the heaviest lifts ever.

In both cases, specially-designed diamond-wire cutting systems were used to slice the wrecks into manageable sections – two for *Kursk*, nine for *Tricolor*. These systems were like gigantic chain saws, stretched between platforms on either side of the wrecks and cutting upward from below the hulls.

Kursk had lifting holes cut by high-pressure jets of water loaded with abrasives. Cables were then lowered from the pontoon and anchored by huge butterfly fasteners which opened inside the hull. Lifting was computer-controlled to minimize tension on the hull and compensate for wave surge. *Tricolor*'s sections were much larger, each reaching the height of a six-storey building and weighing some 3,000 tonnes.

Once raised, the sections were transported to Murmansk and Zeebrugge respectively by three huge 140-metre (460-foot) pontoons, each appropriately named *Giant*. However, the methodology was slightly different. The raised parts of *Kursk* were suspended under one of the pontoons, whose bottom had had been cut to accommodate the conning tower. *Tricolor*'s sections were lifted and placed on top of the pontoons by a pair of huge floating cranes – ocean-going heavy-lift catamaran *Rambiz* and floating shearlegs *Asian Hercules II* had a combined lifting capacity of more than 6,400 tonnes.

Notes

1. All quotations are paraphrased from *The Bible*: *Acts 26-27*.
2. The name Descharges was highly appropriate, since it translates as 'volleys' or 'salvoes'.
3. For information on *Mary Rose*'s salvage, see Appendix A.
4. For more on the composition of both the Armada and the English fleet, see Appendix B.
5. In 1916, during construction of the New York subway system, some of the prow, keel and frame timbers of *Tijger* were uncovered. The waterfront had been filled in, so they lay some six metres (19.5 feet) below the surface. They are now preserved in the New York City Marine Museum.
6. See Appendix C.
7. Almost 333 years later, *Vasa*'s remains were raised and reconstructed. See Appendix D.
8. Press-ganged crews were kept in line by harsh discipline and, when at sea, they understood that, without navigators, they would never know where they were. Hence, any seaman who could calculate position could facilitate mutiny, making 'Subversive Navigation' a crime in the British Royal Navy.
9. Latitude, longitude and navigation by dead reckoning are briefly discussed in Appendix E.
10. For a brief history of these experiments, see Appendix F.
11. Durschmeid's account substitutes van Kinsbergen for Reyntjes, but records indicate that the *Luitenant-Admiraal* was not with the fleet at the time.
12. For an interesting sequel to *Philadelphia*'s capture, see Appendix G.
13. This incident inspired Herman Melville to write *Moby Dick,* his 1851 symbolic study of good and evil.
14. The Sperm whale is well equipped for ramming, which is its method of fighting for females. Its heavy blunt head has a huge oil-filled cavity which acts as a shock-absorber. Modern males are usually killed before reaching full size, but in the late eighteenth and early nineteenth centuries they grew to eighty-five to ninety feet. Hence *Essex*'s 87-foot-long underwater profile was almost exactly the size and shape of a bull whale, and experts theorize that, in the manner of his species, he was attacking what he perceived to be yet another challenger seeking to take over his harem.
15. *Reis* means sea-captain and *Pasha* means general. Hence an admiral is a *Reis-Pasha*.
16. No-one seems to know why a Buffalo-registered American vessel had been named in honour of the wife of Canada's British Governor General, especially at a time when US-British relations were strained.

17 The trunk can be seen in the Wisconsin Marine Historical Society's Museum.

18 Appendix H describes professional resistance to developments in naval architecture.

19 See Appendix I for an extravagant newspaper report of one *Thingvalla* survivors' story.

20 A cable is 720 feet, or just under 220 metres.

21 See Appendix J for theories of what actually caused the explosion.

22 See Appendix K for brief explanations of Rules of the Road, Navigation Lights, and Fog Signals.

23 The damage to *Seydlitz* taught Germany the need to reduce the quantity of propellant stored in turrets, and also to ensure that turrets were insulated from each other. These important lessons were not learned by the British, to their considerable cost at the Battle of Jutland sixteen months later.

24 See Appendix L for discussion of the secondary explosion and other questions raised by the sinking.

25 Another thirty-six disasters – those involving more than 1,000 deaths – are listed in Appendix M.

26 Prien and *U-47* made ten more patrols, sinking twenty-eight ships. They disappeared on the night of 7–8 March 1941 while attacking Convoy OB293.

27 As for Scapa Flow, the four eastern entrances were belatedly sealed with 250,000 tons of concrete, known as the 'Churchill Barrier'.

28 The United States Navy used *Normandie* as a training ground for over 2500 divers, who removed 10,000 tons of rubble and broken glass, and sealed over 2,000 underwater openings. In September 1943, after a complex $4,740,000 recovery operation, she was finally righted and towed to Brooklyn Navy Yard, where it was determined that the cost and time required to put her back into service were prohibitive. Instead, she was stripped of everything useful to the war effort. When the war was over, France came to the same conclusion and, in October 1946, the hulk was sold for scrap, bringing in a mere $161,680.

29 British Admiral Ramsey calls the naval airmen's useless sacrifice 'a major tragedy of this war', adding 'Had I known that the fighter escorts might not keep their rendezvous I would . . . have forbidden the flight.' Wing Commander Tom Gleave creates a precedent by officially reporting: 'Lt-Cdr Esmonde is well worthy of the posthumous award of the Victoria Cross.' Never before has an air force officer recommended a naval officer for Britain's highest decoration. It is awarded.

30 German Admiral Ciliax's diary entry speaks of Esmonde and his naval aircrews as 'men whose bravery surpasses any other action by either side', while *Fregattenkapitän* Helmut Giesler, *Scharnhorst*'s navigator writes 'Such bravery was devoted and incredible. One was privileged to witness it . . . they knowingly and ungrudgingly gave their all.'

31 Even though Bomber Command had achieved little success, Admiral Ciliax was also impressed by the RAF airmen, writing of their 'massed and individual air attacks . . . dogged aggressive spirit, very plucky flying, (and) great powers of resistance.'

[32] *Tirpitz*, sister ship of more famous *Bismark*, was a symbol of the resurgence of German naval power under the Nazis. At this time she was the largest and most powerful warship afloat, with a speed in excess of thirty knots, displacement of 42,000 tons, and 380-mm (15-inch) guns which fired faster and outranged those of all comparable Allied warships.

[33] It has been suggested that Pound reached this extraordinary decision because his judgement was already impaired by the undiagnosed brain tumour which killed him less than a year later. In fairness, it should be mentioned he had previously tried to resign on grounds of ill-health, but had been persuaded to stay on by Prime Minister Churchill.

[34] Anglophobic Fleet Admiral Ernest King was furious that merchantmen had been abandoned to their fate and, for the rest of the war, was even more reluctant to place American vessels under British control.

[35] TBS = Talk Between Ships, a short-range radio-telephone system.

[36] The Utah Beach exercise was code-named *Operation Tiger*. American, British and Canadian assault forces destined for the four eastern beaches, which had different topography, held similar training exercises known as *Operation Fabus*.

[37] 'Friendly fire' was responsible for killing ninety per cent of all Allied POWs lost at sea during the Second World War.

[38] Reported in his book *SOS* Wilhelm Gustloff – *Die Grösste Schiffenkatastrophe der Geschichte (*SOS *Wilhelm Gustloff* – The Greatest Ship Catastrophe in History).

[39] The broken-off bow section was later recovered by a fleet tug, which signalled: 'Have sighted the suburb of *Pittsburgh* and am taking it in tow'.

[40] Paperwork to court-martial Lieutenant Marks, for disregarding standing orders and losing an aircraft, was making its way through the naval chain of command when someone realized who he was and why he had landed on the open sea. Charges against him were withdrawn, but Captain McVay was not so lucky, as can be seen in Appendix N.

[41] In August 2001, fifteen of the survivors, who were still living, sued the Japanese government for compensation for slave labour and attempted murder. After winning the lawsuit, each was awarded a paltry $2,000.

[42] One firefighter describes dealing with a shipboard inferno: 'It's like fighting a house fire by going down the chimney or smoke stack. That steel box conducts heat like you wouldn't believe.'

[43] See Appendix O.

[44] The Swedish ship seems to be immortal – See Appendix P.

[45] The foregoing is the 'official' version of the incident, which continues to be a subject of much controversy as outlined in Appendix Q.

[46] *Saratoga* (CV60), was commissioned in 1956 as the second carrier in the Forrestal class and fifth US Navy ship to bear that name. She had a crew of 2,700 and an air wing of 2,480. The ship displaced 78,200 tons, and her length of 325 metres (1,067 feet) was comparable to the height of New York's Chrysler Building which reaches 336 metres (1,103 feet) including its tall spire.

47   Once the gasket was replaced, '*Sara*' continued in active service. She was modernized in 1968, and served in the Vietnam War. Between 1980 and 1983, she underwent a 'Service Life Extension Program' and in 1991 joined the Gulf War, in which one of her aircraft was the first to be shot down. In 1994, after thirty-eight years in service, she was decommissioned and transferred to Newport RI, where she remains as a museum and memorial.

48   Formerly USS *Phoenix,* re-named after a hero of the Argentine War of Independence.

49   At the time of writing, twenty-one years after the event, controversy continues to rage. The official British contention, that it was a legitimate Act of War, is supported by *Armada Argentina*, but disputed by victims' relatives and some *Belgrano* veterans. They continue to demand the arraignment of former Prime Minister Thatcher before the International War Crimes Tribunal at The Hague.

50   See Appendix R.

51   HTP = High Test Peroxide. Used to provide oxygen for kerosene-fuelled diesel propulsion engines.

52   ASW = Anti-Submarine Warfare.

53   See Appendix S for salvage and recovery details.

54   On 14 April 2003, *Agence France-Presse* announced that French prosecutors had launched an inquiry into the *Joola* disaster. It was to investigate charges of 'Involuntary Homicide, Involuntary Injury, and Lack of Assistance to People in Danger.'

55   To paraphrase Lady Bracknell in Oscar Wilde's *The Importance of Being Earnest,* ' . . . to be struck once is misfortune, to be hit four times looks like carelessness.'

56   See Appendix S for details of the *Tricolor* salvage plan.

57   This account was written as contemporary reportage, based on newspaper and radio reports. No doubt Courts of Inquiry will be convened and more information should then become available. There will certainly be civil litigation, and there could be criminal prosecution as well. These would probably take years to complete. Meanwhile, it seems to the author that *Kariba* was culpable of the initial collision, since she had the Norwegian ship to starboard and collided with its port side, apparently having failed to give way as required under International Law.

Index

PEOPLE